THE SELLING OF FIDEL CASTRO

THE SELLING OF FIDEL CASTRO

The Media and the Cuban Revolution

Edited by

William E. Ratliff

Transaction Books
New Brunswick (U.S.A.) and Oxford (U.K.)

The original conference on the Media and Castro was sponsored in part with a grant provided by the Tinker Foundation to the Cuban American National Foundation.

Prepared in cooperation with the Cuban American National Foundation, 1000 Thomas Jefferson Street, N.W., Washington, D.C. 20007

Library of Congress Catalog Number: 86-20055
ISBN: 0-88738-104-9 (cloth); 0-88738-649-0 (paper)
Printed in the United States of America

Library of Congress Cataloging in Publication Data
The Selling of Fidel Castro.

    Presented as part of a conference held on
November 16–17, 1984, in Washington, D.C.
    "Prepared in cooperation with the Cuban
American National Foundation . . . Washington, D.C."—
Verso t.p.
    1. Cuba—History—Revolution, 1959—Journalists—
Congresses.   2. Castro, Fidel, 1927–   —Public
opinion—Congresses.   3. Foreign news—Congresses.
I. Ratliff, William   II. Cuban American National
Foundation (U.S.)
F1788.S44   1986   972.91'064   86-20055
ISBN 0-88738-104-9
ISBN 0-88738-649-0 (pbk.)

Contents

Preface

Even today, the press continues to treat Fidel Castro as something of a mystery. This is due, in part, to the widely accepted myth that left-wing dictatorships are superior to right-wing, a myth clearly refuted by the historical evidence: no left-wing dictatorship has ever evolved toward democracy, while some right-wing dictatorships have done so. The myth, however, nourished by propaganda, persists; and the perceptions of journalists are correspondingly distorted. Instead of seeing in Castro a man primarily intent on personal power, the press listens to, debates and propagates statements about Cuba which if made, say, by or about one of the Somozas, would never have reached print.

In reality, there is nothing mysterious about Castro. The questions have been answered. He can be explained much more easily than other leaders. Who, for instance, can explain the courage, idealism, political ambition and staying power, immense patience and insight of El Salvador's Jose Napoleon Duarte? And who knows what success he will have in ending the violence and strengthening the complex processes of democracy in his country? These are much profounder questions than can be asked about Castro.

In a sense Castro fascinates us not because he is intrinsically interesting but because he is dangerous. Apparently a natural deceiver, he has improved with practice. Castro is dangerous because he has traded away the hopes of Cubans for national independence, and to secure support for his position as dictator has made his country a tool of the Soviet Union.

The media's reluctance to describe Castro as he really is can be explained. The various pieces in this book provide much of the explanation, and trace the history of the media's fascination with Castro. If he is, by this time, an explainable phenomenon, he is nevertheless a complex one. We must take into account not only the forces behind him, but also the combination of personality cult and a nation organized along totalitarian lines. There are totalitarian societies whose leaders lack the animal magnetism, the slyness and intelligence, the hypnotic long-windedness, the seemingly endless ability to twist new theories out of old failures, and the insight into enemies that characterize Castro. Nicaragua's Daniel Ortega, for instance, is a kind of Castro without the charisma. There are also strongmen, *caudillos* as they are called throughout Latin America, who have never tried, much less succeeded, in imposing totalitarian regimes on their people. With Castro we have the combination of *caudillos* and insular Big Brother, a combination that has proved, for the media of other nations, peculiarly fascinating and bamboozling.

For instance, consider a question still seriously asked, and which reporters still journey to Cuba to answer: is the Cuban revolution a success or a failure? Are the Cuban people better off now than they were in 1958?

If anything proves that democracy is worth not only declaring for but fighting for, it is the current state of affairs in Cuba. Going from partial dependency on the United States, Cuba is now totally dependent on the Soviet Union, which subsidizes it at a rate of about $4 billion a year. Despite these subsidies, Cuba's foreign debt continues to grow, and after 25 years of Castro, new austerity measures have been announced so that the country can meet these debts.

Claims of growth in the Cuban economy are, then, close to meaningless. The economy is stagnant, more dependent than ever on the Soviet Union. Cuba's economic makeup is more colonial than it has ever been. In 1960, 95 percent of Cuba's exports consisted of primary commodities, with sugar by far the largest. Manufacturing accounted for only 5 percent. Twenty years later, the percentages were unchanged. Cuba's manufactured exports were still 5 percent.

During this period El Salvador, without help from the Soviet Union, but with modest assistance from the Alliance for Progress, increased its percentage of manufactured exports from 6 to 39 percent; Mexico from 12 to 39 percent; Nicaragua from 2 to 14 percent. It is difficult, in fact, to find any country except Cuba whose percentage of manufactured exports has *not* grown. Other countries have significantly developed their industrial base, thereby offering more varied and profitable sources of income for their people, but Cuba has diversified only in one way. Once dependent on a single major export crop, Cuba is now dependent on two, because the Soviet Union can use only two crops from Cuba—sugar and soldiers. To play its role in the Soviet design, Cuba maintains the largest armed force per capita in the hemisphere, and its soldiers fight as mercenaries on foreign soil, the footsoldiers of the Soviet Foreign Legion.

The Soviet Union also wants from Cuba the strategic advantage of having bases near the United States. Cuba maintains a network of airfields for the most advanced Soviet aircraft and a base for Soviet submarines, as well as a massive intelligence center that is capable of monitoring telephone conversations all over the United States and the Caribbean.

The Cuban people do not benefit from being the pawns of Soviet belligerence. Their standard of living has declined. GNP per capita has dropped from third highest in Latin America to fifteenth. The Cuban suicide rate is one of the highest in the world.

Cuban apologists claim a medical revolution under Castro, but this claim has been refuted by a number of distinguished scholars. In 1958, Cuba's health services were among the most advanced in the region, in some respects comparable with those of Europe. Since then, they have grown more slowly than those in nations which started even with Cuba or behind it. Cuba's infant mortality rate, for instance, fell 32 percent between 1960 and 1974. Taking this at face value, we may note that during the same period, infant mortality declined even more dramatically in Panama (40 percent), Puerto Rico (46 percent), Chile (47 percent), Barbados (47 percent) and Costa Rica (55 percent). Life expectancy in Cuba, once superior to that of Spain, Greece and Portugal, has fallen behind these nations, and has increased less than life expectancy in 9 other Latin American nations.

Serious outbreaks of typhoid and yellow fever, diseases which had once been wiped out in Cuba, have occurred in recent years. These and other regressions are the obvious result of Cuba's dependence on the Soviet Union and the economic strains imposed by Cuba's obligation to fulfill the Soviet Union's objectives in Africa and Central America.

The media's fascination with Castro outside Cuba is not shared by the residents of his country: since the revolution a tenth of the population has fled. Castro has forfeited the independence of his nation to the Soviet Union, the welfare of his people to a personally mismanaged economy, and their very lives to his thirst for power and military adventurism. How has Castro managed to maintain his media image of the charismatic revolutionary hero?

Part of the answer lies in his reputation of having defied the United States and lived to tell the tale. However, as the 1962 Cuban missile crisis proved, it is not Castro that threatens and strikes deals with the United States, but his Soviet bosses. The U.S.-Soviet understandings of 1962 were reached over Castro's head, and have been slowly eroded by the Soviet Union at its pleasure, not at the pleasure of its puppet.

Another part of the answer lies, as I suggested in the beginning of this article, in a combination of personal magnetism and totalitarianism. One does not hear protesting voices from inside Cuba—indeed one does not hear any independent voices. One hears Castro. One does not see, as one might within a right-wing dictatorship, an armed opposition. There is not even an opposition party. Individual critics and opponents of the regime receive long, hard prison terms. The educational system is in reality a system of indoctrination. The neighborhoods are in reality spy networks. Thus, unrest and dissent—two phenomena that create news—are disguised or stifled in Cuba. The only story to cover is Fidel.

Castro does not lack for personalities. He is a master at choosing and projecting the most useful image for the media, and at manipulating individual reporters. Numerous anecdotes in the pages that follow illustrate this. From the image of the intense, daring and visionary revolutionary in the hills of the Sierra Maestra, an image which captivated the imagination of American journalists in the early days of the Revolution, to that of the maximum leader who at one moment inflicts humiliation, and at the next offers flattery and comradeship, Castro has an instinctive talent for personal and media manipulation. Many reporters find themselves unable to hear the whispers of the Cuban people. They can only try to assess the behavior of a bearded figure out of a Freudian fairy tale.

Castro has, in addition, the benefit of all that the vast Soviet propaganda apparatus can teach him, and the support for him that it can generate. His own slanting of the news and disinformation play a part in, and in return receive the benefit of, a wider apparatus.

The papers and responses that follow were presented as part of a Conference, The Media and the Cuban Revolution, held on November 16-17, 1984, in Washington, D.C. They represent an important contribution to the body of work dealing with this issue. They are of exceptional value if they help us to see clearly, not the media image of Castro, but the mechanism that projects that image: a manipulative personality; a nationalism fronting for the aggressiveness of an international empire; a *caudillo* whose methods are no less totalitarian for their being Leninist rather than fascist.

John R. Silber

1

The *New York Times* and the Cuban Revolution

William E. Ratliff

A brief look at *Times* reporter Herbert Matthews's views of and reporting on the Cuban revolution, which first opened the door to criticism of *Times* coverage of Cuba. An examination of the positions of *Times* columnists and particularly editorial writers at key times and on key issues since Castro's march into Santiago and Havana. Finally, the paper concentrates on the op-ed pieces printed in the *Times* since that page was inaugurated almost fifteen years ago.

> *If in the American press there are apologists for Fidel Castro—and there are—then we ought to analyze what there is inside ourselves as Americans that leads us to look for the "revolutionary hero." Why has Cuba been such a charismatic experience for so many people and why has the revolution's development not been critically analyzed?*
>
> —Georgie Anne Geyer

Introduction

Why a study of Cuba and the *New York Times*? For those who have followed the history of contemporary Cuba, the question hardly needs to be asked. It is not simply that the *Times* is the most influential paper in the United States—in political matters, at any rate—for that would suggest papers also on Mexico or Brazil or whatever country and the *Times*. But those studies are not likely to be forthcoming.

No, there is quite another reason for the frequent juxtaposition of this particular paper and Fidel Castro's revolution.

In 1959 an artistic wit took a swipe at *Times* coverage of Cuba by playing on the paper's advertising slogan, "I got my job through *The New York Times.*" In this cartoon, the happy, successful job finder was Fidel Castro.

There is a long story behind the point made by that cartoon and the many interpretations that have been made of the unique relationship between the *Times* and the Cuban revolution. Indeed, the question of *Times* influence on U.S. policy toward Cuba—or at least *Times* efforts to influence U.S. policy—is still a living, and for some a burning, issue.

This paper is divided into three sections. In the first I will look briefly at Herbert Matthews's views of and reporting on the Cuban revolution, which first opened the door to criticism of *Times* coverage of Cuba. In the second section I will touch on the positions of *Times* columnists and particularly editorial writers at key times and on key issues since Castro's march into Santiago and Havana. And finally, and primarily, I will look at the op-ed pieces printed in the *Times* since that page was inaugurated almost fifteen years ago. (I have provided a methodological note as Appendix I, and summaries of thirty-four op-ed pieces dealing with Cuba as Appendix II.)

Herbert Matthews and the Cuban Revolution

When the cartoonist said Fidel Castro got his job through the *New York Times,* he meant, more specifically, through the help of *Times* correspondent and editorial writer Herbert Matthews. After all, it was Matthews who had visited Castro in the Sierra Maestra in mid-February 1957 and written three articles (24, 25, 26 February 1957) for the *Times,* the first two beginning on page one.

There is little question that these articles, and their impact in Cuba and abroad, played an important role in advancing Castro's cause. The U.S. ambassador to Cuba, Earl E.T. Smith, was among the first to draw attention to the importance of Matthews's articles. Long before the publication of his book *The Fourth Floor* (Random House, 1962), he went so far as to charge that the *Times* writer had excessive influence on the important middle echelons of the U.S. State Department.

Smith and other early critics of Castro and the *Times* were not the only ones to draw a link between the articles and Castro's success. On the other side of the spectrum was the *Times* itself. Harrison Salisbury, who founded the op-ed page, remarked on the power of the *Times*—without specific reference to Cuba—in his book *Without Fear or*

Favor: An Uncompromising Look at The New York Times (Times Book, 1980). Salisbury wrote:

> I was decrying the state of the world to Clifton Daniel, then in training to become managing editor of *The Times*. "If I had the power," I said, "I would really do something about this." Daniel smiled in a worldly way. "But," he said "you do have the power. You are on *The Times*."

Matthews himself proudly proclaimed his historic role in Castro's rise to power, not least in his last article as a *Times* staff writer on 31 August 1967:

> I will not deny that as I sat with Fidel Castro, his brother Raúl, Che Guevara and others up in the Sierra Maestra on the chilly morning of Feb. 17, 1957, Clio, the muse of history, touched me with her hand—or whatever she uses. The resulting publicity in *The Times* gave Castro and his guerrilla band a nationwide and even a worldwide fame that, chronologically, was the start of the most fantastic career of any leader in the whole course of Latin America's independent history.

In his monumental history, *The Cuban Revolution*, Hugh Thomas noted that the *Times* articles had been critically important to Castro and went on to say why:

> Matthews' article on his visit to the Sierra published on 24 February immediately made Castro an international figure. Since the censorship was by chance lifted in Cuba the very next day, the news that Castro was alive became known quickly in Cuba also. The imprecise overestimate of the size of Castro's forces helped attract urban Cubans to his cause. It was supposed that Castro was winning, that Batista's reports could not any more be relied on, and that his side was therefore the right side to be on; Castro's morale was raised. The morale in Batista's army was further depressed, and afterwards, when the Minister of Defence, Santiago Rey, denied both that Matthews could have penetrated the army's ring round the Sierra and that Castro was alive, the government was made ridiculous, since Matthews next published a photograph that he had taken of himself with Castro.

Even if the fact of influence is granted, as I believe it must be, there is more to be considered, and that "more" is what causes the most dispute among those interested in the development of Castro's movement and the Cuban revolution—whether or not *Times* writers, and above all Matthews, harbored a bias in favor of Castro, before and after the guerrillas took power in January 1959. Seldom has a single writer so influentially set the tone—at least as perceived by a broad cross-section of its interested readership—toward a person, movement, or historical phenomenon.

Matthews saw the problem this way in his 31 March 1967 article in the *Times:* "When Cuba's Jefe Máximo and his Government turned Communist and later almost brought on a nuclear war, somebody had to be blamed. I was."

It was a good bit more complicated than that. Matthews and some others at the *Times* were criticized long before Castro "turned Communist" and "almost brought on a nuclear war."

On 14 May 1961—more than six months before Castro publicly declared himself a Marxist-Leninist and almost a year and a half before the missile crisis—a *Times* headline read, "Castro Foes Protest: Picket *The Times* to Register Objection to Cuba Coverage." The article stated that about 150 people "were protesting editorials on Cuba and editorial writings of Herbert L. Matthews in *The Times,* and information in the news columns that they interpreted as favorable to Fidel Castro and therefore to communism." This was not the first protest against the *Times,* nor indeed, the first time the paper had reported protests against its editorials and news reports. But this short article laid out most of the issues with particular clarity. Indeed, the *Times* management evidently recognized the Matthews problem very clearly, for the journalist who had "discovered" Castro was not sent back to Cuba to report on the revolution after Castro took over—though he did return and comment as a columnist and independent writer.

Was Matthews one of the world's foremost reporters? Was he taken in and used by Castro? Did he consciously promote Castro's cause? Ironically, the answer to all three questions is, in varying degrees, yes. Matthews was an eccentric but often resourceful and informative writer. He could be taken in, or he could repeatedly give the benefit of every doubt, if he sympathized with the cause he was covering or if he concluded that the people of the country in question supported what was going on in their land. Matthews filed some partisan reports from the Spanish Civil War long before he did so again from (and on) Cuba.

Matthews wrote that he was "at odds with scholars" like Theodore Draper, Boris Goldenberg, and Andrés Suárez because their studies were two-dimensional. He added a third dimension, he wrote in his book *Fidel Castro* (Simon and Schuster, 1969, p. 10), which "comes from the solidity and impact of life," the "I've been there" one-upmanship the journalist sometimes flings at the scholar. Firsthand observation certainly does add a critical dimension to reporting, and is sought by many scholars as well, but it is often accompanied by debilitating pockets of ignorance and the propensity for superficial analysis. (Scholars are often equally guilty of superficial analyses, and perhaps more often guilty of partisanship, especially when causes they strongly support or oppose are at stake.)

In Matthews's writings, the "Fidel and I" or "Fidel told me" line became overbearing—he certainly did not listen with equal attention to Castro's critics—and at times overcame the degree of detachment he needed to remain an effective correspondent. Matthews developed something of a "stake" in Castro's revolution and, while critical of some of the Cuban leader's policies, repeatedly pointed out that, as he said in the first and last lines of his 1969 book, the Cuban revolution is "Fidel Castro's revolution." The headline to one of his last articles in the *Times* (18 January 1976), "Forward, With Fidel, Anywhere," pretty much summed up Matthews's own position that Castro had every right to do almost anything he wanted.

Once he had taken power, Castro himself told Matthews how the guerrillas had deceived the *Times* correspondent on troop strength—as Matthews related in *Fidel Castro* (pp. 108-9)—a deception of critical importance, as Hugh Thomas pointed out in the above quotation.

As the years passed and the direction of Castro's government became increasingly clear, Matthews continued to tilt toward Castro, to the point where he would reach patently absurd conclusions to justify Castro's policies. "If Fidel Castro brought some tragedy to some families," he wrote in his 1969 book, "I believe that it is demonstrable that he brought a better life to a majority of Cubans—if now always today and for the older generations, then for tomorrow and for the youth." Never mind whether his judgement on the present is correct. Is it *demonstrable* that he brought a better life *tomorrow*? Surely that is going beyond the evidence.

As Matthews was writing his book, Castro's international policies were, in fact, demonstrably failing throughout the hemisphere. The 1970 ten-million-ton sugar program, which virtually destroyed the entire Cuban economy for some years to come, also was well under way. These two major setbacks were instrumental in vastly increasing Soviet involvement in Cuban domestic and foreign policies in the years ahead, yet they were seemingly ignored by Matthews.

Matthews's critics, however, have not always been adequately informed or quite fair in their criticisms of his writings. If Matthews often had a romanticized view of Castro, much of his reporting and analysis proved to be essentially correct. When he was mistaken, his views were shared by some noncommunists in the United States and many in Cuba who had independent sources of information. Indeed, some of Castro's severest and most articulate critics over the past twenty years have been exiled Cubans who themselves expected Castro to be more democratic than he turned out to be and who even worked for several years in Castro's government before leaving or being effectively forced into exile.

In his first (24 February 1957) article on Castro, Matthews waxed eloquent over the guerrilla leader's commitment to liberty, democracy, social justice, the restoration of the Cuban constitution, and elections. He reported that Castro's revolution was anticommunist and its leaders had "no animosity toward the United States." Many democratic Cubans working with Castro evidently would have agreed with Matthews when he wrote on 11 January 1959 that it was "highly unlikely he [Castro] could today formulate a coherent social and political philosophy," though fewer would have gone along with his comment, as late as 16 July 1959, that Castro was "not only not Communist but decidedly anti-communist." (Only three months after this article was published Castro ordered the arrest of Huber Matos, the military governor of Camagüey, who had resigned because of communist influence in the government. Matos was given twenty years in prison and defamed around the country.)

It might be added that Matthews was not blind to the security issues in the Caribbean, as he demonstrated when he wrote on 26 April 1959, "Without bases in the Caribbean islands and without the Panama Canal, the United States would be wide open to invasion." He also did not deny Castro's penchant for revolution—indeed, he stressed it more than most writers—but he tended to play down, as he did on 14 December 1972, the potential danger to other countries of Cuban and Soviet policy in the area.

Matthews was in good company, then, when between 1957 and early 1959 he expected a democratic revolution under Castro's leadership. His personal contacts with Castro, however, seemed to blind him to some ominous developments that began in 1959, or led him to excuse whatever happened, even when he disagreed with it personally. For him, the Cuban revolution was Castro's revolution, and after all, how does one second-guess the Creator?

Times Columns and Editorials on Cuba

It is not my objective here to provide anything like a complete survey of *Times* writings on Cuba over the twenty-seven years since Matthews's articles made Cuba and the *Times* an issue of increasing concern in some quarters. I will look briefly at a few of the *Times* staff columns, to suggest that there was more variety than is sometimes recognized, and I will examine in slightly more detail the paper's editorials on Cuba, since in a sense they overlap or complement the guest columns on the op-ed page. I will not examine the *Times* reporting on Cuba, beyond the points already made on Matthews, and the comment that not all *Times* reporters writing on Cuba, even in the early years, were as mesmerized by Castro as was Matthews.

Times *Columns on Cuba*

Predictably, columnists in the *Times* have most often written on Cuba when it seemed to them they could shed some light on an issue relating to the country or when they had a hole to fill and Cuba was one of the issues of the day. Columnists who wrote most on Cuba during different periods were Matthews, whose efforts were noted above, Hanson Baldwin, James Reston, Tom Wicker, William Safire, Anthony Lewis, Flora Lewis, and others.

In general, columns on Cuba, true to the ways of journalism, have tended to follow events and even to cluster around major (or what are perceived as major) developments. For example, three *Times* staff members wrote five pieces touching on Cuba between 25 February and 26 March 1976 (immediately after Cuba sent troops to Angola), and five writers turned out nine columns between 6 September and 7 October 1979 (after President Carter charged the Soviet Union had an "unacceptable combat presence" in Cuba).

In the first cluster a variety of positions were advanced. C.L. Sulzberger (25 February 1976) suggested that the involvement of Cubans in Africa was a harbinger of renewed Cuban involvement in Latin America, though he did not see that Cuban cooperation with the Soviet Union in Africa might well mean more of the same in the Western Hemisphere. By way of contrast, Wicker on 26 March 1976 used Cuba as a springboard for digging into U.S. policy toward Rhodesia. James Reston wrote three times on Cuba and U.S.-Cuban relations during the month. On 3 March he said that the United States government under President Ford and Secretary of State Kissinger was on the brink of accepting Castro and his system when the Cuban leader deliberately provoked the United States by engaging in anti-United States activities in Puerto Rico and sending 12,000 troops to Angola. On 17 March he picked up a point from his previous column and argued that because of these Cuban activities, the United States and other hemisphere governments would now have to pay more attention to their own security matters. Finally, on 24 March he warned Kissinger that under the circumstances of the day it would be difficult to back up threats that "the United States will not accept further Cuban military intervention abroad," and concluded that a threat not backed up would simply encourage more "Cuban-Soviet adventurism."

While the bulk of *Times* columns over the years have been "liberal" in orientation, many have been highly critical of Castro and many Cuban government policies.

Times *Editorials on Cuba*

Over the years *Times* editorials have sometimes been devoted to Cuban domestic matters, ranging from economic developments to selective blasts at Castro's suppression of human rights. The primary concern of *Times* editorial writers, however, has been U.S. relations with the Castro government.

Times editorials during the anti-Batista war tended to be critical of the Batista government and supportive of Castro, except when the latter kidnapped Americans. In early 1959 editorials were in general very friendly toward Castro, though disapproving of the summary executions. The *Times* reached a peak of praise and optimism on 25 April, after Castro's visit to the United States, when the paper concluded that Fidel was pro-Western, that neither he nor anyone in his government "was communist or in agreement with communism," and that both Castro and U.S. leaders should feel much better about living with each other. But things began to change in the months ahead. On 12 May the paper, noting communist praise of Castro, warned that if Castro "does not repudiate the embrace of the Communists he will be smothered by them."

The *Times* frequently praised U.S. policy toward Cuba during 1959 and 1960, and blamed the deterioration of diplomatic relations on Cuba (29 October 1959), though at times suggesting that Castro was sincere, if mistaken, in his belief that "the United States is trying to frustrate the Cuban Revolution or even to overthrow the Castro Government" (27 January 1960). The *Times* was upset by the departure from the Cuban government of Rufo López-Fresquet and Felipe Pazos, but with impeccable Herbert Matthews reasoning, concluded: "It can be argued that it was logical within the framework of the requirements of carrying out the Cuban revolution" (19 March 1960).

On 5 August 1960 the paper remarked on the departure of many obviously patriotic Cubans, noting that "in every case the break came over the issue of communism." On 28 August the *Times* stated that Cuban ties to the Soviet Union were potentially dangerous and "would provide a base to strengthen the communist and revolutionary forces in all the Latin American countries."

After two years of Castro, the *Times* (1 January 1961) concluded that "today we see a Cuba that is a complete dictatorship, without any freedoms, economically dependent on the Sino-Soviet bloc and heavily influenced by Communists internally."

When U.S.-Cuban relations collapsed in January 1961, the *Times* concluded that President Eisenhower "was given no other choice" than to break ties with Cuba. Castro provoked it, according to an editorial on 5 January: "Let it be clear that this was his [Castro's] decision and nobody else's."

After the Bay of Pigs, the paper concluded that "the Castro regime is now so firmly entrenched and so completely allied to the Soviet bloc that there is no possibility of overthrowing or displacing Castro, short of sending the American marines—which is unthinkable except in the most unlikely event of establishment of a Russian base there." This meant the United States was left with "the unpleasant necessity of finding it possible to live with a communist-type regime in Cuba so long as the latter does not try forcibly to spread its ideas" (21 June 1961).

Following the turbulent middle and late 1960s, when Cuban revolutionary activities in Latin America were at their highest level, the *Times* advocated a rapprochement between Cuba and the United States within the same basic framework as expressed in the June 1961 editorial. On the tenth anniversary of the Bay of Pigs, the *Times* (20 April 1971) played a theme that was to dominate its editorial pages thenceforward. Recognizing that Cuba "remains tightly under Fidel Castro's control [and is] economically viable only because of heavy Soviet subsidy," the paper concluded that "the passage of time has shown that Castro Cuba and the United States can coexist peacefully. . . . The time for reconciliation is now."

The *Times* formula was repeatedly stated in the years ahead: the process will take time; there should be no dramatic moves at first, just a "quiet passing of the word that the Administration will no longer bar Cuba's return to the inter-American system if and when Mr. Castro wishes to lessen his dependence on the Soviet Union" (29 January 1973).

On the twentieth anniversary of the Moncada attack (26 July 1973) the paper concluded that Castro's "mistakes have been costly to the Cuban people both in economic welfare and in personal freedom, while his policies have led Cuba into an even greater dependence on the Soviet Union than pre-Castro Cuba was on the United States."

By 11 January 1974 the *Times* no longer insisted on a lessening of dependence on the Soviet Union as a prerequisite to improved relations.

In mid-1975 the Ford administration went along with the OAS, as the *Times* had suggested in 1971, when it voted to abolish what the paper (31 July, 22 August 1975) called the "tottering system of political and economic sanctions" imposed against Cuba, to fulsome praise from the *Times* editors.

The *Times* continued to push for still closer relations, which came early in the term of President Carter, noting that "normal diplomatic relations should not in any case be confused with moral or even political approval" (31 March 1977). The *Times* praised the moves of the Ford and Carter administrations and found both likely and feasible within the framework of "a long period of Cuban-American détente and negotiation with increased travel and trade leading, ultimately, to normal diplomatic and economic relations" (19 August 1977).

Subsequent Cuban involvement in Africa, however, complicated matters. For a while the *Times* argued (23 November 1977) that the Cuban-Soviet relationship "is far more complex than the simple servant-master image" some critics proclaim. But when word came that Cuban pilots were flying air strikes in Ethiopia while Soviet pilots manned Cuban air defenses, the *Times* proclaimed (15 February 1978), "This news brands the Cubans the tools of Soviet imperial purposes . . . it turns the Cubans into the world's foremost intercontinental force of mercenaries"; and all this came just when Castro had gained a "grudging acceptance in the United States."

Still the *Times* pushed for closer relations, arguing (13 October 1979; 20 April 1982) that U.S. domestic politics prevented gradual normalization. Even if Cuba is "the source of inspiration of regional insurgency," the *Times* argued on 28 May 1983, "it makes no sense to mark it off limits to diplomacy."

As part of its call for easing tensions with Cuba, the *Times* opposed the formation of Radio Martí, which it branded (1 January 1983) as a "gimmicky proposal to wage air war against Fidel Castro." *Times* editorials argued that the mission set for Radio Martí was already being carried out by existing stations, namely the Voice of America and U.S. stations heard in Cuba. But diplomacy is not personal grandstanding, the *Times* asserted after the Reverend Jesse Jackson's visit to Cuba in January 1984. That visit was "political opportunism in reckless disregard for American diplomacy," according to a *Times* editorial, which concluded by quoting one of the Cuban prisoners released during Jackson's visit—poet and diplomat Andrés Vargas Gómez: "To go to Cuba to join in a moral offensive with Fidel Castro is more than morally offensive, it is a moral offense."

Cuba on the Op-ed Page

The Op-ed Editor Looks at His Page

Between early 1971 and late 1984, the *Times* published nearly three dozen op-ed pieces devoted in large part or entirely to Cuba. The objective of the op-ed page according to its founder, Harrison Salisbury, was "to publish views and opinions that are different from those on the editorial page and in editorial staff columns." In a telephone interview on 5 November 1984, Salisbury added that though most op-ed pieces were intended to be "contrary, oblique opinions," some "may be the same as and reinforce opinion in the paper." The current editor of the page, Robert Semple, said that he sees as the objective of the page "to provide a window on the opinions of the outside world, from as broad a perspective as possible. And not incidentally," he added in a telephone interview on 17 October 1984, "it is intended to be educational. We hope it will be provocative enough to make people think." (The third op-ed editor, during the middle years, was Charlotte Curtis.)

How are the op-ed pieces selected? Thousands come "over the transom," which is to say unsolicited, both Salisbury and Semple affirmed. "I am issue-oriented," Semple continued, "and there is no shortage of highly-qualified people who come to me prepared to comment." But Salisbury added, "If we get a bright idea we might go out and get someone." The editor may commission a piece from a specialist known to the *Times* or request a piece on a topic following an outside recommendation or after a letter to the paper has caught the op-ed editor's attention. Semple estimated that between 30 and 40 percent of the op-ed articles as a whole published in the *Times* in recent years have been commissioned. The *Times* receives some 25,000 manuscripts annually, he added, of which about 1,000 are printed. What relationship is there between the op-ed page and the editorial page? "Zero," according to Semple.

Salisbury does not recall paying any particular attention to Cuba during his tenure. "We haven't had many recently on Cuba," Semple concluded. "What we have had has been of the Wayne Smith sort, commentaries on U.S. policy." He added that most people in this country who are interested in Cuba want to write on U.S.-Cuban relations. Cubans in Cuba are not free to write candidly, he concluded, and most visitors who go to the island are subjected to formal guided tours.

Op-ed Themes Between 1971 and 1984

Op-ed pieces on Cuba have fallen into three main categories: (1) a few on Cuban domestic conditions, mostly by Cuban exiles or visitors to the island; (2) a few primarily or partly on Cubans in exile, by exiles and those responsible for dealing with them in the United States; and (3) the vast majority on U.S.-Cuban relations, with ties into U.S.-Cuban/Soviet and general hemispheric relations as well. Within the third category two main themes stand out—that since at least 1974 there have been "signals" from Castro that he wants to improve relations and that it is "time for a change" in U.S. policy toward Cuba.

By year, a breakdown by subject of the op-ed articles dealing with Cuba turns up the following: 1971 (2 op-ed pieces; 1 mainly on foreign affairs, 1 mainly on domestic affairs); 1972 (1; 1 and 0); 1973 (none); 1974 (4; 4 and 0); 1975 (1; 0 and 1); 1976 (1; 1 and 0); 1977 (4; 3 and 1); 1978 (none); 1979 (4; 2 and 1, with one by/on Cuban exiles); 1980 (4; 1 and 1, with two by/on exiles); 1981 (4; 3 and 1); 1982 (5; 5 and 0); 1983 (2; 2 and 0); 1984 (2; 2 and 0). Totals: 34 op-ed pieces, 25 mainly on foreign affairs, 6 mainly on Cuban domestic affairs, and 3 by/on Cuban exiles.

Op-ed Articles on Cuban Domestic Conditions

Six pieces have dealt primarily with aspects of life in Cuba; two by Cubans, one of whom is a well-known New York professor, all highly critical of political repression in Cuba; three by non-Cubans, two of whom were travelers and one a Marxist-Leninist newspaper editor, all largely to entirely positive in their evaluations of conditions on the Caribbean island. One other piece written by a U.S. Latin American specialist was sharply critical of Cuban human rights policies.

The first op-ed piece was by Cuba's best-known political prisoner, Huber Matos, a leader of the anti-Batista revolution. Matos served nine months in 1959 under Castro as military governor of Camagüey Province. He resigned in October because of increasing communist influence in the government and was imprisoned for twenty years on Castro's personal order. Matos's article (12 November 1975) was in fact excerpts from a letter (dated 20 March 1975) that had been smuggled out of prison to his family in the United States. It is a crushing indictment of Castro's inhumanity, pointing out how the Cuban leader imprisons his political enemies and then smears their reputations among the Cuban people.

In a short op-ed piece Professor Irving Howe (22 June 1977) urged the U.S. government to try to get the Cuban government to release

Matos, noting that Castro led "a military attack" against the Batista government—which resulted in many deaths, though Howe does not mention this fact—but served only twenty months in prison. Matos was being required to serve a full twenty years for expressing his political convictions. The prominent use of the word *mercy* in the article is unfortunate, for that word means compassion (by Castro) to an offender (Matos) who has no claim to kindness or forgiveness. This actually is the whole hideous matter stood on its head, as the bulk of Howe's article made clear.

Roger Fontaine's "Dealing with Fidel" (28 June 1977) also dwells in part on the "20,000 political prisoners in Cuban jails making Cuba, on a prisoner-per-thousand population basis, one of the world's leading police states."

Cuban poet Heberto Padilla, who also had experienced political repression in several ways, wrote a more broadly based critique. (The Cuban government had refused to allow Padilla to accept a literary prize awarded him in 1968 by a specially invited panel of foreign intellectuals serving as judges in a Cuban Writers' Union [UNEAC] competition. The poet was imprisoned in March 1971 and released, more than a month later, only after he had signed a "confession" of his "counterrevolutionary" attitudes and activities.) After being exiled from Cuba in 1980, Padilla wrote an op-ed piece (17 September 1981) that scored repression under Castro's rule specifically and went on to indict more generally the nineteenth-century utopian "thinkers" whose modern socialist successors brought us the forced labor camps of the communist world. He concluded by lamenting that people who live in freedom often have little concept of oppression abroad or appreciation of the freedom they take for granted at home.

Two impressionistic, chit-chat articles round out the op-ed pieces that focus on domestic matters. James Higgins, identified as a former editor of *Gazette* in York, Pennsylvania, wrote the first, entitled "Welcome to Cuba—Yanqui" (12 March 1971), an adulatory little tract that grinds away in a chatty fashion at some old saws—e.g. that Cubans don't dislike the American people but rather their government, and that sexual equality has been achieved in the new Cuba.

The second impressionistic article is "Snapshots from Cuba" (1 September 1979) by Mark Scheinbaum, identified as a writer and teacher on Cuban affairs who lives in Key West, Florida. This writer is almost as supportive of the situation in Cuba, noting in his verbal "snapshots" that children have educational opportunities, adults have parks and many benefits beyond people in the United States, as in health and child-care facilities, and that revolution has become part of the nation's routine. He also quotes two seventeen-year-old boys as saying they have been taught all the things "the Yankees have done to try to destroy our country," but they have talked with enough North Americans to conclude "that we mostly have things in common; maybe more than with other countries."

Robert Dobrow, managing editor of *Workers' World,* wrote "Cuba's Problems" (4 June 1980) to proclaim that everything that has gone wrong in Cuba—much is going very well indeed, he says—is because of the policies of United States imperialism. In a little tract devoted mainly to foreign policy (3 August 1971), Higgins returns with more comments on domestic developments, including the assertion that the United States is responsible for the failure of the 1970 sugar harvest.

Op-ed Articles by and about Refugees

Four articles by and/or about refugees were published between mid-1979 and mid-1981, a period during which there were refugee visits back to Cuba and the Mariel exodus. In "Back, but Not Home" (13 July 1979) María Muñiz, editor of *Catalyst,* tried to explain how it feels to have lived one's life in exile with no intention of returning permanently to Cuba but living with the gnawing feeling that part of one's life is back in one's homeland waiting to be recovered.

Jorge Fierro of Union City wrote "For the Comunidad, the Visit Is a Sad Show-and-Tell" (20 January 1980) to apprise the public at large of differences within the Cuban exile community and to dispel any misconception that all Cubans support terrorism and violence. Also, he stresses the desirability of pluralistic, nonauthoritarian means for achieving development and change.

In "Miami's Explosion Isn't Miami's Alone," Florida International University professor Marvin Dunn calls for legal reforms to handle racial problems that arise in communities around the country. The only refugee article, by Heberto Padilla, has been reviewed above.

Op-ed Articles on U.S.-Cuban Relations

Most op-ed commentaries in the *Times* over the nearly fifteen years the page has been in existence have dealt directly or indirectly with U.S.-Cuban relations, and sometimes with broader U.S.-Cuban/Soviet or other hemispheric relations. All have urged U.S. policymakers to reconsider portions or all aspects of U.S. policy toward Castro's government. A few have been openly critical of Castro and his probable receptiveness to constructive change. Many authors have charged that Cuba has repeatedly flashed "signals" indicating Castro's inclination to improve relations with Washington, which they argue most U.S.

administrations have either ignored or mishandled. Op-ed critiques of U.S. policies sometimes come in broad, generalized terms or focus on specific activities, such as those of the Central Intelligence Agency. Many have urged changes on the grounds that the thrust of U.S. policy during Castro's twenty-five years in power has been counterproductive, forcing Cuba into the Soviet camp and sacrificing U.S. relations with other governments in the hemisphere.

On 19 April 1971 Castro said the United States was "almost longing for a gesture from Cuba" that would make improved relations possible, but that no such gesture would be forthcoming, only unconditional demands and intransigent attitudes, as I reported in "Cuba and Hijacking and You" (30 December 1972). The next piece on Cuba, Ben Meyer's "A Signal, Perhaps, from Havana" (13 February 1974), was the first commentary charging that Castro has made gestures after all, but that the United States has rejected them.

This line did not reach a fever pitch until Reagan administration policies inspired a series of pieces on this theme: Tufts University professor Peter Winn's "Don't Say No to Havana" (8 July 1982); former interest section chief Wayne Smith's "It Is Not Impossible to Deal with Castro: Realism Is Required" (5 September 1982); and Smith's "Reagan's Risky Cuban Policy" (1 October 1984). On 29 July 1984, the *New York Times Magazine* published a much longer article by Smith—who by late 1984 seemed to have become a regular nonstaff commentator on U.S.-Cuban relations—entitled "Cuba: Time for a Thaw."

Every article that touched on U.S.-Cuban relations suggested some form of change. A few argued that the United States was not meeting the revolutionary challenge posed by Cuba and the Soviet Union; a few were essentially sympathetic to Washington's policy; but more were, in varying degrees, hostile.

The most important articles that warned that the United States was not responding to Cuba-Soviet probing and challenges came during the Ford and Carter administrations when, on the surface, bilateral relations were improving. Among the first of these articles was "U.S. Policy and Soviet Subs" (22 October 1974), by Brookings Institution staff members Barry Blechman and Stephanie Levinson. This piece argued that the Soviet Union had been "gradually but deliberately encroaching upon" the U.S.-Soviet arms agreements and that the failure of the United States to respond could "bring into question [U.S.] credibility in world affairs."

Ernest Lefever argued in "The Paralysis of Power" (18 January 1976) that the U.S. failure to respond to the Soviet-Cuban military intervention in Angola suggested that the United States was unable or unwilling to support the self-determination that was being challenged by elite dictatorship and coercion.

Roger Fontaine's "Dealing with Cuba" (28 June 1977) came during Carter's opening to Cuba, and warned that "mindless moralizing about human rights" is not a productive policy. Fontaine wrote, "My purpose is not to question the wisdom of talking to Fidel Castro, but to suggest how we should go about it." He then offered a step-by-step agenda for combining human rights and other issues in an integrated negotiating program.

An op-ed piece I wrote was among the few that were more skeptical of Castro than of U.S. policymakers (30 December 1972). It called upon the United States to go along with the majority of American states on the maintenance or lifting or sanctions while reassuring our allies who still feared Cuban intervention in their domestic affairs. I said that we should be willing to talk to Castro if he showed interest but that we should not rush into new relations until he became more open and less contemptuous of U.S. interests.

"Test Castro to Learn If He Would Negotiate" (1 August 1983), by Joseph Sisco, a former under secretary of state, argued that "the heart of the problem is Fidel Castro's unwillingness to keep his hands off other countries." Sisco doubted Castro's sincerity in wanting to improve relations, but argued that the United States should test his commitment, "if for no other reason than that it will strengthen the United States standing in the Western Hemisphere."

Among the articles adopting something of a middle ground was "The Rightist brigade" (16 September 1979) by former State Department officer Leslie Gelb. Gelb reacted to the furor about the "Soviet brigade" in Cuba by warning against the extremes in politics—the "scared and ambitious" politicians, the rightists with their anti-Soviet "holy war," and the naive left-wingers who think we can respond to growing Soviet military strength with "business-as-usual." President Carter must formulate a coherent policy that Moscow will find compelling and the American people will understand, counseled Gelb.

Harvard professor Jorge Domínguez anticipated a deterioration of relations between Cuba and the United States after Reagan's inauguration, and in "On U.S.-Cuban Ties" (26 February 1981) said the two sides should continue to work on their common interests.

Among the more critical pieces were James Higgins's "A Little Red Book" (3 August 1971), which blasted a 1964 speech by Under Secretary of State George Ball that, Higgins was told, still represented U.S. policy toward Cuba. Ball sought to clear his name with "Your Evil

Embargo: Our Purity of Purpose" (21 March 1974), a defense of isolating Cuba while Castro was trying to "spread the Communist gospel by force and subversion" during the mid-1960s. Now that Castro's policies have changed, he wrote, economic sanctions have become counterproductive.

Brazilian journalist Henry Raymont argued in "Washington's Futile Policy Toward Havana" (29 April 1974) that the U.S. "obsession with the Castro regime" has thwarted U.S. business in the area and alienated potential Latin American allies. Abraham Lowenthal of the Woodrow Wilson International Center for Scholars called for an end to the total embargo of Cuba in "It's Time to Talk Turkey with Cuba" (13 July 1977). Washington holds the "trump cards," he concluded, and should have "nothing to fear from negotiating."

The volume of criticism increased in late 1980, after the election and inauguration of President Reagan. Most contributors between then and late 1984 either did not accept the Reagan administration's arguments that Cuba posed a serious strategic challenge to the United States or believed that such threat as there was could best be met by a more conciliatory policy.

Most of the articles maintained that substantive change is necessary, many bringing in the argument that the U.S. policy of hostility toward Castro simply keeps him in the Soviet camp. I had emphasized the critical nature of the Soviet-Cuban relationship back in December 1972, but Ben Meyer in February 1974 was the first to argue that U.S. policy "patently forces Havana to remain under Moscow's domination and gives the Soviet Union a splendid geographical base for military, economic, political and subversive activity in this hemisphere."

Just as the Carter administration was beginning to be concerned about Cuban involvement in Nicaragua and Nicaraguan support for guerrillas in El Salvador, issues that became even more intense for the incoming Reagan administration, Carla Anne Robbins of American University and Pamela Falk of the Center for Inter-American Relations argued in "Avoiding a Hard Line on the Cubans" (16 December 1980) that "Cuba is no longer interested in exporting revolution to the region" and urged the new administration to compete with rather than confront Cuba.

William LeoGrande, also of American University, wrote in "Getting Cuba" (17 November 1981) that the Reagan administration should not be tempted to "go to the source" because "military options available for use against Cuba are severely limited" and are either unacceptable or not productive.

Op-ed articles calling for a modification of U.S. policy continued with "Warm Up to Cuba" (4 March 1982) by Saul Landau of the Institute for Policy Studies. Landau argued that the U.S. "obsession with the East-West conflict" actually "lies at the heart of the United States' bad relations with Cuba." The "vituperative and vindictive" policy of the U.S. has only strengthened the Cuban government and its ties to the Soviet Union and thus should be abandoned.

Ellen James of the *Baltimore Evening Sun* (7 April 1982) suggested that Soviet aid to Cuba may be decreasing and thus the time is right for the United States to move closer to Castro. Peter Winn of Tufts University wrote in "Don't Say No to Havana" (8 July 1982) that though Castro will not "surrender his revolutionary vocation or sunder his Soviet ties, he seems willing to compromise his goals in the interests of regional peace and Cuban autonomy." The United States, he continued, is "tightening the screws in response to Cuban concilia-tion" and thus forcing Havana to "move even closer to Moscow."

In the fall of 1982 the journal *Foreign Policy* published "Dateline Havana: Myopic Diplomacy" by Wayne Smith, chief of the U.S. Interests Section in Havana from 1979 to 1982. The article, excerpted in the *Times* under the title "It Is Not Impossible to Deal with Castro: Realism Is Required" (5 September 1982), charged that the United States has "rebuffed Cuban overtures." The U.S. should follow the same "cautious yet realistic" approach adopted toward the Soviet Union, said Smith, and with clear, realistic objectives, such as reduc-ing Soviet influence in Cuba, move toward these objectives by "grad-ual engagement" with Castro's government.

Lawyer Jean Zorn criticized travel restrictions imposed on U.S. citizens in "Bad Tack on Cuba" (26 February 1983). After Sisco's less sanguine call for negotiations (9 August 1983), the *Times* published McGeorge Bundy's "To Kissinger Commission: History Warns Against Threats to Invade Nicaragua" (6 January 1984). The most recent op-ed piece on Cuba was another by Smith, "Reagan's Risky Cuban Policy" (1 October 1984), which suggested that the Reagan administration's disregard for the 1962 and 1970 U.S. military agree-ments with the Soviet Union implied that the administration may be considering an invasion of Cuba.

In a subcategory on U.S.-Cuban relations are those articles devoted to the Central Intelligence Agency. The first, by John Marks, called "The C.I.A., Cuba and Terrorism" (28 June 1977), charged that "for the last 35 years our Government has made regular use of terrorism as an instrument of foreign policy." He concluded that the U.S. govern-ment seemed to have stopped promoting terrorism but still needed to crack down on anti-Casto Cubans trained by the CIA whose "violent actions have seriously interfered with the current policy of better relations with Cuba."

In "Torture's Teachers" (11 June 1979) A.J. Langguth wrote that "in our hearts we cannot believe that Americans have gone abroad to spread the use of torture," but he has seen testimony that Daniel Mitrione did just that in Uruguay. Langguth "wants to believe" that no American who taught or condoned torture is still with U.S. intelligence agencies. Lawyer Floyd Abrams, in "Naming Covert Agents" (11 June 1982), argued that a new law making it illegal to name covert agents has been correctly described as "the clearest violation of the First Amendment attempted by Congress in this era."

Conclusions

On balance the op-ed pieces on Cuba do inform readers on certain critical issues and at times force them to consider or reconsider problems that would be more easily ignored. Occasionally, they have focused on the oppressive nature of the Cuban government by giving space to such Cubans as Huber Matos and Heberto Padilla. Far more often they have directed the reader's attention to U.S. policy toward the Cuban government and the relationship of Cuban-U.S. ties to Cuba's international alliances and commitments around the hemisphere and the world.

But there have been problems with op-ed coverage.

1. The educational function of the op-ed pieces has been hampered by the nature of the news business in the United States. Thus op-ed pieces do not fill an ongoing educational role because they are crisis-oriented. It is, of course, particularly important to help readers understand issues during moments of tension, and indeed many readers, even of the *Times,* would skip over an article that was not related to a critical issue of the day. But as a result, the effort to educate is dictated less by rational consideration of basic issues than by the flow of events, which sometimes does not draw out commentaries that confront basic issues.

2. Although it seems admirable to aim at as broad a representation of views as possible, that is a better thereotical than practical goal. There simply is not enough space to do it with any consistency. Given this constraint, many opinions do not warrant the wide exposure of this forum, at least when the publication of marginal pieces means the rejection of more substantial, if perhaps less "oblique," articles. For example, many Americans, some of them very well informed on Latin American affairs, support the essential thrust of current U.S. policy

toward the Caribbean Basin. But the articles of these individuals, who have substantial national support, are very seldom found on the op-ed page of the *Times,* though pieces presenting their views are submitted for consideration. It is no good to argue that such positions are put forward often enough by the government, for surely those who happen to see things more or less the same as the government does should not for that reason lose their opportunity to speak to the public on the op-ed page of the *Times* or any other paper. Nor is the literary quality of some of their submissions markedly inferior to many the paper uses.

On the other hand, what we might loosely term "liberal" criticism of U.S. policy abroad abounds, criticism that tends to parallel positions taken by editorials in the *Times.* Indeed, one sometimes feels that op-ed pieces are intended more to lecture government leaders than to enlighten readers, though the two objectives are not mutually exclusive. There is no reason to attribute this to an anti-administration conspiracy at the *Times,* nor to one part of the paper's dictating policy to another. Rather, it is probable that most *Times* editors tend to agree much of the time on which issues are "hot" and to believe that certain issues—e.g. that the United States is ignoring "signals" from Cuba—most need to be prominently expressed. In any event, these positions are vastly overrepresented, particularly in view of the stated objectives of the page.

3. Why are some pieces not worth the space they take? Because they do not contribute sufficiently to the discussion of issues to justify displacing more serious commentaries. For example, while anecdotal commentaries sometimes can be enlightening, several carried on the op-ed page—say, Higgins's "Welcome to Cuba—Yanqui"—have not been so. With all the serious issues needing consideration, why should *Times* readers care about the relative trivia in Higgins's piece, much less that he ogles beautiful Cuban women? Or, if the *Times* wants a statement of the Cuban position vis-à-vis the United States, why not get one from Havana rather than from Dubrow, the editor of a line-toeing Marxist-Leninist paper in the United States that has no significant U.S. constituency.

4. The reliability of other articles is open to serious question. Dobrow's "Cuba's Problems" is packed with nonsense, as most *Times* editors would be among the first to acknowledge. Or consider *Torture's Teachers* in which Lagguth quotes a former double agent at great length to "prove" his argument that the United States promoted the use of torture in Latin America. But it is not immediately obvious why we should believe "a former double agent, a Cuban named Manuel, who was said to have information" on U.S. intelligence activities. Why

should we believe this double agent who is "said to have information"? The author admits, though it does not seem to bother either him or the *Times* editors, that he could not even meet to cross-examine the former double agent since he was "out of the country the entire time I was in Cuba." One is tempted to marvel at how wonderfully convenient it was for Cuba that Manuel was not around to be cross-examined and that Lagguth was so uncritically receptive of the information from a book whose source is clearly questionable.

Other commentaries focus on points that are either demonstrably false or extremely unlikely, while arguments to the contrary are not published. In Higgins's "Little Red Book" in 1971 and Dobrow's "Cuba's Problems" in 1980 we are told that the United States was responsible for the failure of the 1970 sugar harvest. Even the Cubans do not try to claim that; on 26 July 1970 Castro admitted the disastrous harvest and collapse of the economy were due to failures of the Cuban leaders. Then just as the Carter administration was finally becoming concerned over Cuban involvement in Central America, Robbins and Falk wrote (December 1980) that Cuba "is no longer interested in exporting revolution to the region." And just as Soviet assistance to Cuba increased in the early 1980s, Ellen James wrote (April 1982) that Soviet aid evidently was being cut back. Or take Peter Winn's suggestion in "Don't Say No to Havana" (8 July 1982) that U.S. economic pressures on Cuba in the 1960s were a major cause of Castro's active support for guerrilla movements during those years. Perhaps something was lost in the editing, but as it stands this is almost as far off the mark as Dubrow, and seems to reflect a fundamental misunderstanding of the Cuban leader's commitment to revolution.

In summary, Herbert Matthews generated a storm of criticism with his sometimes ill-informed and biased reporting and commentary on what he termed "Fidel Castro's Revolution." Not all reporting, commentary, and editorials in the *Times* have been similarly slanted, however, though the basically liberal editorial staff of the paper is at odds with most Cuban-Americans and a substantial percentage of the American people. The op-ed contributions since that page was set up almost fifteen years ago have ranged from thought provoking and educational, which is what they should be, to trivial, petty, and ideological, these latter playing games with commentary, information, and disinformation. "Liberal" critiques of U.S. policy toward Cuba—which largely parallel *Times* editorials—have far outweighed all other commentaries. Op-ed pieces on Cuba in the *Times* in recent years generally lecture the Reagan administration on its alleged failure to respond to what certain commentators consider conciliatory signals from Cuba. When it comes to covering Cuba, there is too little effort to present a variety of information and views to educate and stimulate *Times* readers as a whole.

Appendix I. Methodological Note

Although I have read the *New York Times* for most of the twenty-eight years covered in this report, and was one of the first contributors on Cuba to the op-ed page, I did not have most of the op-ed articles on Cuba in my files. I asked a member of the indexing department at the *Times* if it had listings of op-ed pieces, and was advised that it does not, that the only way to find these articles is to read all of the papers for the years in question or consult the index. All op-ed articles, I was told, would be listed under the heading "Cuba" in the extensive annual index. I found, however, that most of the pieces were not identified as "op-ed," but were mixed in the (sometimes) dozens of pages of news reports and other items, and often were very difficult to distinguish in the index listing from those other contributions. What is more, I discovered that not all op-ed articles dealing to a major extent or entirely with Cuba were listed in the index under "Cuba," for example, "The Paralysis of Power" (18 January 1976) by Ernest Lefever and "Getting Cuba" (17 November 1981) by William LeoGrande. I found "missing" articles from citations in indexed letters and references in other articles. Thus I cannot guarantee that I have found all of the op-ed pieces in question, though I believe the patterns that have emerged are representative of coverage as a whole. I interviewed the founder and first editor of the op-ed page, Harrison Salisbury, by phone on 5 November 1984, and the present op-ed editor, Robert Semple, by phone on 17 October 1984.

Appendix II. Summaries of Articles

1. James Higgins, "Welcome to Cuba—Yanqui," *NYT,* 12 March 1971. (Author identified as former editor of *Gazette* in York, Pennsylvania, and a student of the Cuban Revolution.)

Attended 7th Congress of International Organization of Journalists at Habana Libre (former Hilton) Hotel. While waiting for the meeting to start, an unnamed director of the Cuban Film Institute told him that Cubans do not disagree with the American people, but with their government, and explained that women now have equal rights in Cuba. The director and Higgins both foresaw a revival of "faithful romantic love" and Higgins found himself studying the "incredibly attractive young Cuban women" "even more keenly than before."

2. James Higgins, "A Little Red Book," *NYT,* 3 August 1971. (Author identified as a former editor of the *New York Gazette and Daily* of York, Pennsylvania, and a student of the Cuban revolution.)

Critique of State Department's booklet "U.S. Policy Toward Cuba," a 1964 speech by Under Secretary George W. Ball. Cites comments at IOJ conference by Paul Roa and reporter for Juventud Rebelde, paper of the Cuban Union of Young Communists. Reporter said U.S. attacks on Cuban "areas of vulnerability" "had been primarily responsible for the sugar defeat." What is the moral basis of U.S. policy? Who is United States to tell Cubans what government to have? And who are the real economic determinists? Remember that almost half the Cuban population are under sixteen; their condition and spirit are the "human indicators of the future." Are Americans too blind to discard the notions of that policy statement?

3. William Ratliff, "Cuba and Hijacking and You," *NYT,* 30 December 1972. (Author identified as research associate at Stanford University.)

Article on anti-hijacking talks maintains press coverage has been extensive but superficial, leading to uncritical enthusiasm for anticipated pact and overly optimistic speculation on the easing of tensions between the United States and Cuba in the near future. The two sides have not been moving toward each but, rather, the United States has been moving toward the Cuban proposal of 1969. Problem of U.S.-Cuban relations is actually one of U.S.-Cuban/Soviet relations, though Castro himself remains the main obstacle to improved ties. The United States should go along with the majority opinion in the Organization of American States (OAS) and be prepared to talk to Cuba, but not adopt a new relationship until Castro becomes less contemptuous of U.S. interests.

4. Ben F. Meyer, "A Signal, Perhaps, from Havana," *NYT,* 13 February 1974. (Author identified as retired AP correspondent who has written about Latin America for thirty years.)

The United States may have missed a signal from Havana, and not for the first time, that Cuba is ready to negotiate better relations. Cuban ambassador to Mexico said, "We would be willing to talk to the

United States," though foreign minister Roa "indicated no enthusiasm for the idea." Support for subversion has diminished. The ideal development for United States would be for Latin American countries to get their act together, but they are split over Cuba. We should have closer relations; at present our policy "patently forces Havana to remain under Moscow's domination and gives the Soviet Union a splendid geographical base . . . in this hemisphere."

5. George W. Ball, "Your Evil Embargo: Our Purity of Purpose," *NYT*, 21 March 1974. (Author identified as investment banker, was under secretary of state in Kennedy and Johnson administrations.)

U.S. embargo of Cuba made sense as effort to isolate Cuba and stop "spread of Communist gospel by force and subversion." It does not make sense any more, except to make us feel virtuous; it is hurting our prestige with Latin American countries, particularly Argentina and Canada. We should end the embargo and reopen trade with Cuba.

6. Henry Raymont, "Washington's Futile Policy Toward Havana," *NYT*, 29 April 1974. (Author identified as writer for Rio de Janeiro paper *Jornal do Brasil*.)

None of the Nixon administration's "professed foreign policy assumptions—a lower profile and a world of ideological pluralism, consensus and reduction of differences with former adversaries—seem to apply when it comes to Cuba." The trade embargo is "obsolescent," has been challenged by corporations and even has provoked Argentina, which "had little interest or inclination to espouse the Cuban cause . . . into militant advocacy of Mr. Castro's reintegration into the Latin American family." The policy of isolation is futile, though as in the past Washington readily sacrifices its relations with all South America because of an obsession with the Castro regime.

7. Barry Blechman and Stephanie Levinson, "U.S. Policy and Soviet Subs," *NYT*, 22 October 1974. (Authors identified as staff members of the foreign policy studies program at the Brookings Institution.)

In 1962 the Soviet Union agreed it would "no longer deploy strategic offensive weapons in Cuba." In 1970 it constructed a facility for servicing submarines at Cienfuegos, and a secret agreement was reached with the United States; in 1971 President Nixon said, "In the event that nuclear subs were serviced in either Cuba or from Cuba, that would be a violation of the understanding." Since 1971 the Soviet Union has sent in submarines ranging from a nuclear-powered tactical missile submarine to a diesel-powered strategic missile submarine. "The Soviet Union is gradually but deliberately encroaching upon the agreement" as a "test of United States willingness to take risks in its broad relations with the SU." The lack of U.S. response is "essentially an endorsement of the Russians' conduct" and U.S. "reluctance to insist on compliance with the accord could help bring into question its credibility in world affairs." "Only by demonstrating a willingness to make issues of single events that in isolation appear relatively insignificant can the United States cause the Soviet Union to understand that normalizing our relations requires mutual concessions."

8. Huber Matos, "Letter from a Havana Prison," *NYT,* 17 November 1975. (Author identified as a leader of the anti-Batista revolution and former military chief of Camagüey Province.)

Deprivations of prison lessen happiness but do not impoverish the spirit. Those of us in prison here are certain it is for life. National and international developments do not seem to affect our lives. What pains me more than imprisonment "is to be labeled and treated as an enemy of the People, knowing as I do that I am part of the People, and that their cause is my cause." "If the spiritual state is holding up, I cannot say the same for my physical state."

9. Ernest Lefever, "The Paralysis of Power," *NYT,* 18 January 1976. (Author identified as senior fellow, Brookings Institution.)

While Washington is suffering from "creeping policy paralysis induced by breast-beating on Capitol Hill and in the media," Soviet colonialism is in motion. The Soviet Union has undertaken a "far larger and more brazen" intervention in Africa than ever before; the one in Angola, with the help of a "political mercenary force of 7,500 heavily armed Cubans." (Mercenaries because the Soviet Union is "subsidizing the Castro regime to the tune of about $2 million a day.") And Angola is just part of an ongoing Soviet plan. "Cuban intelligence agents and military men have been used to train, lead or otherwise support terrorist groups in a dozen countries." Congress refuses to support the more moderate Angolans, partly because the president has not made clear what is at stake in Angola: "A testing ground between two radically different ways of organizing society—one emphasizing self-determination and consent and the other elite dictatorship and coercion." The United States is not the world policeman, but "we have a responsibility, commensurate with our power and consistent with our interests, to resist the forcible imposition of totalitarian power." Angola is a test case for détente; the United States must tell Moscow to withdraw its Cuban forces or else we stop shipments of grain and break off strategic arms limitation talks. The "illusion of American omnipotence is giving way to an even more dangerous malady—the paralysis of power."

10. Irving Howe, "Mercy," *NYT*, 22 June 1977. (Author identified as professor of English at Graduate School of City University of New York.)

Matos was sentenced to twenty years in prison in 1959 because he quietly differed with the growing influence of communism in the Cuban revolution and submitted his resignation from government office. So far he has served more than seventeen years. By way of contrast, Castro led a military uprising against the Batista government but was sentenced to only fifteen years and was released after less than two. Even if you leave justice and human rights aside, Matos should be released out of mercy.

11. John Marks, "The C.I.A., Cuba and Terrorism," *NYT*, 28 June 1977. (Author identified as associate of Center for National Security Studies.)

The U.S. government has placed a high priority on stopping international terrorism, but for the past thirty-five years has regularly used terrorism as an instrument of foreign policy. "At present terrorism seems to have been eliminated from America's bag of dirty tricks," though anti-Castro Cubans trained by the CIA continue to operate and "their violent actions have seriously interfered with the current policy of better relations with Cuba." The United States must now "turn the full force of the Government against these Cubans."

12. Roger Fontaine, "Dealing with Fidel," *NYT*, 28 June 1977. (Author identified as director of Latin American studies at Center for Strategic and International Studies, Georgetown University.)

Negotiating with Cuba has begun. It is now "vital to know precisely what we want and how we plan to get it." The Carter administration's "mindless moralizing about human rights" is likely to "worsen the lot of the Cuban people." Generally agreed there are about 20,000 political prisoners in Cuba. First we must get precise information on prisoners, have prisoners visited by neutral parties, and get freedom for long-time prisoners like Matos. Castro is not likely to go along with these demands, so we must have leverage, "employ linkage diplomacy by making a direct trade-off between human rights and business." The United States should agree to lift the embargo by stages in exchange for meeting our human rights demands. Next step, begin a second round of negotiations linking trade and human rights. But special trade preferences only after Cuba passes additional tests: trade in good standing; join IMF; not be dominated or controlled by international communism; provide prompt, adequate, and effective compensation for expropriated property of Americans.

13. Abraham Lowenthal, "It's Time to Talk Turkey with Cuba," *NYT,* 13 July 1977. (Author identified as head of Latin American program at Woodrow Wilson International Center for Scholars.)

The Carter administration is substituting a stance toward U.S.-Cuban relations that is "both right in principle and sound in practice for one that was self-defeating." Both countries will gain politically and economically. The United States should "bargain hard on specific issues," and "skillful negotiations by American diplomats should produce a favorable balance in the process of compromise." Each country must accept the other as "a sovereign equal with a legitimate right to differ." Each should drop its hostility toward the other. The decision to drop the embargo "would clearly signal the end of an era."

14. A. J. Langguth, "Torture's Teachers," *NYT,* 11 June 1979. (Author identified as author of *Hidden Terrors,* a book about the CIA in Latin America.)

People in the United States cannot believe that "Americans have gone abroad to spread the use of torture." But they have. The author tried to contact Cuban double agent, Manuel Havia Cosculluela, who "was said to have information about United States involvement with torture in Latin America." Manuel was "out of the country the entire time I was in Cuba," Langguth reports, but the government gave visitors a copy of Manuel's book on the subject. The book contains an account of a talk with U.S. adviser Dan Mitrione—which Langguth believes is accurate—who was executed by the Tupamaros in Uruguay, in which Mitrione allegedly told Manuel all about the virtues and tactics of torture. The U.S. police advisory program has since been abolished but "few of the accomplices in torture have ever been brought to account." The Carter administration has no ties to that past and should investigate, weed out, and punish those who have engaged in torture.

15. María L. Muñiz, "Back, but Not Home," *NYT*, 13 July 1979. (Author identified as editor of *Catalyst*.)

Autobiographical piece by a woman who came to the United States from Cuba with her parents at the age of five. She is a U.S. citizen and most of her friends are Americans. Memories stand in the way of her viewing the Cuban revolution "with detachment or objectivity," and she has no intention of moving back to Cuba. Still, she says she is "outside American, inside Cuban," and her life will remain somehow incomplete until she can talk to her family members who are still in Cuba. Politics has become less important to her over the years as she increasingly feels the need to preserve and renew her cultural heritage.

16. Mark Scheinbaum, "Snapshots," *NYT*, 1 September 1979. (Author identified as a writer and political scientist who lives in Key West, has taught Cuban and Caribbean politics at Florida State University, and written two books on Cuba and Cubans.)

A first-time visitor to Cuba talks with two seventeen-year-old Cubans who like the music they hear on Miami radio stations and feel they may have more in common with North Americans than other nationalities. But, when told problems U.S. parents have paying for child and health care, they affirm they are very fortunate to have many of the benefits they do have. Author comments on educational and recreational opportunities, on Cuban enthusiasm for Nicaraguan revolution, and Cuban incredulity that the United States would admit Somoza, even though it encouraged him to leave Nicaragua.

17. Leslie H. Gelb, "The Rightists' Brigade," *NYT*, 16 September 1979. (Author identified as senior associate of Carnegie Endowment for International Peace and former director of Bureau of Politico-Military Affairs in the State Department.)

On the Soviet brigade in Cuba: "Before the facts could be established, a number of scared and ambitious political leaders, legislation and a few Administration policy makers went off like firecrackers." Also because of the near hysteria about the Soviet Union's military capability and international designs. Right-wingers are right that we need increased defense spending in order to maintain the military balance, but they went farther and declared a "holy war," so that moderates are afraid to say that though Soviet power presents us new and serious problems, the Soviet Union has problems too. To point out Soviet problems would make them seem apologists for Moscow. But beyond this, Carter "has no overall policy for dealing with the now more-powerful Soviet Union that either Moscow finds compelling or the American people can begin to understand and support. Carter must "take on the right wing frontally," but "he also has to deal with the naivete of some left-wingers who think we can respond to growing Soviet military strength with business-as-usual. Mr. Carter has to convince Moscow and Missouri that he has a coherent way of maintaining and managing a world of military parity between the superpowers."

18. Jorge Fierro, "For the Comunidad, the Visit is a Sad Show-and-Tell," *NYT*, 20 January 1980. (Author identified as living in Union City.)

Cuban exiles and their supporters must "apprise the public at large of some of the concerns and controversies within the Cuban community so as to dispel a perhaps monolithic conception of terror and violence," as is fostered by the activities of the Omega 7 terrorists who "reinforce the stereotyped conception of Latin American politics." Also, "our general community imprudently exhibits a total lack of philosophical or moral orientation with regard to political behavior," seen partly in the parade of Cubans to Cuba. Cubans must learn to "highlight political considerations without resorting to authoritarian tactics or piecemeal cosmetic efforts," all "within the scope of democracy."

19. Marvin Dunn, "Miami's Explosion Isn't Miami's Alone," *NYT*, 20 May 1980. (Author identified as professor at Florida International University who has directed several federally funded programs to improve racial and ethnic relations in Dade County.)

President Carter's open door to Cuban refugees has been harmful to the already ethnically explosive Miami community. Justice is difficult to achieve under these conditions, so two reforms are needed: there must be "a continuing mechanism of early intervention" by the U.S. Department of Justice "in extreme cases of local abuse of police power," and there must be a federal revamping of the methods of selecting a "jury of one's peers."

20. Robert Dobrow, "Cuba's Problems," *NYT,* 4 June 1980. (Author identified as a managing editor of *Workers' World,* weekly paper of the self-styled "independent Marxist-Leninist" Workers' World Party.)

"The setbacks, difficulties and problems that exist in Cuba are not the results of the 'failure' of Cuban socialism, but rather the policies of the United States imperialism." The United States has tried invasion, assassination, sabotage, and blockade, but in spite of everything the Cuban revolution has "taken great strides forward" since the days of Batista, and the vast majority of Cubans constitute a "revolutionary and class-conscious population that is more determined than ever to overcome all obstacles and reconstruct Cuba as a strong, socialist country." The "tiny fraction" of the population that seeks exile finds mounting unemployment, double-digit inflation, and racism as the "opportunities" awaiting them in the United States.

21. Carla Anne Robbins and Pamela S. Falk, "Avoiding a Hard Line on the Cubans," *NYT,* 16 December 1980. (Robbins identified as teacher of political science at American University, and Falk as a program associate at the Center for Inter-American Relations in New York.)

Cuban international activities are causing grave concern in Washington, but typically the United States is overreacting. In many cases our efforts to defend Latin American democracies from "the communist threat" have prompted military coups and the demise of those democracies, as in Chile, Brazil, and Uruguay, which make "the cure seem deadlier than the disease." "Cuba is no longer interested in exporting revolution to the regions"; rather, Cubans "seem more interested in providing technical and political advice than military support," even "suggesting that the Nicaraguans adopt a moderate course." The Cubans' own "economic failures at home and the painful reality of their complete economic dependence on the Soviet Union have made them realistic about alternatives open to small states." "The United States can afford a tempered response. . . . There may be more opportunities for the United States in the region if the new administration adopts a course of active competition rather than reactive return to military containment. . . . While the Cuban presence in the region is clear, it is not necessarily a present danger to the United States. The real danger to both democracy and long-range peace may well lie in choosing military strength over the strength of democracy, both at home and in Central America."

22. Jorge I. Domínguez, "On U.S.-Cuban Ties," *NYT,* 26 February 1981. (Author identified as professor of government at Harvard University, author of *Cuba: Order and Revolution.*

We can expect relations between the United States and Cuba to deteriorate in coming months, but U.S. policy must recognize that despite areas of conflict, "there is an important aspect of the bilateral relationship that should be preserved." The United States and Cuba have some common interests: combating international terrorism, including airline hijacking; regulating and controlling the flow of people across borders; mutual exchanges of tourists, artists, scholars, and others; international drug traffic; weather services; "interest sections"; even some international crisis areas, such as Nambia and Gulf Oil operations in Angola.

23. Vladimir Solovyov, "The Cuban Triangle," *NYT,* 14 April 1981. (Identified as author of *Russian Paradoxes;* emigrated to the United States in 1977.)

President Reagan will try to "neutralize Cuba as a military and political ally of Moscow," and "where there's a will, there's a pretext." "If the Russians' concern for Cuba can be ascribed to their national vanity, the United States' inclination toward a Cuban adventure can be attributed strictly to its national wealth: the ability to make money, and the inability to spend it. The competition is for a burden." Cuba costs Russia $8 million per day and no other "Soviet possession makes the Soviet Union so vulnerable, politically and strategically." The United States would be doing the Soviet Union a favor by taking responsibility for Cuba. Author argues that ideological and strategic concerns are decidedly secondary to the economic. Indeed, "Mr. Reagan should let the Soviet Union acquire a few more such forward posts in the Western Hemisphere—if not El Salvador, then Nicaragua—so as to make the Soviet Union even more vulnerable economically, politically and strategically."

24. Heberto Padilla, "After 20 Cuban Years," *NYT,* 17 September 1981. (Author identified as exiled from Cuba in March 1980.)

Over the past twenty years, living in his native Cuba, and in Moscow, Prague, Budapest, and Warsaw, the author "lived in a world made up of ideas painted in black and white." Everything related to the United States was anathema; Latin American writers like Mario

Vargas Llosa, Julio Cortázar, and Carlos Fuentes are condemned (or ignored) as antiprogressive and/or proimperialistic. The author cannot take slogans seriously and feels "betrayed by many intellectuals who, I once thought, were sages, our moral superiors," among them Marx, Engels, the nineteenth-century utopian socialists, Georg Lukacs, Herbert Marcuse, and Theodor Adorno. Now he sees that they represent "Empty Scholasticism." "Communism is no longer the exemplary challenge of our epoch. Rather, it is the ugly summation of everything that has been and is." "During the last 20 years I have lived in frightening laboratories of social experimentation . . . where the same experiment always ended with the same chemical result: tyranny." "It is difficult to ask anyone born into freedom to realize exactly what she or he possesses."

25. William M. LeoGrande, "Getting Cuba," *NYT,* 17 November 1981. (Author identified as director of political science at the American University.)

The Reagan administration "has repeatedly threatened to contain the crisis in El Salvador by 'going to the source,' " but it will find that "the military options available for use against Cuba are severely limited." Cuba, which Brezhnev has called "an inseparable part of the Socialist community," is very well defended and a U.S. invasion would require so many forces we would have to strip every other theater of operations of its conventional forces. A naval blockade would face the same problems of concentrating U.S. forces and challenging the Soviet Union; at the time of the 1962 "blockade" the United States had a 5-to-1 nuclear weapons superiority, whereas now there is "relative nuclear parity." A "limited blockade," interdicting arms shipments to Central America "offers several advantages to the Administration, but has its costs"; it would "shatter what little remains of the United States' relations with Cuba." But above all it would accomplish little because Cuban arms are not the critical factor in the Salvadoran revolution.

26. Saul Landau, "Warm Up to Cuba," *NYT,* 4 March 1984. (Author identified as senior fellow for Institute for Policy Studies.)

Washington's hostility toward the Castro government has strengthened the Cuban revolution, made Cuba dependent on the Soviet Union, and given Moscow a friend in the Western Hemisphere. After 1973 Nixon and Ford took "small steps" toward a thaw; Carter took more and "allowed the United States, for the first time since the Cuban Revolution, to regain some informal influence in Cuba." It is the U.S.

"obsession with the East-West conflict that lies at the heart of the United States' bad relations with Cuba"; the "preoccupation with Cuban troops in Africa and Cuban aid to revolutionary forces in Central America is both exaggerated and unworthy of a great power." The United States should lift the economic embargo, which Castro considers an act of war, and then discuss other issues. "Both common sense and geography argue against the existing alignment in which the Soviet Union, not the United States, is Cuba's most important partner and ally."

27. Ellen L. James, "Is Moscow Reducing Assistance to Cuba?" *NYT,* 7 April 1982. (Author identified as reporter for *Baltimore Evening Sun,* and fellow in economics and business at Columbia University.)

The Soviet Union may be reducing its aid to Cuba. The rate of increase of Soviet-Cuban aid has declined, the composition of aid "appears to be changing dramatically, with more assistance coming through trade-deficit credits, which are repayable, and less through trade subsidies, which are not." The UN's ECLA reports a change in the "formula by which Moscow subsidizes the price of Cuban exports" so that "the Soviet Union is absorbing less of the Cuban trade deficit than it has done." Analysts suggest that "the proportion of Cuba's total trade with Socialist bloc countries is going to decrease, despite Soviet efforts to persuade Eastern Europe to carry more of its Cuban burden." The Soviet Union has had some international advantages from the Cuban connection. If Soviet support is declining, Cuba could try to make its economy more efficient or seek a new patron, but as one diplomat said, "Cuba might be put up for auction, but there's only one bidder."

28. Floyd Abrams, "Naming Covert Agents," *NYT,* 11 June 1982. (Author identified as partner in law firm Cahill Gordon & Reindel who has represented the *New York Times,* and a lecturer in law at Columbia University School of Law.)

The Intelligence Identities Protection Act just passed by the Senate has been described as "the clearest violation of the First Amendment attempted by Congress in this era." It follows the murder in Greece of a CIA agent identified in the Greek press, and is intended to protect other agents by making anyone who identifies a "covert agent" run the risk of criminal prosecution. The language meant to limit its scope—that the disclosure must be part of a "pattern of activities intended to identify and expose" covert agents—is cloudly.

29. Peter Winn, "Don't Say No to Havana," *NYT,* 8 July 1982. (Author identified as professor of Latin American history at Tufts University, and senior fellow at Columbia University's Research Institute on International Change.)

"The troubled history of American relations with Castro's Cuba has been paved with mutual misperceptions and missed opportunities." Three months ago a "senior Cuban official told a group of visiting Americans that Cuba was prepared to offer the United States a new relationship based upon mutual restraint," but the Reagan administration responded by tightening the screws." A State Department spokesman says Reagan's policy "is to make Cuba totally dependent upon the Soviet Union to punish Cuba for its overseas adventures and to raise for Moscow the cost of its empire," with the result that the administration "is forcing Fidel Castro deeper into the Soviet embrace." Just when "Cuba has signaled its readiness to compromise, the Administration is insisting upon capitulation," possibly convincing Castro there is no incentive for restraint. Alas, that Reagan policymakers "show little understanding of historical process and less still of Mr. Castro and the Cuban Revolution." "During the 1960s, similar economic pressures only made Mr. Castro more defiant, as Cuba's active support for other guerrilla movements demonstrated."

30. Wayne S. Smith, "It Is Not Impossible to Deal with Castro: Realism Is Required," *NYT,* 5 September 1982. (Author is identified as chief of U.S. diplomatic mission in Havana from 1979 until his recent retirement from Foreign Service; a senior associate at Carnegie Endowment for International Peace. Article adapted from *Foreign Policy.*)

"Objective analysis" of Cuba is "extremely rare" in the Reagan as in earlier U.S. administrations. When he came to office, Reagan "faced serious problems in Central America that involved the Cubans," but "firm but careful admonitions aimed at pointing the Cubans, the Sandinistas, and others in the direction of real negotiations and peaceful solutions . . . [were] not the Administration's purpose." We have turned down offers for discussions. Having turned our backs on diplomacy, "we are left in the same blind alley we have been in for the past 20 years." In the future "we must overcome emotionalism. Our policy must be geared to clear, realistic objectives . . . a principal objective should be to reduce Soviet influence in Cuba." "Our best hope of moderating Cuban foreign policy is in demonstrating over a period of time that compromise is in Havana's interest," though "no quick fix is possible. Mr. Castro is a convinced revolutionary and many of his objectives are antithetical to our own. Relations are likely to remain adversarial for a long time to come." In short, "the United States should apply to Cuba the same cautious yet realistic approach used toward the Soviet Union."

31. Jean G. Zorn, "Bad Tack on Cuba," *NYT,* 26 February 1983. (Author, identified as a lawyer specializing in international business, recently visited Cuba.)

The U.S. government seems to want "to prolong its cold war with Cuba into the indefinite future," though to do so works to the disadvantage of the Cuban and particularly the American people by means that "tear at the basis of the constitutional foundation upon which this country was built." With the imposition of the embargo in 1962, trade between the United States and Cuba stopped, and "Cuba turned to the Soviet Union instead." The government asserts that the ban on travel "is not to deprive Americans of information but solely to deprive Cuba of hard currency." But the policy also "denies to Americans the right to travel freely and to learn about the culture, politics and economics of one of this country's closest neighbors."

32. Joseph J. Sisco, "Test Castro to Learn If He Would Negotiate," *NYT,* 9 August 1983. (Author identified as former career diplomat; was under secretary of state for Political Affairs from 1974-76.)

The United States and Cuba have expressed interest in the Contadora peace process. This is the time for broadly based and realistic negotiations with Castro to find out if he is posturing, as the author suspects, or serious. If progress is made, so much the better, but if it is not, let the onus be on Castro. The legacy of the past will have its impact. We tried to overthrow Castro in the 1960s, but Castro is where he is today by his own choice, not because we pushed him there. The U.S. display of power has "not gone unnoticed in Havana," and the Cuban economy has not yielded promised benefits. Castro has much to gain by U.S. trade and tourism and by changing "his status as nearly total hostage of Moscow." We cannot expect him to give up his revolution in Cuba; the "heart of the problem is Fidel Castro's unwillingness to keep his hands off other countries, in the Caribbean, Central America and worldwide." Poverty, injustice, and inequality make fertile ground for revolution in Latin America, but Castro must withhold his active intervention in the affairs of those nations.

33. McGeorge Bundy, "To Kissinger Commission: History Warns Against Threats to Invade Nicaragua," *NYT,* 6 January 1984. (Author identified as professor of history, New York University, and national security adviser to presidents Kennedy and Johnson.)

The author relates his experience during the 1962 missile crisis. In the Kennedy and Khrushchev messages of 27 and 28 October 1962, Kennedy offered to give assurances against any invasion of Cuba if the Soviet Union removed and did not reintroduce missiles to Cuba. The Soviet assurances were never fully carried out because Castro did not allow UN inspection of Cuba, though the removal was verified by intense aerial photography. But "in the absence of the extreme provocation of the missiles, he [Kennedy] had no intention whatever of invading Cuba . . . the assurances . . . not a concession but a statement of position he already held." The American people would not support an invasion of Cuba, which makes "any threat of invasion self-defeating, unless and until Cuba presents a direct military threat to the United States itself." Kennedy said United States would not abandon "political, economic and other efforts of this hemisphere to halt subversion from Cuba nor our purpose and hope that the Cuban people shall some day be truly free." Neither the Cuban precedent nor the Grenada experience, where conditions were different, would justify an invasion of Nicaragua, where such an action would not have the political support of the American people nor be politically effective in the country itself.

34. Wayne S. Smith, "Reagan's Risky Cuban Policy," *NYT,* 1 October 1984. (Author identified as senior associate at the Carnegie Endowment for International Peace.)

The terms of the Kennedy-Khrushchev agreement were clear: "If the Russians would remove their offensive weapons systems from Cuba, the United States would lift its naval blockade and promise not to invade." The Nixon and Carter administrations were committed to abiding by this understanding. The Reagan administration, however, evidently wants to free the United States from that commitment: "Must we assume, then that it wishes to remove any obstacles to an American invasion of Cuba?"

Respondent: Ms. Georgie Anne Geyer

Fairness is something that's very much needed when dealing with this whole area. I have interviewed Castro on several occasions and

when I was in Cuba in 1966, I was told that Matthews was also in town
waiting to see Castro. A couple of days later I was told that he was still
in town and hadn't yet seen Castro and that Castro was deliberately not
seeing Matthews. So after waiting and waiting, Matthews went to the
airport and then Castro called him back.

I always remembered that because it was so very Fidelista—the
attempt at humiliation of somebody who had been very close to him.
That should be remembered, too; that it doesn't pay to be too elabo-
rately affectionate toward Castro because a man like that really hates
it.

We ought to think of things other than the popular questions such as
did the *New York Times* bring Fidel Castro to power?

To me this is just absurd. What about all the Cubans who fought and
worked to bring Castro to power, many of them now in the opposition?

We ought to think more of "Who is Fidel Castro?" Who is this man
that is such a manipulator of the images of our times? How does he
come to this position? And why do we see other Fidel Castros, like
Quadaffi and others, all over the world?

How did Cuba become communist? That's something that I've never
really totally understood. How do you take a Western, democratic,
Catholic people of the New World and turn them into an Eastern,
totalitarian, atheistic people?

We ought also to think of what came before. There were mistakes
made. It's a very easy out for a very complex theme to blame the *New
York Times* for the communist takeover of Cuba. Today we have not
only Nicaragua but also the Philippines facing us with an almost exact
configuration of elements.

2

The World According to *Granma*

Kevin Greene

An analysis of *Granma,* Cuba's daily newspaper and
official publication of the Central Committee of the Communist Party of Cuba. The paper examines both the daily
version of *Granma* published for domestic consumption and
the *Granma Weekly Review,* intended for international dis-
tribution and published in English and French in addition to
Spanish. *Granma*'s language, format, coverage and political
perspective on international events are analyzed.

> *Western journalists pride themselves in a language of objectivity,
> detachment, lack of partisan passion and of independence from
> government. The language of* Granma *aims to sell the government
> to the reader or at least to deny him an alternative viewpoint
> and to encourage a systematic contempt for adversarial points
> of view.*

> —Suzanne Garment
> *The Wall Street Journal*

Introduction

Granma, Cuba's daily newspaper and the official organ of the
Central Committee of the Communist party of Cuba, reflects the
opinions and outlook of Fidel Castro's regime. Intended for internal
consumption, the paper serves as an outlet for Castro's propaganda
while maintaining the appearance of a daily newspaper offering both
domestic and international news. Another of Havana's official news
publications, the *Granma Weekly Review,* is distributed worldwide as
the medium for spreading Castro's message that Cuba is the model for
successful anti-Western, pro-Soviet revolutions around the globe.

Granma domestic edition offers readers an unadulterated dose of the official party line and worldview of Castro's regime. The *Granma Weekly Review* is published in English and French, as well as Spanish, and the daily edition only in Spanish. *Granma* chronicles Castro's prevailing party line as faithfully as *Pravda* does the Soviet one—but with greater clarity and less subtlety.

A regular reader of *Granma* would have learned early on of Havana's support for the Sandinistas in Nicaragua and of the material support lent the Sandinistas once they were in power. The reader would have learned of the close cooperation between the Castro government and the rebels in El Salvador, of regular meetings between these rebels and Castro, of Castro's bitter denunciations at the election of Salvadoran president José Napoleón Duarte and his utter contempt of that nation's electoral process, and of Castro's intransigent opposition to any negotiations between the Salvadoran rebels and Duarte's administration. Although the views expressed in *Granma* are the official views of the Cuban government and may not necessarily represent the specific views of the Sandinistas, the Salvadoran rebels, or any other group on which the newspaper is "reporting," foreign policy strategists should be interested in what Havana is saying about these groups.

The regular reader of *Granma* would also be aware of Castro's unbounded hatred of the state of Israel, his fealty toward the Soviet Union and the Eastern bloc nations, and his government's warm relations with the Palestine Liberation Organization and its leader, Yasir Arafat. Apparent throughout *Granma*'s reporting is Castro's devotion to Marxism-Leninism and his government's contempt for the capitalist way of life and for most things Western.

Some items, however, one would never find in *Granma*. For example, the newspaper frequently reports on Havana's close ties to several left-wing, pro-Soviet nations in Africa but hardly ever mentions the presence of active Cuban soldiers there. Although there are about 35,000 Cuban soldiers fighting in Angola and 10,000 Cuban soldiers fighting in Ethiopia, *Granma* emphasizes the success of "cooperation councils" in these nations. Similarly, one reads only of rebel successes in El Salvador, never of rebel defeats; of guerrilla refusals to negotiate in Colombia, rarely of guerrillas' agreeing to negotiate.

Also absent from *Granma* are any reports of political executions in Cuba, cultural repression, the jailing of anti-Castro dissidents, the poor shape of the Cuban economy, the deaths of Cuban soldiers in Africa, or the absolute dependence of Castro's regime on the Soviet Union. Absent is any mention of the successes of more than a million Cuban-

Americans, one-tenth of the entire population of Cuba, who have fled their homeland since Castro's coming to power in 1959.

Recurrent themes in *Granma*'s message are

1. that the United States and all such capitalist countries generate greedy, corrupt, crime-ridden, disease-infested, and drug-plagued societies—the United States in particular, *Granma* maintains, directs most of the evil in the world and is itself a racist, Nazi-like regime;
2. that Cuba and its revolutionary and socialist brethren, by contrast, are moral, forthright, healthy, and progressive societies standing at the cutting edge of all scientific, cultural, and social advances in the world;
3. that due to this fundamental opposition between the forces of good and evil in the world, Marxist-Leninist revolutions must succeed globally—with material aid and moral guidance from Havana's revolutionary government in conquering the Western, capitalist way of life. At the same time, the United States stands ready to halt the forces of change at any moment. Thus, Cuba must remain ever-vigilant of the inevitable invader, and be able to demand of its people endless sacrifice to promote and spread the revolution.

A noticeable change in *Granma*'s message over the years lies in its accusations against the United States. They have become more shrill, and the portrayal of a simplified battle between good and evil has become more pronounced in the past decade as Castro has fallen more deeply into the Soviet embrace.

The principal source material for this paper was *Granma* itself, both the daily edition and the *Weekly Review*. Seventy-eight issues (a full eighteen months) of the *Weekly Review* were examined, along with more than two hundred issues of the daily newspaper. The period investigated covered a ten-year span, but the focus of this work is primarily the period from August 1982 to August 1984. The purpose of the study is to summarize and detail *Granma*'s style and content, but mostly to allow the Cuban paper to reveal itself through its own words.

Typical Editions

The front page of the daily *Granma* reflects a style of journalism far different from that to which most Western readers are accustomed. Frequently the lead article is an exhortation to exemplary revolutionary behavior, or a report on the stalwart efforts of some group or province in completing production goals. Periodically, a criticism of

Western (particularly U.S.) behavior dominates the front page. The front page also includes a report on the well-being or solidarity of a Cuban ally, or some evidence of chaos in a Western country.

Often, a front-page article concerns a recent speech by Fidel Castro. Frequently, his speeches last more than an hour, sometimes several hours, in which case photographs of Castro speaking, or of an approving audience listening, appear with just the headline on the front page, and the full text of Castro's remarks are printed inside without commentary or summarization.

Immediately inside the daily edition of *Granma* one can usually find a group of articles describing the failings and inequities of pre-Castro Cuba. These articles always serve to justify, and to exalt, the current revolutionary regime and are subject to the biases of Castro's government censors. In addition, some display of past "Yankee arrogance" toward Cuba may be revealed.

World events—major news events covered by most of the world's news organizations—are absent from the front pages of *Granma*. As in the Soviet Union, unless news has significant ideological value, it is not reported. If reported, the news is buried deep within the newspaper.

Omission of world news items occurs daily. Examples would include any news on arms control progress between the United States and the Soviet Union, regular news on Angola, news of any Latin American debt renegotiation if United States banks might appear in a favorable light, unfavorable action against Cuba at the United Nations or by any country or multilateral organization, Havana's own debt renegotiations with European banks, or news of any Western cultural or scientific accomplishment.

What *Granma* does cover are official international, socialist events such as conferences, meetings between Castro and leaders of other socialist or nonaligned nations, or trade agreements with friendly nations. Other exceptions to the general exclusion of current news events are *Granma*'s coverage of the civil war activity in Central America and occasional reports of attempts at negotiations between rebel factions and ruling regimes throughout Latin America. The limitation in both cases is that the rebels can be depicted only in the best possible light (by Havana's standards), often appearing more radical and militant than they themselves might wish to be portrayed.

When it is inevitable that news negative to the Castro regime be printed in *Granma,* it is invariably foreshadowed several weeks or even months beforehand by the selection of stories to set the tone. For example, news of Havana's debt renegotiation with Western banks (called the Paris Club) was preceded by little or no coverage of the

Latin American debt crisis in 1982 and 1983. At the same time, the debt crisis was being covered widely in the West, particularly by the U.S. press. In the fall of 1983, it also became widely known that Castro had a sizeable foreign debt problem with Western bankers (to say nothing of Cuba's large debt to the Soviet Union). Still, none of this was being reported in *Granma*'s pages.

Early in 1984 *Granma* began to devote significant attention to the Latin American debt problem, which was already more than a year old, casting the issue in terms of high U.S. interest rates doing unjust damage to Latin economies, and with cartoons of a cruel Uncle Sam and the International Monetary Fund accompanying the articles.[1] But the criticism of the United States and the IMF was still comparatively tame.

Finally, in April 15, 1984, nearly nine months after the rest of the world had learned of Castro's debt problem, *Granma* officially revealed that a Cuban debt problem existed. The article ran under the title "In 1984, Cuba Hopes to Renegotiate Its Debt under the Conditions Dictated by the Crisis in the Sugar Market."[2] The article claimed that the weak world price of sugar had caused Cuba an external debt problem. This news was previously unknown to Cuban readers of *Granma* but was a well-known fact in nations with a free press. The information was duly supported by an accompanying one-and-a-half-page interview with the minister-president of the National Bank of Cuba, and was replete with charts and photographs. Yet, because Cuba sells nearly all of its sugar to the Soviet Union and Eastern bloc nations, at about four times the international rate, the world price of sugar and the world market are conditions irrelevant to Cuba's debt problem with the West.

Once the news about the Cuban debt had been reported in *Granma,* full disclosure of the entire Latin American debt problem was necessary, to shift the focus of the crisis away from Havana. Equally important to Castro's censors were vehement denunciations of the alleged United States role in creating and maintaining the crisis. Suddenly, coverage of the Latin debt issue had evolved from an issue described in sober, restrained language to one of tremendous rhetorical magnitude as evidenced by such dramatic headlines as: "Strangling the Debtor, a Strange Way of Collecting Debts"; "IMF, U.S. Banks and U.S. Attempt to Bring Venezuela to Its Knees"; and "Latin America's Foreign Debt Will Double by 1990."[3] Adroitly disguising the truth about Cuba's debt, Castro could now exploit all the discontent that could be aroused by the debt crisis, and by the austerity measures that would inevitably be required to reduce the debt.

Castro's message in *Granma* regarding the debt was that any Latin government so afflicted was the exploited victim of U.S. and other Western banks, and therefore worthy of his support and guidance. The most blatant example of this was the case of Argentina, then ruled by an anticommunist military government that despised Castro, and that Castro equally despised. As had happened during the Falklands/ Malvinas crisis, when Castro eagerly championed the cause of Argentina against Great Britain, the Cuban dictator gave tremendous (rhetorical) support to the military regime when it appeared that the regime might seriously consider reneging on paying the interest on its debts.[4]

In an article entitled "The CIA's Many Private Businesses," *Granma* resorted to a rarely matched level of inventiveness in explaining the roots of the Latin debt crisis. The article's thesis was summarized in the following lines:

> The roots of the companies set up by the [CIA] during the decades of the '50s and '60s spread into such a complex network that given the normal flow of capital it grew to such economic heights that not even the CIA itself exercised full control over it. . . . Like Mafia money, CIA funds (which rightfully belong to U.S. taxpayers) have wholly permeated U.S. finances.[5]

The article goes on to note a book by a former CIA insider in which it is alleged that the CIA once took over an ailing airline company for use in the event of an armed intervention in Central America. The article reaches the following astonishing conclusion: "It is for the above reasons that U.S. capital penetrating the Third World cannot possibly be seen as a purely economic phenomenon. Rather, it is a time bomb ready to explode the day a button is pushed at CIA headquarters in Langley, Virginia."[6]

The debt issue provided the reader of *Granma* with a look at two characteristics of virtually every *Granma* story concerning the United States: (1) the United States is to blame for any and all international crises covered in *Granma,* and (2) if the event can be exploited for political gains, it will be frequently reported about, ever emphasizing the sinister motives of the United States.

Another example of how *Granma* sets the stage for potentially bad news was its reporting on the Cuban boycott of the 1984 Olympic games in Los Angeles. Early in January and leading up to the Olympics, *Granma* reported on alleged United States violations of international Olympic rules and the U.S. State Department's reluctance to grant visas for certain Soviet athletes. Notice of the Soviet boycott was briefly noted in *Granma* as well. On May 22 the newspaper noted that nine more countries would not be participating in Los Angeles, although this information had already been announced to the outside world long before.[7] Finally, on May 24 when the Castro regime made the decision not to attend the 1984 Olympics, *Granma* carried little more than the official statement of the Cuban Olympic Committee, and the comments of two Cuban athletes, Teófilo Stevenson and Alberto Juantoreno, who expressed support for the decision and no disappointment at not being able to compete.[8]

Granma's two-page international section carries a banner headline emphasizing some foreign policy perspective of the regime, for example, "The 24th Year of the Bay of Pigs," that is, the twenty-fourth anniversary since Castro defeated the Bay of Pigs invasion in 1961. In the *Granma Weekly Review* a banner headline reads, "From the Río Grande to Patagonia," signifying the Cuban regime's intention to eliminate U.S. influence from all of Latin America.

By continuously insulting the United States, exalting the policies and intentions of Cuba's communist and Third World allies, and glorifying Cuba's activities around the world (with little if any mention of Cuban troops abroad), the international section promotes specific foreign policy objectives of the Castro government. The United States is repeatedly portrayed as the enemy of the entire world, and as about to invade Cuba, Nicaragua, El Salvador, or even Guyana. Often reports from rebels in El Salvador or Guatemala, as well as other pro-Cuban insurgency groups, are printed in the international pages of the *Weekly Review*. For example, demonstrating that Castro considers the rebels in El Salvador the legitimate government of that nation, the *Weekly Review* reprinted in its entirety the FMLN/FDR proposal for a provisional Salvadoran government.[9] Similarly, other rebel factions throughout Latin America, however small, are often given higher visibility than the officials of those nations.

A frequent news item in *Granma* is a visit by Castro or one of his ministers to an allied nation, or a visit to Cuba of a representative from a friendly government. To depict Cuba's alleged importance on the world stage, these events are given high visibility. No third-party description of what the two parties discussed is ever reported. Any issue discussed is reported only in a communiqué released at the end of several days of talks. Formal expressions of communist solidarity either by the reporter or one of the subjects of the article are frequent, but no spontaneous or particularly notable comments are published.

Another frequent characteristic of articles appearing in *Granma* is what might be described as a national paranoia, a considerable sensitivity to actual or imagined criticism. One example of this phenomenon is the article entitled "Reply to Yankee Slander: More Proof of Imperialist Insolence." The subject of this article was a University of Miami study by Dr. Caroline Macleod, in which she proposed the hypothesis that acquired immune deficiency syndrome (AIDS) in the United States may have originated from sexual contact between U.S. and refugee Cuban or Haitian homosexuals recently arrived in the United States. Despite the fact that Macleod's hypothesis received little attention in the United States, it nonetheless provoked a half-page response from *Granma* that appeared on the cover of the *Weekly Review* on April 3, 1983.[10] *Granma,* charging that Macleod's results were merely fabricated by the CIA, viewed her hypothesis as a U.S. government plot to discredit the Castro regime, ending its lengthy denunciation with the statement, "These are our arguments and this is our answer to the new act of insolence by the imperialists."

A second example of *Granma's* sensitivity to criticism, as well as a reflection of the paper's zeal to discredit the United States, was an article bearing the headline "Cuban Veterinary Service Becomes the Target of U.S. Slander."[11] The article focused on the claim that U.S. embassies in several Latin American countries had initiated a slander campaign against Cuba by spreading the rumor that aphthous fever, a fatal disease that attacks cattle and can be fatal to humans as well, existed in Cuba.

A front-page article entitled "Right of Response" detailed *Granma's* objection to a French television series of the same name *("Droit de Réponse")*. The program referred to in the article was "Cuba Yes, Cuba No," which aired on June 2, 1984. On that occasion, *Granma* wrote: "The title of the program was "Cuba Yes, Cuba No" in an attempt to present an image of objectivity and professionalism to conceal a campaign based on vulgarity, lies and the intellectual poverty of its orchestrators."[12] The article continued:

> At a time when the First Havana Biennial is being held—an event which reflects the most varied samples of Latin American and Caribbean arts, and at which the vast majority of the talent on our continent is represented, thus turning Cuba into a modern art center; at a time when the Cuban cultural festival in Venice has just been held with great success and made a deep impression on broad sectors in Italy; when a retrospective is being held in Paris . . . the small groups that control the information monopolies in France have undertaken a far-reaching slander campaign against our country. They are responsible for a scandal on a totally anti-Cuban television program and level all sorts of charges in various mass media against our culture and policy in the arts.[13]

Several far-fetched assertions are made in the above paragraph: (1) by holding its first biennial exhibit in Havana (after twenty-five years in power), the regime in Havana could thus transform Cuba into "an important modern art center"; (2) an exhibit that excluded many Latin American artists and showed no North American artists represented "the vast majority of talent on our continent"; and (3) there exist in France "small groups that control the information monopolies," whose chief aim is a "far-reaching slander campaign" against Cuba. *Granma,* in reporting on the exhibition, attempted to depict the Havana Biennial as an event of the highest international magnitude.

In spite of *Granma's* claims, many Cuban writers and intellectuals fled Cuba because they did not find the atmosphere conducive to cultural and creative endeavors. Cuban writers abroad are treated as "traitors" and "fakers" who are "guilty of treason" against Cuba. But, according to the "Right of Response" article, the position of Cuban artists and intellectuals currently living in Cuba is as follows:

> The Cuban Revolution and the writers and artists of the country are not prepared to become ensnared in a gross controversy promoted and encouraged by the United States, nor will they agree to debate under allegedly equal conditions set up beforehand with traitors or fakers, some of whom are not really artists. They will not do this for the same reason that the French might refuse to debate with those who are guilty of treason against France. This is a principle we cannot renounce and whose validity we are willing to discuss at any level and at any international event.[14]

The article concludes that any debate on Cuban cultural policy must take place in Cuba with "genuine" French intellectuals, handpicked by the Castro regime, and must exclude the "traitorous" writers who once practiced their art in Cuba but who are now in exile.

> It must be made clear to these reactionaries that Cuba is an heir to and follower of the intellectual and moral traditions of French socialism, classical German philosophy and British political economy, the foundations for historical and dialectical materialism which are the true pillars of Marxism-Leninism.[15]

Finally, *Granma* asks for "a calm analysis," a "debate without insults," but ends by stating that the Western media "ignore the value of the arts in underdeveloped countries. This arrogant, vulgar and ignorant tyranny does not want to recognize what is happening in Latin America and the Caribbean."[16] So much for debate without insults.

The world view projected in *Granma* is also shaped by news organizations other than Cuba's own *Prensa Latina* and the *Granma* staff, whose reports are published in the daily and weekly editions. These news organizations include the pro-Cuban, pro-Soviet FRELIMO

Party Press of Mozambique and the government press of the Cuban-backed regime in Angola, which report on African affairs; Latin American reporting from El Salvador's rebel radio station *(Radio Venceremos);* the government-controlled Sandinista press in Nicaragua; occasional reports from the M-19 in Colombia; and reporting on Asia from the Vietnamese and North Korean press. Stories from these sources are dominated by the ideological and radically militant nature of the groups reporting. Other sources of news and commentary are the Communist parties of virtually any country, including the United States, and, of course, the Soviet Union's news organizations: TASS, *Pravda,* and *Izvestia.*

During its examination of the Polish crisis in late 1981, *Granma* relied primarily upon official government reports, ignoring the relatively independent Polish News Agency (PAP), which the *New York Times* and the *Washington Post* used regularly as a source of information.

Noticeably absent from *Granma's* list of sources are the major news organizations of western Europe, Asia, and the Americas. Exceptions to this practice occur for articles critical of Western society, the United States in particular.

A final, important distinction should be made between the style, format, and content of the daily issue of *Granma* and the *Weekly Review.* First, the daily *Granma* is published in a small tabloid usually not more than eight pages in length. The *Weekly Review* is published on a scale equal in size to the *Washington Post* or the *New York Times,* and is normally twelve pages long. Frequently, the *Review* includes a pullout section featuring a single topic, such as a day in the life of the average Cuban, the Cuban sports world, or Guyana as a target of U.S. imperialism.

The *Weekly Review* includes many photographs; the photographs in the daily are fewer and less impressive. Banner headlines and imaginative layouts are used liberally in the *Weekly Review;* such practice is mostly confined to just the front page of the daily edition. Visually, the *Weekly Review* is much more aesthetic and impressive than the daily *Granma.*

It should also be noted that although the *Weekly Review* is primarily a summary of the week's articles that appeared in the daily, it also includes articles from other publications, such as the Cuban magazine *Bohemia.* The *Weekly Review* also maintains its own reporting staff, whose members write some independent articles or expand upon themes first discussed in the daily *Granma.*

In terms of content the two publications often exhibit further dissimilarities. Both are stridently anti-Western in tone and outlook, but the *Weekly Review* devotes much more space, proportionally, to foreign affairs, and the daily is more domestically oriented, with foreign news generally restricted to pages six and seven. The international section of the *Weekly Review* is targeted at a foreign audience, particularly at the revolutionary movements of the world. The message conveyed by this section is one of harmony among communist nations, the integrity and honesty of the Soviet Union, and the decadence, greed, and hostility of Western culture.

The following excerpt is an example of how the United States is portrayed by the *Weekly Review:*

The Medical Mafia in Action

The general decline of the health of broad sectors of the U.S. population (as revealed by official statistics) due to the high cost of health services, public health budget cuts, etc. is further aggravated by the "medical mafia."

We're talking about the widespread gangsterism present in the public health sector where an unscrupulous group goes so far as to make up diseases in healthy patients in order to treat them for handsome profits.

According to a western news agency, six powerful transnationals own the best 40 private hospitals in the United States and make annual net profits of some 1000 mln. *[sic]* dollars With a yearly income of over 65,000 mln. dollars, the six are at the top of the "medical industry" and employ over 5 million people.[17]

Such is the stuff of daily life according to *Granma*. These exaggerated reports are taken as indicative of the life of an average American, and are conveyed by the *Weekly Review* to the Third World.

Cultural events abroad and in Cuba involving Cuban artists are covered extensively in the *Weekly Review,* more so than in the daily. The Havana Biennial, mentioned above, was broadly heralded in the *Review,* as was the First Annual Fashion Show in Havana that claimed to make Cuba the "fashion capital" of the world for its duration. In the *Granma* daily, notices of the events were far more subdued, and the photographs fewer. Perhaps the events were staged to counteract growing world attention on Cuba's cultural repression, and thus were lavishly reported in the *Weekly* Review. Similarly, Cuban writers and artists living on the island today are so blatantly repressed and controlled by the Castro regime that such protestations of a free and vibrant artistic community would not have been believed by the Cuban readers of the daily *Granma,* although such claims would undergo less scrutiny by a more remote and sympathetic readership in the *Weekly Review*.

Cuba is always portrayed as industrializing and diversifying its economy, principally with Soviet, Bulgarian, and East German technical assistance. In 1984 the industrial plant at Cienfuegos was the topic of several articles, although it still appeared to be unfinished. The high quality of cattle raising and milk production is also emphasized in the *Weekly Review*. In fact, however, Cuba is all but completely dependent on a single crop, sugar, and beef and milk are strictly rationed on the island.

Castro's political rationale for having the *Weekly Review* portray Cuba in this light is clear: the Cuban leadership desires to be seen as the model for all "liberation" movements around the world. Furthermore, the Soviet Union reaps the benefits of favorable writing about its international prestige, while *Granma* furthers anti-Western and anti-U.S. propaganda and sentiment around the world.

This study draws equally from both *Granma* and the *Weekly Review*, but the reader should not lose sight of the fact that each is directed to a vastly different audience. In the United States several thousand college libraries and presidents of college student governments receive the *Weekly Review* free of charge on a regular basis.

Granma's View of Events in Angola

In early March 1984 a headline in *Granma* announced, "South Africa Forced to Hold Talks with Angola on Troop Withdrawal from Southern Africa and Namibian Independence." The first paragraph of this article read:

> In view of world condemnation, repeated UN Security Council resolutions and the military strengthening of the People's Republic of Angola, which is firmly supported by Cuba and the Soviet Union (as was shown by the recent tripartite meeting in Moscow), the racists in Pretoria and their allies in Washington have been forced to start talks on a negotiated solution to the withdrawal of South African forces from Southern Angola and to Namibia's independence.[18]

The *Washington Post* offered a different reason for the beginning of negotiations on the withdrawal of Cuban troops. On March 16, 1984, quoting from an interview with Portugal's Prime Minister Mario Soares, the *Post* reported:

> Battlefield reverses of the Angolan government against the anti-communist UNITA have forced hard choices on the Soviets and the Cubans,

according to Soares: "either a deeper engagement militarily," or "a gradual disengagement." He added, "It seems they have opted for the second." Soares, calling the war in Angola "interminable," said he believed that the Soviets and Cubans had calculated that "to continue and increase their presence, would place them in a Vietnam situation."[19]

The same *Washington Post* report also noted that public statements in Havana and Luanda (Angola) had given the reason for disengagement negotiations as "forced by Angola's growing strength."

The *Granma* report gave no indication whatsoever of Cuban or Angolan willingness to ease tensions; the initiative had to appear to be South Africa's alone. Nor was there ever any mention in *Granma* of the ceasefire agreement between South Africa and Angola that preceded attempts at negotiations, or the good services of the United States during these talks.

On March 19, following the visit to Havana of Angolan President José Eduardo dos Santos, Reuters reported that Castro had agreed to "a gradual withdrawal of its estimated 25,000 troops in Angola provided certain conditions are met," citing a communiqué issued jointly by both nations.[20] The conditions were the widely publicized request for the unilateral withdrawal of South African soldiers from Angola, acceptance of the UN's rulings calling for a withdrawal of South African troops from Namibia, the granting of full independence for Namibia, the cessation of all acts of aggression against the Angolan government by South Africa and the United States, and an end of all aid to the Angolan insurgents. The tone of the Reuters report was diplomatic and sober.

The tone of *Granma*'s publication of the full joint Cuban-Angolan communiqué, on the other hand, was bombastic. After noting Cuba's "principled" alliance two years earlier with dos Santos's MPLA, the communiqué stated:

> The heroic resistance of the Angolan people, firmly supported by their international allies, has persuaded the imperialist aggressors that it is impossible to break down the People's Republic of Angola and wipe out its revolutionary process, forcing them to accept negotiations on a new basis.[21]

The *Granma* story concludes:

> The Cuban government, on behalf of the Cuban people, pays deserved tribute to the courage of the Angolan people, who for nearly a quarter of a century have been engaged in a war of liberation against the colonialists, racists, their imperial masters and their lackeys, paying a high price

in blood to achieve full independence and to give international aid to other people.[22]

Reuters examined the joint communiqué closely; for *Granma* it was a secondary item. The lead article that day read, "President of Angola Visits Cuba," and carried the subtitle, "Delegation by Fidel and José Eduardo dos Santos Hold Talks on Bilateral Relations and the Situation in Southern Africa."[23] This lead article gives the usual ceremonial appraisal of the meeting, noting that the talks were held "in a climate of mutual understanding and friendship," and lists the Angolan and Cuban ministers who participated in the meeting. A brief note is made of the joint communiqué printed below the article, but no attention is paid in the lead article to the substance of the talks or to the content of the communiqué. Thus, in *Granma's* view, it seems that the ostensible solidarity of the Angolan and Cuban leaders is more of a substantive international news story than one pointing to the possibility of a cessation of hostilities in southern Africa.

One interesting aspect of the communiqué does appear in *Granma*.

> The Cuban and Angolan governments reiterate that they will resume, by their own decision and in the exercise of their sovereignty, the gradual withdrawal of the *Cuban internationalist military contingent* as soon as the following three conditions are met [emphasis added].[24]

What was astonishing about *Granma's* treatment of that story, particularly to anyone who followed the newspaper closely, was the reference to the Cuban "internationalist military contingent" in Angola, for mention of any Cuban troops in Angola was at the time virtually nonexistent. To someone whose only access to information was the daily *Granma,* an "internationalist military contingent" might mean merely a group of military or technical advisers. On the other hand, someone on the island whose friends or relatives were fighting in Angola or Ethiopia, or had died there, might be aware of some Cuban combat troops in Africa. It is Castro's policy, however, that families are not told where their sons in the military are stationed, and Cubans almost never know the extent of Cuban military commitment overseas.

Likewise, Cubans are not likely to read in *Granma* any regular reporting of Cuban troops engaging in combat in Angola, nor of an Angolan army defeats, nor of any Cuban battle deaths. Instead, *Granma* runs such articles as "Brutal Imperialists and Racists Act againat Cuban Civilian Cooperation Personnel in Angola." The report explained the incident in the following, "acceptable" terms:

On April 19 [1984], agents at the service of the U.S. imperialists and the South African racists carried out a criminal explosives attack on Cuban civilian cooperation personnel in Huambo, Angola. . . .

Once again, a number of dedicated Cuban construction workers have laid down their generous lives while contributing to the economic and social development of other peoples. . . .

In an exemplary response that is the pride of our people, many Cuban internationalist workers in Huambo village, whose assignment had been completed, have requested that their stay be extended, and the men and women wounded have said that their greatest wish is to recover as soon as possible so as to be able to resume their work in construction and in the schools and hospitals of Huambo.[25]

Another aspect of battle reports from Angola (as well as El Salvador, Nicaragua, Ethiopia, or any other location where Cuban or pro-Cuban forces are fighting) is that *Granma* will mention only the enemy's killing of civilians, never that the enemy has inflicted casualties on Cuban combat troops, or Cuba's allies. The picture is clean and simple, and often repeated elsewhere: pro-Castro forces win all battles and can route the enemy; enemy forces, who kill only civilians, can defeat no pro-Castro troops and always lose battles quickly. The most striking thing is that no Cuban soldiers are ever involved, because all Cuban personnel are "civilian workers," like those killed at Huambo.

The average Cuban, therefore, can rely neither on *Granma* nor on the official reports from the Castro government to learn of military deaths in Angola. Thus, the Cuban people are never made fully aware of either the extent of Castro's military involvement overseas or the price paid by Cuban citizens in lives lost or money spent in Castro's support of rebel insurgencies around the globe. Much more information about Castro's initiatives in Angola, Ethiopia, Mozambique, and elsewhere is reported by the Western press, but the Cuban people have no access to Western newspapers and magazines.

The early March announcement in *Granma* that South Africa was willing to negotiate a troop withdrawal from Angola because "its policy of using force had failed" is another example of how Cuban propaganda prepares its readers for a coming event—in this case, the joint communiqué with Angola of March 19 announcing a possible Cuban troop withdrawal.[26] The earlier report also planted the seed for Castro's later justification of a possible cease-fire (announced in the joint communiqué): South Africa's military weakness.

One final point of interest arises from the story on South Africa's willingness to negotiate. In the first paragraph *Granma* mentions "the military strengthening of the People's Republic of Angola, which is firmly supported by Cuba and the Soviet Union (as was shown at the recent tripartite meeting in Moscow)." This is interesting because (1) it is the first reference to any meeting held between Angola, Cuba, and the Soviet Union; and (2) *Granma* almost never explicitly cites Soviet support for the cause of a Third World government allied to Castro. *Granma*'s report of the tripartite meeting was noted in the *Washington Post* on March 16, 1984, and although the timing of the meeting was not known, the *Post* reporter speculated, with the help of official U.S. sources, that the meeting must have taken place in late January.

Crisis in Poland

Granma's coverage of the events leading to the imposition of martial law in Poland—through the establishment of the Military Council of National Salvation—on December 13, 1981, provides an example of how the Castro regime cautiously handles civil unrest in a sister Soviet satellite.[27] A comparison of *Granma*'s coverage with Western press reports is instructive.

In early November 1981, while the Western press was closely following the increasing pressure building up in Poland, *Granma* reported very little unrest there. A piece dated November 5 and carrying the headline "Predictions of a Worsening of Internal Markets in Poland" quoted a government economist's forecast that the domestic economy in Poland had continued to weaken for the fourth quarter of 1981, and that "some informed sources report continuing strikes in various regions of the country."[28] The report credits these strikes, which occurred in Jarnobrzez, Konin, and Katowice, as one possible cause of the weaker domestic demand for goods. At the time the article surprised many analysts with its frank accounts of abuses perpetrated by the Communist party leadership in Poland. In retrospect, however, it may be that the article was designed to foreshadow the purging of former and current Polish government officials at the time General Jaruzelski declared a state of siege in December.

Granma's portrayal of the situation in Poland was one of a temporary viral disease that was slowly being cured, rather than a deep-seated problem with which both government leaders and members of Solidarity were struggling. The November 5 article closes with mention of a topic that became the focus of the paper's coverage of the crisis from that date until the final two and a half weeks prior to the imposition of martial law:

The news agency PAP said that the leadership of the parallel trade union "Solidarity" created a special group to analyze the Government's proposal to form a Front of National Accord. . . . The "Solidarity" leadership estimated that such proposals [from the Government] opened the possibility of negotiations.[29]

The following day *Granma* reported that Polish Premier Wojciech Jaruzelski, Archbishop Jozef Glemp, and Lech Walesa met to discuss a national front for understanding. The article was entitled "The Possibility of Creating a National Front for Understanding Is Discussed in Poland," but, as is usually the case, few details and no speculation on the substance of the talks were included.[30]

On November 7 *Granma* reported on a meeting between Jaruzelski and a Polish Communist group called the Liberty Fighters about the possibility of a front for national accord. The article also included the following information:

Meanwhile, the strikes directed by sectors of "Solidarity" continue in many regions of the country [like] Lubgora, Province of Zielona Gora, in spite of their rejection by the agrarian workers of [the orthodox] branch trade unions. . . . Those workers agreed to create brigades to work in the factories where strikes continue.[31]

On November 9 *Granma* reported "The Leadership of 'Solidarity' Affirms It Is Disposed to Compromise with the Polish Government":

The maximum meeting of the parallel union "Solidarity" today approved a three-part declaration that sent a sign of its willingness to compromise in the coming negotiations with the Polish government. . . . With this decision of the parallel union, the formation of a Front of National Accord seems imminent in which the Agriculture Union, the Youth Union, the Fighters for the Liberty and Democracy, among other political forces, proclaim their support for the creation of a common platform.[32]

On November 11 *Granma* printed "The Polish Government Approves the Results of Jaruzelski's Conversations with the Catholic Primate and Walesa."[33] The next day *Granma* reported that the Politburo of the Polish Communist party had also approved of attempts to form a new national front in Poland.[34] No actual agreement had been reached between Solidarity and the Polish government as of mid-November (nor would it happen at any time before the imposition of martial law), but the impression conveyed by *Granma* through its single daily article on Poland was that forces were working inexorably toward a national rapprochement in a climate of general unity and social calm.

An article run by *Granma* on November 17, "Jaruzelski Visits Various Labor Centers in Warsaw and Explains to the Workers Poland's Political and Socioeconomic Situations," once again attempted to depict a prevailing national unity and calm that was becoming increasingly difficult to believe, even for those whose only information came from *Granma*.[35]

During this period of daily coverage of Poland, Solidarity was treated deferentially, and its actions portrayed as mostly positive. The crisis was attributed to just a few radical, antisocialist members who exploited Poland's economic crisis. Although Solidarity's name always appeared in quotation marks, somehow questioning the legitimacy of the group and its name, and was always referred to as a parallel union subservient to the Communist party's own branch unions, it is clear that *Granma* wanted to show the trade union in a positive light, cooperating with the Polish leadership in an attempt to create a front of national accord.

In contrast to *Granma*'s reporting, the Western press presented a far different picture of the relations between the Polish Communist leadership and Solidarity. The *New York Times* began November with a piece entitled "Parliament Bids Polish Workers Stop All Strikes," which read as follows:

> Parliament today acceded to the wishes of Poland's Communist Party leader, Gen. Wojciech Jaruzelski, and passed a resolution appealing for an immediate halt of all strikes. If the strikes continue, Parliament said it will consider "providing the Government with such legal means as are required by the situation." This was a reference to a law banning strikes outright.[36]

The front-page article also announced that in two days the national leadership of Solidarity would meet in an attempt "to regain control over the rebellious locals, if necessary by means of disciplinary measures."[37]

The following day, November 2, the *Times* reported "Solidarity Chapters Continue Strikes; 250,000 Workers Still Idled."[38] The Polish cities identified as the main center of strike activity were Zyrardow, Tarobrzeg, Zielon Gora, and Sosnowiec. The issues highlighted were food shortages and opposition to certain unauthorized activities practiced by the security forces.

On November 13, 1981, the *New York Times* reported:

A special Government economic commission issued a gloomy report today describing what is called "growing chaos" in Poland's economy and warning that drastic measures may be necessary to get through the winter.[39]

After two consecutive weeks of making daily reports on Poland (it is rare for the Cuban press to dwell on any single issue for a period of time), *Granma* suddenly stopped coverage of Poland for nine days. Thus, from a story receiving tremendous play, albeit buried in the middle of the international pages, Poland suddenly disappeared from the *Granma* reader's view altogether.

On November 26 the subject of Poland reappeared in *Granma* in an article with a very different tone. Earlier in the month Solidarity had received only occasional mention, and most of that favorable; it was now the focus of the article as the scapegoat and irresponsible agitator of all of Poland's problems.[40] This shift in reportorial tone presaged the imposition of martial law, which occurred two weeks later. This event was reported on December 13 in the front-page article "General Jaruzelski Is Made Head of a Military Salvation Council That Assumes Control in Poland."[41]

On November 27 in a front-page article headlined "Tranquility in Poland after the Declaration of a State of War," *Granma* reported that the Polish capital of Warsaw was "absolutely tranquil," and that although there were rumors of some strikes in the country, they remained unconfirmed as the pace of life returned to normal.[42]

What is curious is that while *Granma* ceased reporting on Poland, from November 17 to 26, the *New York Times* was reporting that tensions in Poland were gradually easing. They did not begin to rise again until late November. By the time *Granma* returned to its coverage of the Polish crisis, it was clear from the *Times* that the political situation in Warsaw had significantly worsened. On November 28, for example, a *Times* story revealed the following:

Poland's Prime Minister and Communist Party leader, Wojciech Jaruzelski, said today that the Politburo had instructed the Government to seek legislation banning strikes. He told the Party's policy-making Central Committee that the move is needed because of the mounting economic, political and social crisis. . . . The initiative is focused at the heart of last year's agreement between the Government and the trade union movement Solidarity that gave the union the right to strike.[43]

Granma did not mention any of this; in particular, the newspaper never acknowledged that Solidarity had been guaranteed the right to strike.

Therefore, it would have been difficult to explain why the Politburo was seeking a measure to ban strikes.

Finally, on December 13, the *New York Times* reported "Poland's Military Leader Puts Military in Charge After Union Chiefs Call a National Vote on the Future of the Communist Government," and "Premier Declares 'State of War' to Insure 'Law and Order in Crisis.' "[44] Neither the call for a vote on the legitimacy of the Communist party, nor the call for the removal of various party organizations in twenty-one Polish provinces, was ever mentioned in *Granma*.

The situation in Warsaw immediately following the imposition of martial law represents another example of the discrepancies between the news as expressed in *Granma* and that in the Western press. While, as previously mentioned, the Cuban paper depicted a calm and "tranquil" atmosphere in the Polish capital, the *New York Times* report of the same day was strikingly different. Under the headline "Poland Restricts Civil and Union Rights: Solidarity Activists Urge General Strike," the *Times* stated:

> Poland's new military leaders issued a decree of martial law today, drastically restricting civil rights and suspending the operations of the Solidarity union. The union's activists reacted with an appeal for an immediate general strike to protest. . . . There were no immediate reports of any violence, but opposition seemed in the offing. Union activists, in dozens of leaflets being circulated in the streets, called for an immediate general strike.[45]

Two days later, on December 16, *Granma* stated that "a climate of calm and normality predominated in the capital [Warsaw] and in the majority of the regions in the country, indicating the wide diffusion of Poland's measures."[46] The same day, the *New York Times*, quoting Solidarity sources, ran the article "Widespread Strikes Reported in Defiance of Polish Regime; U.S. Postponing All Pending Aid." It said:

> As Poland's military leaders tightened their controls, defiant workers protesting martial law mounted strikes throughout the country yesterday. . . . A clandestine information service of the Solidarity trade union reported strikes and worker resistance in factories, shipyards, steel mills, coal mines, and even academic institutions in Warsaw and other major cities and regions.[47]

The next day *Granma* reported "Poland's Economic Activity Continues to Recuperate: Factory Work Normalizes":

> The situation in Poland continued tranquil today and the majority of factories and other institutions worked normally while the Military

Council of National Salvation adopted other measures to deal with the acute national crisis.[48]

The *Times* reported on December 17 that the Polish authorities broke up strikes already in progress, not merely plans for strikes, as *Granma* had reported, and that strikes and disruptions still continued.[49]

On December 18 *Granma* reported that Polish Politburo member Stefan Olszowski said the only measure authorities could have taken was to declare a state of war:

> In a press conference held at the Foreign Ministry in Warsaw, Olszowski said that the implementation of a state of war frustrated the plans of the counterrevolution to take power.[50]

Furthermore, while the *Times* was writing about reports of food shortages and hoarding in Warsaw,[51] *Granma* ran the article "The Military Council for National Salvation Continues Implementing Measures Against Anti-Socialist Elements":

> In the streets of Warsaw, where the populace had become accustomed in the last few months to apocalyptic announcements by the illegal union "Solidarity" and other subversive groups—divulged by the press—the city was progressively recuperating towards normality.[52]

The Polish crisis, downplayed from the beginning by *Granma*, was at an end, and calm had returned. No strife or protest against the Polish government existed, according to the Havana paper, and the Solidarity opposition element had been contained and declared illegal, although *Granma* reported no arrests of union leaders. Nor was there any mention of the subsequent government repressions, the demonstrations of popular support for Solidarity, or any of the other unrest. Since 1981 periodic articles in *Granma* have attested the tranquility and the absence of any conflict in Poland.

The Invasion of Grenada

On Monday, October 24, 1983, the *New York Times* under the headline "Grenada Radio Warns of Attack," reported, "As U.S. diplomats consulted with Americans in Grenada, 16 military officers who recently seized power there warned the nation that they expected an invasion by forces from neighboring Caribbean states."[53] On the following day both the *New York Times* and the *Washington Post* reported fifty marines had landed in Barbados the day before as a possible "option" for an evacuation of U.S. citizens in Grenada.[54]

On October 26 the *Washington Post* gave the following report about
the U.S. invasion of Grenada:

> An American force of up to 1900 Marines and Rangers invaded the leftist
> nation of Grenada at dawn yesterday, seizing two airfields and an
> American-run medical school in an action President Reagan had ordered
> to protect more than 1,000 citizens living on the small island.[55]

Granma's handling of the Grenada story began on October 26, when
it printed, in its entirety, the "Statement by the Cuban Party and
Government on the Imperialist Intervention in Grenada." The statement begins by noting the "painful" events that took place at the time
of the assassination of Grenadian Prime Minister Maurice Bishop on
October 19, 1983. It said that the Cuban government had made clear its
"unequivocal" position on the assassination at the time, and warned
that "imperialism would try to derive the utmost benefit from this
tragedy [Bishop's death]."[56] There is, however, no public record of this
Cuban position until the October 26 statement, although analysts
generally agree that Castro preferred Bishop over Bernard Coard and
Hudson Austin, and that the Soviet Union pushed Coard and Austin
and pressured Castro to accept them.[57]

The October 26 statement on the invasion of Grenada directly
addresses the question of why Havana's personnel on the island were
in possession of offensive weapons and appeared well prepared for
combat:

> The merits of such a policy [of nonintervention] can be noted now more
> than ever, since it has become evident that the Cuban personnel in
> Grenada had the combat capability with which they could have at-
> tempted to influence the course of [Grenada's] internal events. The
> weapons in the hands of the Cuban construction personnel and coopera-
> tion workers in Grenada had been given to them by Bishop and the
> Grenadian Party and Government leadership so that they could defend
> themselves in the event of foreign aggression against Grenada, as has
> unfortunately been the case. These were mainly light infantry weapons.
> Our own personnel kept custody over those weapons in their living
> quarters. They were not meant to be used in any domestic conflict and
> they were never and will never be used for those ends.[58]

Havana's statement further explains that Grenada's ruling regime
asked Cuba for military assistance just a few days before the invasion
by the joint U.S.-Caribbean force, but the Castro regime responded as
follows:

> That Cuba cannot send reinforcements not only because it is materially
> impossible in the face of overwhelming U.S. air and naval superiority in

the area, but also because politically, if this were to be merely a struggle among Caribbeans it [Cuba] should not do so in order not to justify U.S. intervention.[59]

The Cuban communication to Grenada's leaders prior to the invasion also said that "Grenadian revolutionaries themselves are the only ones responsible for this disadvantageous and difficult situation for the revolutionary process politically and militarily."[60] On Saturday, October 22, the statement asserts, Castro sent the following message to the Cuban officials in Grenada:

> A large-scale Yankee aggression against us can take place at any moment in Grenada against our cooperation workers; in Nicaragua against our doctors, teachers, technicians, construction workers, etc.; in Angola against our troops, civilian personnel and others, or even in Cuba itself. We must always be ready and keep our morale high in the face of these painful possibilities.[61]

Granma's mention of troops in Angola is rare, and noteworthy, although it probably would not have been mentioned had it not been part of an official intragovernmental communiqué.

The October 26 statement also includes a communication from the Castro regime to the government of the United States. The Cuban government states that it tried to assure the United States of the safety of its citizens in Grenada, but felt that its intentions had been completely ignored, given that a U.S. response did not arrive in Havana until two and a half days later, ninety minutes after the invasion of Grenada had begun.[62]

The October 26 statement published in *Granma* closed with a battle cry, a typical method used by the Cuban newspaper to elicit emotional reaction to a particular story. In this case, the article ended with the phrases "Grenada may become for the Yankee imperialists in Latin America and the Caribbean what the Moncada prison meant to the Batista tyranny in Cuba. . . . Eternal Glory to the Cubans who have fallen! My country or death! We will be victorious!"[63]

U.S. government evidence, reported in the *Washington Post* and the *New York Times* during the week following the Grenada invasion, pointed to a large store of armaments discovered by the U.S. marines during the operation. Although reference to the "weapons in the hands of our construction personnel" was made in the October 26 statement published in *Granma,* no specifics as to the magnitude of the Grenadian cache were given, and the subject was never mentioned again by the paper. The marines also discovered Castro's plans to expand his operation on Grenada by as many as 6,800 Cuban personnel, as well as an alleged plan to capture U.S. citizens there and hold them hostage.[64] A treasure trove of "Grenada documents" also pointed to Soviet and Cuban plans to route Soviet arms through Cuba and North Korea to Grenada.[65] *Granma* continued to try to score ideological points regarding the Grenada invasion, maintaining a steady stream of criticism of the "imperialist operation" for a full six weeks, but the paper never addressed itself to the specific allegations raised in the Western press, nor did it mention the cache of weapons and documents.

Granma's handling of the invasion was an attempt to repudiate the U.S. action in three discernible ways. First, the paper printed stories that spoke to the illegitimacy of the operation. On the evening following the incident, *Granma* published a message from the Castro government to the United States, in the form of a ten-point memorandum, that claimed the invasion was "totally unjustifiable." The fourth point of the message stated:

> That we [Cuba] have no soldiers, but actually construction workers and civilian advisers in Grenada, with the exception of a few tens of military advisers who were working with the army and security forces before Bishop's death. Our personnel had been instructed to fight back only if attacked and they were not the first to shoot. Furthermore, they had been given instructions not to obstruct any action for the evacuation of U.S. citizens in the area of the runway near the U.S. University. It was evident that if any attempt were made to occupy Cuban installations, they would clash with them.[66]

Second, the newspaper tried to show the geopolitical failure of the U.S. operation, and its "disastrous" consequences for U.S. foreign policy. An early November article in *Granma* reported "Incalculable Political and Moral Defeat."

> A completely isolated Reagan administration, probably more so than any other U.S. government in history, has suffered a severe international defeat with the unanimous condemnation of the U.S. forces' invasion of Grenada. It is hard to say where the outrage has been greatest, but one of the regions where U.S. isolation should be singled out must surely be Latin America.[67]

Finally, for purely rhetorical value, reports in *Granma* during the five weeks following the Grenada invasion carried such headlines as "All of Cuba Repudiates the Brutal U.S. Attack on Grenada." That article was accompanied by photos of mass rallies in Cuba, with one showing a large placard reading, "Yankees, If you Have So Much Courage, Try Coming Near Cuba," and another, "We Will Never Surrender."[68]

The November 20 issue contained the following litany of headlines, taken from the "eyewitness" accounts of Cuban survivors:

> I Witnessed the U.S. Plundering of Cuban Construction Workers' Belongings;
>
> They Wanted to Know What Was the Advantage of Being a Member of the Party; "The Honor of Being the Vanguard in Work," I Told Them;
>
> They Asked Me Whether I'd Like to Leave Cuba and My Answer Was I'd Never Betray My Homeland or the Revolution;
>
> The Yankees Kept Their Guns Pointed at the Cuban Women.[69]

A full month after the Grenada invasion, the *Granma Weekly Review* was still reporting "Manacled, Blindfolded, with Yankees Ready to Shoot Us; Further Charges of Yankee Plunder"; and "We Held Our Fire Until They Attacked, But When They Did, the Decision Was to Fight Until the Last Drop of Blood."[70]

To avoid being the only voice for or against a certain point of view, thereby lending increased credibility to a particular pronouncement, *Gramna* often uses the close relations between Fidel Castro and the nonaligned, Third World, and communist bloc countries (the categories greatly overlap) to bolster its own propaganda. In the case of Grenada, for example, Havana solicited disapproval of the U.S. action from all its "friends," and then printed an article in *Granma* entitled "The World Is Their Judge":

> According to the dispatches received in our newspaper up to November 1, a total of 92 governments have made public statements on the U.S. invasion of Grenada. Of these, 79 have repudiated or disapproved of the Reagan administration's criminal action.[71]

Granma maintained its vitriolic coverage of the Grenada invasion through the end of December, although Cuban personnel had returned from the neighboring island at least a month earlier. Stories during that time included reports of Raúl Castro's rallying women's combat groups and local militias in the country in defense of an imminent "Yankee" attack against Cuba.

In early June 1984 *Granma* reported the formation of the Maurice Bishop Patriotic Movement—announced in Saint George's, Grenada, by Kenneth Radix, a former minister in the Bishop government—as a new Grenadian political organization. At the same time the newspaper printed Radix's announcement of the creation of the Maurice Bishop Memorial Fund to perpetuate Bishop's ideas and work, and to be funded by donations from individuals, nongovernment organizations, and other foundations, as well as the group's own activities.[72]

Throughout the remainder of 1984 *Granma*'s stories concerning Grenada took the form of its stories on Honduras, the Dominican Republic, or any other Latin American nation not friendly to the Castro regime in Havana. The paper reported that tourism was off on the Caribbean island, that the Grenadian economy had declined since the U.S. invasion, and that the United States had not found the island as much of a boon to capitalism as it had expected.

Central America, 1984

In early January 1984 *Granma* published a review of Central American political events in 1983. Regarding Honduras, the headline for one story read, "A Country That Has Been Taken Over,"[73] reflecting Havana's anger over the U.S. Big Pine military exercises. Honduras's argument that the exercises were a defensive measure to prevent the exportation of revolution from Nicaragua or El Salvador over the border into Honduras is never mentioned by the newspaper. The U.S. troops in Honduras are seen as merely another example of U.S. arrogance. Throughout the year, *Granma* described disastrous economic conditions in Honduras, which, it asserted, flowed directly from the presence of U.S. troops in the country.

Another story, entitled "1983 Increase in U.S. Military Presence in Latin America and the Caribbean," alleged an increase of U.S. troops in the region from 15,000 to 27,900.[74] How this number compares with the minimum 75,000 armed soldiers in Nicaragua (as well as another 75,000 militiamen) or with the 200,000 under arms in Cuba is never mentioned. In addition, the article's troop count includes troops stationed as a result of long-term agreements or treaties: 9,200 in Panama; 3,800 in Puerto Rico; and 2,400 in Cuba (Guantánamo Bay); as well as 8,700 military personnel at sea in the region.

According to *Granma,* the U.S. troops in El Salvador and Honduras numbered no more than 3,100, including the 2,960 the paper said were added during 1983. It listed only several hundred more for Guatemala and Costa Rica. Yet, it was this U.S. military "might" that was cited throughout 1983 as justification for the mammoth militarization that occurred in Central America, and Nicaragua's 100,000 armed troops were never mentioned.[75] Nor were the additional "friendly" troops from Cuba, Bulgaria, Libya, or the PLO, which supplemented the Nicaraguan forces, ever discussed in *Granma*.

By contrast, the *New York Times* estimated U.S. troops in Honduras at 1,200 in the fall of 1984, having fluctuated between 600 and 1,700 throughout most of the year.[76] It further reported that the U.S. naval task force in the Caribbean had 2,100 personnel on board, not the 8,700 claimed by *Granma*. Using the *Times* totals, additional U.S. troops in Central America could be no more than 3,900, compared with the 11,600 according to *Granma*. Of course, the Cuban paper consistently has accused the United States of threatening Central America and the Caribbean, even with significantly smaller troop commitments.

Regarding Nicaragua, the *Weekly Review* of January 8, 1984, reported:

> The repeated failures of the counterrevolutionaries in their plans to capture a portion of its [Nicaragua's] territory and the mass mobilization to confront direct U.S. attacks were what most characterized Nicaragua during 1983. Throughout the year, members of the Sandinista People's Army, Ministry of the Interior and reserve battalions, along with self-defense militia, displayed extraordinary heroism in foiling escalating attacks from Honduras and Costa Rica. *In the last few months, Nicaragua has been constantly threatened by direct U.S. military intervention, especially since the invasion of Grenada on October 25* [emphasis added].[77]

There were dozens of warnings about U.S. intervention in Central America over the first half of the year, quoting various sources, but most frequetly Nicaraguan Interior Minister Tomás Borge and Junta Coordinator (now President) Daniel Ortega Saavedra. Reports of such a threat are obviously valuable to Castro's and Oretga's propaganda campaigns to obtain international support for their regimes, but by the fall of 1984—a year after the intervention in Grenada—none of their predictions had come true. Although the invasion of Grenada increased the frequency, and perhaps the credibility, of the "imminent invasion" threat, *Granma* has run an invasion forecast for years.

Granma traditionally reports events in Central America (and wherever else revolutionary insurgencies exist) in a spirit of friendship and solidarity with the revolutionary, and usually Marxist, group. It does this in two ways: by printing affectionate messages from the groups to Castro or the Cuban people, and by reporting as favorably as possible on the "gains and accomplishments" of the Marxist groups.

On the occasion of Castro's twenty-fifth anniversary in power, *Granma* published congratulations from Nicaragua's Daniel Ortega and from various rebel commanders in El Salvador's FMLN/FDR. The Nicaraguan greeting was published as follows:

> On the occasion of the 25th anniversary of the triumph of the Cuban revolution, allow me, on behalf of the Junta of the Government of

National Reconstruction, to express the sincere congratulations and fraternal affections of the Nicaraguans for you and the sister Cuban people. . . . Dear Comrade Fidel, accept, along with the Cuban people, government and Party, warm and militant greetings from the people of Sandino. Fraternally, Daniel Ortega Saavedra.[78]

Anniversary greetings from the FMLN/FDR rebel leadership in El Salvador were far more emphatic and bitter than Ortega's. The Salvadoran letter read, in part:

We are grateful to you and your people for the example of unshakable fortitude, readiness to win and staunch dignity in the face of U.S. imperialism, the most powerful enemy of all people, including the people of the United States. . . . The revolutionary and heroic people of El Salvador and its vanguard FMLN celebrate the 25th anniversary of the Cuban Revolution, fighting and beating the army of the genocidal dictatorship, puppet of the Pentagon and instrument of Reagan's bloodthirsty politics. . . . Long live Fidel! Long live the fraternity between the Cuban and the Salvadoran peoples! United to fight until final victory! Revolution or death, we will win![79]

Granma reveals its appreciation of such rhetoric by consistently portraying Marxist groups in the best possible light. The January 29, 1984, *Weekly Review* carries the front-page headline "FMLN Fully Controls One-Third of El Salvador," and the subheadline, "In All Liberated Regions People's Power Is Running Trade, Production, Education, Politico-Military Training and All Other Activities." The story reads:

Samayoa is a leader of the People's Liberation Forces [FPL], one of the five organizations that make up the FMLN. He explained that in regions held by the insurgents there is people's power regulating trade, production, education, politico-military training and economic, political and social life in general. In order to illustrate the progress made by the guerrillas, Samayoa explained that whereas fighting would previously last up to ten days, encounters are now decided in hours. As an example of this, he cited the case of El Paraíso Garrison which fell in two hours, the Cuscatlán Bridge in the same time, and the attacks on the San Miguel Garrison that lasted 11 hours.[80]

Most of the Western press at this time was reporting the situation in terms of typical guerrilla warfare, where the guerrillas were having trouble holding onto their gains, and yet the Salvadoran army could not fully eliminate them. The guerrillas were also reported to have been pressing local Salvadorans into military service to keep the guerrilla forces supplied with recruits.

Cuba's recognizing the FMLN/FDR, reporting only its victories and never mentioning its defeats, and idealizing its leaders legitimizes Castro's vision of an ever-growing revolution in Latin America. Consequently, more sacrifices can be demanded of the Cuban people to support the revolutions, for they are portrayed always victorious, with the United States constantly in retreat. It does not necessarily follow, however, that a majority of the Cuban population believes such a scenario, at least in all aspects.

Granma's reports on revolutionary activity in Latin America are also skewed, in that all such activity must strictly follow the Cuban model. Because virtually all revolutionary movements in Latin America are trained, funded, supplied, and endorsed by the Castro regime, it is not unusual that they would all follow established patterns. Nevertheless, *Granma's* coverage of these movements invariably parallels the way Havana works and wants its protégé governments to work.

The revolutions in Nicaragua and El Salvador draw upon the revisionist version of the Cuban revolution that is portrayed in *Granma*. Ultimately, war is waged in the name of the people and against the Yankee imperialists. The revolutionaries gain a foothold in the countryside and start a massive propaganda campaign to call attention to the countervailing actions of the existing government and its ally, the United States. The insurgents then hope public opinion in the free world will paralyze the opposition and make the United States waiver in its support. Economic sabotage is valid because this is a people's war. People's power methods of tightfisted political control are established in areas controlled by guerrillas, and the propaganda machines, including *Granma,* fabricate stories of economic progress occurring in the rebel-controlled areas. On the other hand, the rest of the country, subject to the more objective scrutiny of outside journalists and observers, is obviously suffering from the war. When the war is over and the rebels are victorious (the theory goes) then a national reconstruction can begin to repair economic damage that was actually caused by the war of liberation itself.

Thus, in the Salvadoran case, *Granma* boasts about acts of sabotage and terrorism perpetrated by the Marxist rebels, and uses the excuse of National Reconstruction in Nicaragua, where the rebels have been victorious, to purge the country of all opposition and remove almost every vestige of civil rights, all in the name of preserving peace. "Building peace," in the propaganda campaign, means repairing the war's damage and the damage done by capitalism's allegedly inferior social and economic structures. What is never mentioned is the political repression that accompanies the process. While "building peace," anything may be demanded of the citizenry, including state control of all economic operations, rapid and unprecedented militarization of the nation, and sacrifice of economic and civil liberties. Havana's model is followed with extensive Soviet aid, initially giving the impression of increasing wealth until the revolution is consolidated and fully "institutionalized." As long as events pass along the plotted course, *Granma* can easily justify the rebels' actions to the people in Cuba and to rebels in other parts of the world while preserving Havana's cherished position as the model for Third World revolutions. Any failures are described as the fault of U.S. military or political presence in the region, or U.S. subversion. Dissident groups, never explicitly mentioned in *Granma,* would upset this picturesque scenario. This dilemma is easily solved by intimating that any group or individual opposing the social harmony of a socialist regime must be in the employ of, or sympathetic to, the United States government.

Along the same lines, *Granma* has been inconsistent in its coverage of the electoral processes in Nicaragua and El Salvador. In December 1983 *Granma* covered the elections in Nicaragua, saying, "In early December, the Nicaraguan Government took concrete steps towards institutionalization by announcing the date for the beginning of the elections and giving thousands of Nicaraguans the chance to return to their country."[81] Of course, institutionalization to the paper in Havana meant the implementation of the National Reconstruction, while to the West it signified an institutionalization of the repressive, Marxist government that would mimic Fidel Castro's Cuba. This article was intended to make the Sandinistas more appealing to would-be voters. (The more people who showed up at the polls, the more credible the Nicaraguan election would seem, despite the lack of real opposition.)

In late March 1984 *Granma* took another step toward making sure there would be good voter turnout and toward ensuring a Sandinista victory at the polls. It published a report on the Sandinistas' decision to allow anyone over the age of sixteen to vote in the upcoming election. The focus of the story was on the Sandinista Communist Youth League, and its support of the government's voting policy.[82]

The ploy made some political sense. Because Nicaraguans between the ages of sixteen and twenty are unlikely to remember any government prior to the current Sandinista regime, which had then ruled for more than five years, and because they were likely to be unsophisticated voters susceptible to Sandinista propaganda, this group represented a large segment of the Nicaraguan population that could be easily manipulated and mobilized for the regime's success. *Granma* accommodated this propaganda campaign whenever possible.[83]

By contrast, *Granma* reported on the elections in El Salvador, in which two candidates with sharply divergent views campaigned vigorously for the presidency, as if it were a *fait accompli* imposed by the United States. The Cuban paper also tried to depict the Salvadoran situation as constantly deteriorating under rebel pressure and its own disorganization. For example, as the election primary in El Salvador approached, the *Weekly Review* ran the story "Half of El Salvador without Electricity, Genuine Chaos during Elections":

> The Eastern section of El Salvador was cut off from the rest of the country as rebel forces destroyed the El Pacayal communication center in San Miguel department.

> With the interruption of electrical power, half the country was blacked out and bus traffic was virtually halted, leaving the Salvadoran east virtually isolated.[84]

It is interesting to note that the eastern part of the country referred to in the article as under attack and isolated is the same area that was said to be under rebel control in the January 29 issue, in which the "people's power" was regulating life peacefully. Following Castro's lead, *Granma* labeled the Salvadoran elections a farce and then raised the rebel disruption and economic sabotage to the level of front-page heroics. Likewise, following the final elections in El Salvador held in May 1984, *Granma* ran a story entitled, "Duarte Proclaimed Winner of Election Farce."

Throughout this period *Granma* maintained the same repetitive message: (1) El Salvador's war is a people's war, with the FMLN enjoying the full support of the population; (2) the Salvadoran government is merely a puppet of the United States; (3) the United States is planning an imminent invasion of El Salvador; and (4) the only group capable of preventing such an invasion is the FMLN-FDR rebels, for El Salvador's puppet government has no say in the matter and might even welcome an invasion (as insurance against giving up power).[85]

The Cuban newspaper's coverage of Nicaragua and the Sandinista regime has been altogether different. Most of its stories deal with Sandinista warnings of a U.S. invasion. These reports never admit to Nicaraguan resistance successes in Nicaragua, nor do they even mention internal dissent to the Managua regime. And the elections in Nicaragua are always treated as "true and honest" reflections of the will of the people.

But *Granma*'s most important function to Fidel Castro is as chronicle of the Havana regime, putting forth its official line verbatim. Such was the case in May 1984, when *Granma* ran a piece detailing Havana's position on a negotiated settlement of the crisis in Nicaragua, which would include the opposition to the Sandinistas. The article was framed as a response to a pastoral letter from a conference of Nicaraguan bishops. It read in part:

> On April 22 a pastoral letter from the Nicaraguan Conference of Bishops was placed in circulation, but from that very moment it has also been refuted and rejected by broad sectors of the population. Its contentions are eminently more political than religious and overtly coincide with the domestic and foreign enemies of the Sandinista Revolution and Nicaragua.
>
> The Bishops called for dialogue between Somoza supporters, counterrevolutionaries, traitors, CIA mercenaries, the Reagan administration and its Central American allies and local reactionaries at the bidding of U.S. imperialism, on the one hand, and, on the other, the Sandinista government, commenting menacingly that "if those who have taken up arms do not participate in dialogue, there is no chance of settlement."
>
> The pastoral letter was quickly rejected by mothers of heroes and martyrs, relatives of the dead, the young in military service facing the killers with weapons in hand, fighters of the Sandinista People's Army, the People's Militia, Sandinista Defense Committees, workers, peasants, students, the media, the government and the Sandinista Front leadership.
>
> In letters to the editor of the daily *Barricada* Mrs. Carlota Paz de Teller wrote, "Yes, Bishop Obando y Bravo, on April 30 it will be a year since my son Daniel Teller Paz was murdered by those beasts and my heart still bleeds for him. How could I have a dialogue with killers?"[86]

It is worth noting the inconsistency between *Granma*'s never reporting on Sandinista casualties, and its strident rejection of the bishop's letter by "mothers of heroes and martyrs, relatives of the dead, [and] the young in military service . . . with weapons in hand."[87] This inconsistency is rampant in *Granma*'s treatment of Castro's military as well.

The above-mentioned article in *Granma* is much more important than Castro's party line, however. It also represents the view of the Sandinista regime toward the place of religion in Nicaragua, facilitating the Sandinistas' institutionalization of their antichurch policy. Take, for example, the comments made by Sandinista Junta member Sergio Ramírez:

> When the Nicaraguan Bishops should have taken a patriotic stand they issued a document running counter to the interests of the country and in favor of the United States.

The pastoral letter is "another mine against the Nicaraguan people, another of the mines which the CIA has been placing on our coasts," because it seeks to undermine unity and confuse the people.

The Catholic people do not refuse to take up arms in defense of the Revolution and there are many thousands of Catholics on the front line as Nicaraguans and revolutionaries.[88]

Quoting an editorial from the Sandinista daily *Barricada, Granma* gives the Sandinista view of the Catholic Chuch's role and the pastoral letter:

It is easier to oppose an enemy who makes his position clear than one who hides behind 2,000 years of ideological domination to conceal his interests. . . . These are the glad tidings brought to us by the pastoral letter.[89]

Finally, the article "No Dialogue with Counterrevolution" concludes with *Granma*'s description of what negotiation would mean:

A new battlefront opens for the Sandinista Revolution as a result of a decision taken by its age-old enemy, U.S. imperialism, and its local allies. Yet in political and ideological battle, as well as armed struggle, the people of Sandino and their vanguard, the FMLN, will win.[90]

Thus, *Granma* defines the Sandinistas' goal as achieving peace only at the cost of total defeat for the "imperialists" supporting the democratic alternative. Nevertheless, *Granma* will never pass up an opportunity to characterize U.S. reluctance to negotiate a political solution with the Sandinista regime as intransigence, posturing, and outright warmongering.

Despite Havana's repetitive admonition that the United States is not willing to negotiate a solution to the crisis in Central America, *Granma*'s coverage of contacts between Nicaragua's leaders and U.S. Secretary of State George Schultz has been very sparse. The *Weekly Review* did publish a photograph of Secretary Schultz with President Daniel Ortega, with only this caption:

Commander Daniel Ortega, Coordinator of the Government Junta of Nicaragua, met with U.S. Secretary of State George Schultz, when he made a surprise visit to the country. Reporting on their two-hour meeting *Barricada* warned that further talks with Washington should not lead anyone to expect that a serious negotiation process is about to start. While in Managua Schultz reiterated the known official stand of the Reagan administration.[91]

Granma and the World

In the previous sections of this paper, I have examined various aspects of *Granma*'s coverage of certain international events. In a real sense *Granma*'s editorials represent the closest available views of Havana's official line on daily events of international import. Although the international relationships already covered are clearly *key* to understanding Fidel Castro's role in the international arena, certain of his other foreign policy views are indicative of Havana's worldview.

It is obvious, from the events already discussed, that Cuba has fraternal feeling toward the Sandinistas in Nicaragua and the FMLN rebels in El Salvador. It is equally obvious that *Granma*'s authors feel nothing but extreme hostility for the pro-Western Central American governments, which they portray as mere puppets of U.S. imperialism, taking a particularly antagonistic position with respect to the Salvadoran and Honduran governments.

Granma, meanwhile, reflecting the wishes of Castro, attempted to utilize its propaganda operation to drive a wedge between the United States and friendly Latin American nations, such as Mexico, Argentina, and Brazil. One such example is the story run during Mexican president Miguel de la Madrid's visit to Washington, D.C., in May 1984, which read in part:

> The differences between Mexico and the United States, or rather between Mexico and the Reagan administration, were made clear during President Miguel de la Madrid's official visit to Washington.
>
> The differences cover a wide range of issues ranging from Mexican opposition to military intervention in Central America, growing U.S. economic protectionism and aggressiveness towards millions of workers of Mexican origin who work on plantations in the southern part of the United States and in other jobs spurned by local workers, to the three recent hikes in interest rates ordered by U.S. banks. The latter development has meant that overnight Mexico's foreign debt has skyrocketed.
>
> The Mexican stand was perhaps best reflected in headlines of the main Mexico City dailies based on statements made by Mr. de la Madrid in Washington: "Mexico Wants to be a Dignified Neighbor and Not a Slave of the United States"; "Mexico Will Not Accept Pressure from Anybody"; "Mexico Will Not Change Its Political Principles for Economic Transactions."[92]

Granma ran the above story in conjunction with other reports on de la Madrid's visit, such as one alleging that the Reagan administration had not sent anyone to the airport to greet the visiting dignitary upon his arrival, humiliating the Mexican leader and embarrassing the administration.[93]

Granma has further accused the United States of imposing a painful IMF plan of austerity on Mexico. In another example, the Havana paper attempted to portray the United States as hostile to Mexican trade interests, and unsympathetic to that nation's burgeoning debt crisis. A fairly typical example was the piece "Hitting below the Belt," which ran in May 1985:

> Blows below the belt are banned in boxing and when they are repeated the wrongdoer is disqualified. But the Reagan administration seems to have forgotten about this rule in its dealing with Mexico, its neighbor to the south.
>
> Recently the U.S. government removed 56 Mexican products from the General System of Tariff Preferences in open violation of measures adopted by the United Nations Conference on Trade and Development [UNCTAD].[94]

The article ends by noting Mexico's objections to the measures described, which *Granma* deemed showed a cruel lack of concern on the part of the Reagan administration.

In South America, as in Africa, the Middle East, and elsewhere, Havana closely follows the movement of leftist guerrilla groups, primarily in Colombia and Peru. *Granma* often cites these revolutionaries' news services as prime sources of information for the countries in which they operate. Virtually all of the ruling South American governments, with the exception of Guyana, Suriname, and occasionally Argentina, receive *Granma*'s antagonistic and negative appraisal. *Granma* gives wide press coverage to political unrest in Chile and focuses on unrest in Brazil whenever possible. Among all the South American nations, Chile receives most of *Granma*'s attention, all of it negative. Venezuela also receives negative comments from *Granma*. These reports often underplay or ignore many facts. In the case of Paraguay, while *Granma* reports on the close relationship between that country and the United States, the *New York Times* has noted the Reagan administration's attempts to distance itself from the regime of Paraguay's dictator Stroessner, despite Stroessner's assertion that he is the best ally United States has.[95]

Argentina, under the anticommunist military junta led by General Leopoldo Galtieri, was a relatively frequent target of scathing articles in *Granma*. By contrast, as Castro tried to improve his overall relations with the Southern Cone countries, *Granma* has given much more favorable reviews to the civilian government of Raúl Alfonsín. Such treatment of Alfonsín's government, however, should not be seen as evidencing a sudden appreciation of liberal democracies on the part of Fidel Castro. Rather, he is happy to see the departure of Galtieri and company and their replacement by a civilian government that might prove a new friend in the region, or that could, at least, be more easily manipulated on such difficult issues as the current debt crisis. Argentina, one of the largest of today's debtor nations, has also proved among the most intractable on debt-related issues.

The Soviet Union

So far, little mention has been made of *Granma*'a views on the Soviet Union, Havana's financial and military lifeline. Castro's relationship to the Soviet Union can be easily gleaned from a survey of *Granma*'s headlines, such as a front-page *Weekly Review* headline that ran in early 1981:

> The Soviet Union and the Glorious Party You Represent Again Emerge as a Hope for Peace and a Guarantee that the Imperialists Will Not Be Able to Impose Their Domination and Aggressive Arrogance.[96]

The Soviet Union is mentioned periodically in *Granma,* but not too frequently; its profile is kept benign and only occasionally in view. These reports are always of an official nature and almost never dwell on the life-styles of the Soviet people. Naturally, the Soviet Union is always depicted favorably.

Relatively unimportant items, such as obituary notices of middle-level Soviet officials, sometimes appear in *Granma,* but major international situations involving the Soviets, such as Afghanistan and the arms negotiations, are regularly neglected. The arms talks are ignored as a matter of course, unless the Soviet Union stands to score against the United States or respond strongly in defense of the fraternity of communist states. It is always ignored when the Soviet Union fails to wholeheartedly support the actions of an ally, such as Syria or the PLO.

Copiously reported in *Granma* were stories regarding the deaths of Andropov and Brezhnev. Most of the attention was paid to Castro's visits with each late premier's successors. The *Weekly Review* articles announcing the deaths of Andropov and Brezhnev were bordered in gray and replete with photographs of a mournful Fidel Castro standing shoulder to shoulder with the highest Soviet officials.

On the occasion of Andropov's funeral, *Granma* ran the story "Living Legacy in Hall of Columns":

> The first activity of Fidel and his delegation after arriving in Moscow was to convey Cuba's tribute of respect, admiration, and gratitude to the memory of Yuri Vladmirovich Andropov.
>
> Even his [Andropov's] political enemies have been forced to breathe an air of respect and peace on the occasion of Andropov's death.
>
> The worldwide repercussion over his death calls for meditating on what socialism has come to signify in our day and age.
>
> The world is not saying farewell to a figure famous by birth or fortune. No one had to spend millions of dollars to make him a political figure. The world is saying farewell to the son of a railroad worker from Satvropol. . . . His fortune is there at the foot of his bier and it consists of the Hero of Socialist Labor Medal and the many other decorations conferred by the Soviet Union. His death marks the end of fruitful life for an experiment of the new world, of the world of ordinary men, a world which measures according to a new yardstick.
>
> A life has ended but a message remains. The intensity with which he lived a communist life, a time of struggle and creativity, is a lesson to all. And it is to that legacy that Fidel and the other members of the Cuban Party and Government pay tribute.[97]

The same issue of *Granma* that eulogized Andropov also reported on the Politburo meeting that selected Konstantin Chernenko as the next Soviet premier, and on the meeting between Fidel Castro and the leaders of Bulgaria, East Germany, and Poland. Subsequent meetings between Castro and the leadership of Asian, African, and European liberation movements were also reported in a later issue of *Granma*.

Although the political relationship between the Soviet Union and the United States is almost never mentioned in the Havana newspaper, an aspect that receives significant attention is Soviet military preparedness. One example is the following story, "The Soviet Union Will Not Allow Military Superiority over It, Says Dimitri Ustinov," which was based on a report in *Pravda* dated November 19, 1983:

> If despite the Soviet Union's peace proposals and the protests of progressive social forces all over the world the deployment is carried out, the socialist countries will take effective countermeasures, says Marshal Ustinov.
>
> If the U.S. missiles are deployed in Europe, we will lift our moratorium on the deployment of SS-20 medium-range missiles in the European zone. In coordination with our allies we will deploy new weapons to create a counterweight to the growing number of NATO nuclear weap-

ons in Europe. We will also take such countermeasures regarding the territory of the United States so that the Americans will clearly feel the difference between the situation which existed prior to and after the deployment.[98]

With stories like this, *Granma* enables the Castro regime to spread the myth inherent in the Ustinov statement, that there are no Soviet missiles in Europe, and only deployment by the United States would force such a Soviet counteraction. This claim could not have been further from the truth.

In another attempt at highlighting Soviet technological advances, Soviet space voyages and related achievements are heralded by *Granma,* while U.S. space activities are seldom reported. The Soviet Union, as leader of the communist bloc, is frequently portrayed as the international leader in science and technology. Members of that bloc, such as Bulgaria and East Germany, are regularly praised in *Granma* for their technical assistance to the Havana regime.

Israel

Granma's coverage of Israel over the years has reflected an unrelenting hatred that has grown steadily, particularly during the last decade or so, as Cuba has drawn closer to radical, Soviet-supported Arab hardliners, such as Libyan strongman Muammar Qaddafi, various Palestinian terrorists, and other Arab allies. Former Israeli prime minister Menachem Begin was routinely referred to as a Nazi, a particularly sadistic way of referring to an individual persecuted by both Nazi and Soviet henchmen during World War II. Political cartoons appearing in *Granma* have portrayed Begin as a skull-and-crossbones figure wearing Nazi swastikas.

One tactic employed by *Granma* in its propaganda campaign is to treat Israel as the world's pariah, publishing stories of mixed facts and falsehoods, often distorting the truth. This happened, for example, during *Granma*'s coverage of the Lebanese slayings in the refugee camps of Sabra and Shatila, when the paper put the entire blame for the massacres on Israel, and inflated the number of deaths that actually occurred.

Granma also concentrates on carrying unfavorable stories about Israel's arms sales to Central American nations and its growing ties with many nations in Africa, both areas of joint Cuban and Soviet commitment. Occasionally, the paper will try to legitimize its reporting by adding references from other international journals, such as an article entitled "Zionism Militarizes Central America":

Israel's relations with Central American regimes such as those of Honduras and Guatemala, characterized by a regular exchange of visits by top-ranking officials, demonstrate that Tel Aviv has agreed to become the United States' covert agent in the matter of sales and donations of weapons to certain Latin American republics.

Gregorie Selser says in an article published in the daily *El Día* that the United States supports Israel's trading in armaments in Latin America because of converging U.S. and Israeli interest in the region.[99]

With the rise of Marxist dictatorships in Africa since the 1960s, Castro has found fertile ground for friendships in that portion of the world. Such regimes as those in Angola, Ethiopia, and Mozambique are guaranteed favorable press in *Granma*. Much of the rest of Africa is ignored, except for South Africa, which is regularly excoriated by the press in Havana.

Coverage of the rest of the world is generally rare. Western Europe, particularly Great Britain, France, Italy, Switzerland, and West Germany are hardly ever mentioned, unless in some negative way, as in a story about economic problems or defense increases. The one exception to that is the disproportionate coverage of Communist party activities in those countries. Reports from members of these parties, as from members of the U.S. Communist party, generally critical of their home governments, frequently find their way onto the pages of *Granma*.

Likewise, *Granma*'s coverage of Asia is sparse. Vietnam regularly receives the approval of the Castro regime, and occasionally stories about North Korea and Cambodia appear. But stories on Japan, Malaysia, South Korea, or Thailand are virtually nonexistent. China, whose relations with Castro have worsened as Cuba has moved closer to the Soviet Union, is not often covered by *Granma*.

Conclusion

The iron hand of censorship as applied by Castro to all forms of journalism in Cuba makes the island's press a mouthpiece for his regime. Although this situation renders it almost impossible for the average citizen in Cuba to learn the truth about Castro's behavior in world affairs by reading Havana's media, it does afford analysts who take the time to read *Granma* a glimpse of what the leadership in Havana is thinking in foreign affairs. This is important because there is very little access to the policymakers in Castro's cadre. By monitoring the way *Granma* covers various international events, Western analysts and policymakers can perhaps better understand, and thus more effectively deal with, the international activities and adventurism of Fidel Castro and his revolutionary regime in Havana.

Respondent: Mr. George Gedda, Associated Press

Many people in the United States complain about the U.S. press, that it's too liberal or too critical. This is nothing compared to what the Cuban people are up against in trying to find out what's happening in the world through the pages of *Granma*.

The basic difference is that in Cuba all news is distributed by the government, resulting in a system that doesn't permit independent viewpoints. In the United States news is distributed by independent news agencies because an "official" news agency could be used too easily by an incumbent president for political gain.

During one of my trips to Cuba, I explained this situation to a high-ranking Cuban official and she was astonished by this revelation. She found it hard to believe that a country that, she had been told, was hell-bent on worldwide domination would not control its own newspapers.

Respondent: Ms. Suzanne Garment, *Wall Street Journal*

It is very easy to say that *Granma* is a communist paper of a totalitarian regime and that therefore it has all the characteristics that one may expect of such a house organ. It's quite another matter to read in detail the language to which the readers are exposed every day and the language in which they are led to conceptualize international relations. That is very frightening.

The hope of Western societies is that, in the end, the pride of Western citizens and the respect that we have for the private press will prove an advantage over the cynicism that a totalitarian press breeds in its citizens. It is not a vain hope.

In circles where it counts, newspapers like *Granma* are seen as the propaganda tools they are and they have a hard time being believed.

I worry more about Western writers who don't have the conceptual arms to recognize the difference between the two kinds of journalism.

Discussion Summary

The Cuban model has been taken up by Nicaragua with newspapers such as *Barricada* and *El Nuevo Diario*. The U.S. and international media should explore the origin of the news in these newspapers. Often Nicaraguan newspapers quote *Granma* as a reputable, legitimate, authoritative source of news. There is also interplay among *Pravda, TASS,* etc. in attempts at credibility.

Notes

Founded in 1964, *Granma* took the name of the boat on which Fidel Castro sailed from Tuxpan, Mexico, in December 1956. With eighty-two men, he landed in Oriente Province, Cuba, to start the guerrilla insurrection that ended with an overthrow of Fulgencio Batista on January 1, 1959. A day later *Revolución,* formerly published clandestinely as the organ of the 26 of July Movement, became the chief daily of Cuba. In 1964 *Revolución* was fused with *Hoy,* the official organ of the old Partido Socialista Popular (Communist party of Cuba), and became *Granma.*

 1. See Roberto Alvarez Quiñones, "The Deficit Bomb," *Granma Weekly Review,* April 29, 1984, p. 9; José G. Guma, "Strangling the Debtor, A Strange Way of Collecting Debts," ibid., p. 10.
 2. "In 1984, Cuba Hopes to Renegotiate Its Debt under the Conditions Dictated by the Crisis on the Sugar Market," *Granma Weekly Review,* April 15, 1984, pp. 4-5.
 3. See, for example, Guma, "Strangling the Debtor"; "Latin America's Foreign Debt Will Double by 1990," *Granma Weekly Review,* April 29, 1984, p. 10.
 4. "Argentina: No to the IMF," *Granma Weekly Review,* June 24, 1984, p. 11.
 5. Reinaldo Lugo, "The CIA's Many Private Businesses," *Granma Weekly Review,* April 22, 1984, p. 8.
 6. Ibid., p. 10.
 7. "Nine More Countries Won't Be at Los Angeles Olympics," *Granma Weekly Review,* May 27, 1984, p. 5.
 8. "Cuba Will Not Attend Los Angeles Olympics," *Granma Weekly Review,* June 3, 1984, p. 3.
 9. "FMLN-FDR Propose Formation of Broadly Based Provisional Government for El Salvador," *Granma Weekly Review,* February 19, 1984, p. 10.
10. "Reply to Yankee Slander: More Proof of Imperialist Insolence," *Granma Weekly Review,* April 3, 1983, p. 1.
11. "Cuban Veterinary Service Becomes the Target of U.S. Slander," *Granma,* June 1, 1983, p. 7.
12. "Right of Reply," *Granma Weekly Review,* June 17, 1984, p. 1.
13. Ibid.
14. Ibid.
15. Ibid.
16. Ibid.
17. Roberto Alvarez Quiñones, "Deterioration of Public Health in the United States: The Medical Mafia in Action," *Granma Weekly Review,* July 17, 1983, p. 2.
18. "South Africa Forced to Hold Talks with Angola on Troops Withdrawal from Southern Angola and Namibian Independence," *Granma Weekly Review,* March 4, 1984, p. 5.
19. Don Oberdorfer, "Portugal's Soares Sees Cuba Quitting Angola," *Washington Post,* March 16, 1984, p. 26.

20. "Cuban Withdrawal from Angola Set—With Conditions," *Washington Post,* March 20, 1984, p. A20.
21. "Joint Statement by the Governments of the Republic of Cuba and the People's Republic of Angola," *Granma Weekly Review,* March 25, 1984, p. 1.
22. Ibid.
23. Ibid.
24. Ibid.
25. "Brutal Imperialist and Racist Act against Cuban Civilian Cooperation Personnel in Angola," *Granma Weekly Review,* April 29, 1981, p. 1.
26. "South Africa Forced to Hold Talks with Angola on Troops Withdrawal from Southern Angola and Namibian Independence."
27. Alcibíades Hidalgo, "Encabeza el General Jaruzelski el Consejo Militar de Salvación que Asumió el Control en Polonia," *Granma,* December 14, 1981, p. 1.
28. "Discuten en Polonia la Posibilidad de Crear un Frente de Entendimiento Nacional," *Granma,* November 5, 1981, p. 6.
29. Ibid.
30. Nelson Marcos García, "Aumentan las Posibilidades de Formar un Frente de Acuerdo Nacional en Polonia," *Granma,* November 6, 1984, p. 5.
31. Nelson Marcos García, "Reúnese Jaruzelski con la Dirección de la Unión de Luchadores por la Libertad para Tratar Sobre la Creación del Frente Nacional Polaco," *Granma,* November 7, 1981, p. 5.
32. "Afirma la Dirección de 'Solidaridad' que Está Dispuesta a Compromisos con el Gobierno Polaco," *Granma,* November 9, 1981, p. 5.
33. Nelson Marcos García, "Aprobó el Gobierno Polaco Resultado de las Conversaciones de Jaruzelski con el Primado de la Iglesia y con Walesa," *Granma,* November 11, 1981, p. 5.
34. Nelson Marcos García, "Aprueba el Buró Político del POUP Gestiones para Crear un Frente de Acuerdo Nacional en Polonia,"*Granma,* November 12, 1981, p. 5.
35. Nelson Marcos García, "Recorre Jaruzelski Varios Centros Laborales en Varsovia y Explica a sus Trabajadores la Situación Política y Socioeconómica Polaca," *Granma,* November 17, 1981, p. 5.
36. John Darnton, "Parliament Bids Polish Workers Stop All Strikes," *New York Times,* November 1, 1981, p. A1.
37. Ibid.
38. "Solidarity Chapters in Poland to Continue Strikes," *New York Times,* November 2, 1981, p. A9.
39. "200,000 Poles End 20-Day Wildcat Strike but Other Protests Go On," *New York Times,* November 13, 1981, p. A3.
40. "Asegura el CC del POUP que 'Solidaridad' Persigue y Aplica el Terror Moral Contra Militantes del Partido en las Fábricas," *Granma,* November 26, 1981, p. 5.
41. "Encabeza General Jaruzelski el Consejo Militar de Salvación que Asumió el Control en Polonia", *Granma,* December 14, 1981.
42. Alcibíades Hidalgo, "Tranquilidad en Polonia Tras la Declaración del Estado de Guerra," *Granma,* December 15, 1981, p. 1.
43. Henry Kamm, "Politburo Passes Antistrike Law," *New York Times,* November 28, 1981, p. 1A.

44. John Darnton, "Premier Declares 'State of War' to Insure Law and Order in Crisis," *New York Times,* December 13, 1981, p. 1A.
45. John Darnton, "Walesa Negotiates: New Army Council Bans Rallies and Sets Wide Grounds for Arrests," *New York Times,* December 14, 1981, p. 1A.
46. "Predomina la Calma en Varsovia y en la Mayor Parte de Polonia," *Granma,* December 16, 1981, p. 6.
47. "Widespread Strikes Reported in Defiance of Polish Regime; U.S. Postpones All Pending Aid," *New York Times,* December 15, 1981, p. 1A.
48. "Va Recuperando Polonia Su Actividad Económica; Normalízase Trabajo Factoril", *Granma,* December 16, 1981, p. 6.
49. "Army Rulers Said to Break Some Major Strikes; Church Challenges Regime," *New York Times,* December 17, 1981, p. 1A.
50. "Expresa Stefan Olszowski, Miembro del Buró Político del POUP, que la Unica Medida Justa que Podían Tomar las Autoridades Era Declarar el Estado de Guerra," *Granma,* December 18, 1981, p. 6.
51. Robert Pear, "A Bread Shortage; U.S. Says the Resistance Seems to Continue in Gdansk and Silesia," *New York Times,* December 19, 1981, p. 1A.
52. "Continúa el Consejo Militar para la Salvación Nacional, en Polonia, Ejecutando Medidas contra Elementos Antisocialistas," *Granma,* December 19, 1981, p. 6.
53. Michael T. Kaufman, "Grenada Radio Warns of Attack," *New York Times,* October 24, 1983, p. A4.
54. See Michael T. Kaufman, "50 Marines Land at Barbados Field," *New York Times,* October 25, 1983, p. 1A; Kernan Turner, "Marines Land in Barbados as 'Option' for Evacuation," *Washington Post,* October 25, 1983.
55. Jim Hoagland, "U.S Invades Grenada; Fights Cubans; Reagan Cites Protection of Americans," *Washington Post,* October 26, 1983, p. 1.
56. "Statement by Cuban Party and Government on the Imperialist Intervention in Grenada," *Granma Weekly Review,* October 30, 1983, p. 1.
57. "Lessons in Grenada," *Problems of Communism* (July-August 1984).
58. "Statement by Cuban Party and Government on the Imperialist Intervention in Grenada," *Granma Weekly Review,* October 30, 1983, p. 1.
59. Ibid.
60. Ibid.
61. Ibid.
62. Ibid.
63. Ibid.
64. Philip Taubman, "U.S. Reports Evidence of Island Hostage Plan," *New York Times,* October 28, 1983, p. A14.
65. Bob Woodward and Patrick E. Tyler, "CIA's Reports Magnify Soviet-Cuban Presence," *Washington Post,* October 29, 1983, p. A10.
66. "Statement by the Cuban Party and Government on the Imperialist Intervention in Grenada," *Granma Weekly Review,* October 30, 1981, p. 1.
67. "All of Cuba Repudiates Brutal U.S. Attack on Grenada," *Granma,* November 6, 1983, p. 7.
68. "U.S. Marines Invade Grenada: Incalculable Political and Moral Defeat," *Granma,* November 6, 1983, p. 10.

69. Ibid., November 20, 1983, p. 5.
70. Ibid., November 27, 1983, p. 9.
71. Ibid., November 6, 1983, p. 7.
72. "Maurice Bishop Patriotic Movement Formed in Grenada," ibid., June 10, 1984.
73. "Honduras 1983: A Country That Has Been Taken Over, More Sacrifices and Problems on the Horizon," ibid., January 8, 1984, p. 11.
74. "1983 Increase in Military Presence in Latin America and the Caribbean," ibid., January 8, 1984, p. 11.
75. Ibid.
76. "Honduras Seeks Looser Alliance and Rise in Aid," *New York Times*, October 9, 1984, p. 1.
77. "1983 Increase in Military Presence in Latin America and the Caribbean," *Granma*, January 8, 1984, p. 11.
78. Ibid.
79. Manuel Guerrero, "The People United Will Never Be Defeated," *Granma Weekly Review*, January 8, 1984, p. 11.
80. "FMLN Fully Controls One-Third of El Salvador," *Granma*, January 29, 1984, p. 1.
81. "Nicaragua Takes Steps Toward Institutionalization," ibid., December 18, 1983, p. 8.
82. Orestes Valera, "Nicaragua Is Sandino," ibid., April 1, 1984, p. 2.
83. Ibid., p. 1.
84. "Half of El Salvador without Electricity, Genuine Chaos during Elections," *Granma Weekly Review*, May 20, 1984, p. 5.
85. Ibid.
86. "No Dialogue with Counterrevolution," *Granma*, May 13, 1984, p. 2.
87. Ibid., p. 10.
88. Ibid.
89. Ibid.
90. Ibid.
91. "Nicaragua," ibid., June 17, 1984, p. 10.
92. José Gabriel Guma, "De la Madrid's Trip to Washington, the Differences Remain," ibid., May 27, 1984, p. 11.
93. Ibid.
94. José Gabriel Guma, "Hitting Below the Belt," ibid., May 8, 1983, p. 11.
95. John Vinocur, "A Republic of Fear: 30 Years of General Stroessner's Paraguay," *New York Times Magazine*, September 23, 1984, p. 20.
96. "We Will Never Harbor Ingratitude, Opportunism, or Betrayal," *Granma Weekly Review*, March 8, 1981, p. 1.
97. Julio García, "Living Legacy in Hall of Columns," *Granma*, February 19, 1984, p. 1.
98. *Granma Weekly Review*, October 11, 1983.
99. Rafael García Breto, "Zionism Militarizes Central America," *Granma*, December 18, 1983, p. 2.

3

The Press in Cuba, 1952-1960: Autocratic and Totalitarian Censorship

Carlos Ripoll

An examination of the elements that characterize auto-cratic and totalitarian censorship of the press in the context of the Batista and Castro regimes in Cuba from 1952 to 1960. Through citations and content analysis, the paper makes the case that under Batista, autocratic censorship impinged on political life but left other aspects of daily life relatively untouched, and that under Castro, totalitarian censorship tries to change the way the people think so that they all say the same thing, as instructed by the press.

> *The difference between the Batista and the Castro regimes is essentially the difference between Ali Baba and his 40 Thieves and Mohammed. During the Ali Baba regime you wouldn't have much trouble unless you interfered with the 40 Thieves; they were only after your money. But under Mohammed you have to worship him every minute of the day.*
>
> —Dr. Luis Aguilar
> Georgetown University

Introduction

There are two types of censorship: one is aimed at sustaining a government and affects only what might have an impact on the government's hold on power; the other reaches much further in its aim, to change the way that people think.

The difference in approach between the two stems from the different

83

concepts of authority that serve as their underpinnings. The first, the selective type of censorship, is likely to be found where the government's self-proclaimed mission is to maintain the established order. Like the autocratic governments that engender it, that kind of censorship impinges on political life, but in other areas it allows some freedom of expression. The second, the all-embracing kind, reflects the totalitarian mentality—the belief among those in power that they have discovered truth. Their governmental mission, therefore, is to make society conform to their dogma, and censorship as imposed by them must pervade all areas of life, not just politics.

The plight of Socrates reflected the lesser of the kinds of censorship. The government that condemned him feared subversion in his teaching of Athenian youth. The Roman emperors used censorship of essentially the same sort; ultimately, death by crucifixion became the penalty for writing or distributing criticism of the emperor. Later on, in the hands of the Catholic church, censorship became progressively more insidious as the goal of the censors became universal acceptance of their dogma. We know, for example, that during the time of Clement Romanus, Saint Peter's successor, Christians were forbidden to read anything by a gentile because church writings were supposed to suffice to shape the ideal world.

Whether we look far into the past or only to this century's lessons for proof, we find that positive change cannot occur if thought and expression are subject to control. Individuals lose the capacity for creative independence when the outside world invades their inner preserves. If the media become instruments of a government intent on converting the public to its brand of truth, citizens can gradually lose hold of themselves. The censored press will remind them daily to conform. It will tell them how to think, it will speak for them, and it will make their decisions. In that anti-Cartesian world, because they *do not* think they exist. The proof is all around them: anyone who thinks or questions reality or marches out of step becomes a nonperson.

The reason for this severity is simple. The strength of thought is such that if it finds a crack in the censor's walls, it can shake the government's foundations. Poland offers a recent example. After the workers' strikes in 1976, dissidents began to publish materials that deviate from the party's line. Forced to accede to labor demands, the Gierek government agreed to workers' access to the media. Shortly thereafter, in April 1981, Solidarity's weekly publication began to appear. Tight press censorship had effectively been smashed, so the government adopted a new law on censorship. But with the relaxation of censorship, the government had lost control of the situation, and only two months later the Jaruzelski government felt compelled to impose martial law and then to declare a state of war.

From 1952 to 1960 Cuba lived through both types of censorship. Under the government of Fulgencio Batista the repression was aimed at shaping opinion to support, or prevent subversion of, authority. When the Castro regime took power, a qualitative change in the censorship occurred: the new government's goal was to impose a different view of society, and the role of the censors went beyond suppression of dissent to forging an exclusive national way of thought. The censorship of the old autocracy had sought to prevent some Cubans from saying certain things; the new totalitarian censorship sought to force all Cubans to say the same thing.

In the final analysis, it was not Castro's guerrillas or popular dissatisfaction with an immoral regime that brought Batista down (although there was plenty of that dissatisfaction). It was, in fact, the press that, notwithstanding the punishment it received, gradually undermined the dictatorship by denouncing its illegal claim to power and its abuses at every opportunity. Batista ignored the people's will and repeatedly, and often brutally, violated his opponents' civil rights, but his regime was timid or inefficient in its use of censorship and it really never could enforce censorship effectively. On the other hand, Castro followed the advice of the old-line Cuban Communists in treating the press as a dangerous adversary. Fearing the truth in Napoleon's maxim that "four hostile newspapers are more to be feared than a thousand bayonets," Castro dealt with press criticism of his government's actions by treating journalists as if they were armies to be defeated. Ultimately, the government seized absolute control over all mass media and other outlets for expression of opinion and culture and placed them all in the service of the Cuban Communist Party.

The following is an overview of the role of the press and censorship in the period from 1952 through 1958 under Batista and in the succeeding two-year period at the outset of the Castro regime. To highlight the Batista years, I have looked particularly to events involving *Bohemia*, which was the most militant of the antigovernment periodicals. I have traced the beginnings of totalitarian censorship through events surrounding the demise of *Diario de la Marina*, which was the most vocal and variant critic of increasing communist penetration in Cuba. Because a key in governmental efforts to control the media at the time was *Revolución*, the official daily, its activities in the process are explored. The report also includes an overview of subsequent legislation adopted under Communist party initiatives. The laws concerned present a good picture of some restrictions that currently apply to the press in Cuba; it is clear that under that set of legal sanctions, the published word can serve no purpose other than progovernment propaganda.

My general guideline in preparing this report was to let the original source materials speak for themselves. They reveal the climate of the historic events described much more eloquently than any commentary a historian could add.

The purpose of my review is simply to illustrate the importance of freedom of expression and access to information, and to show, using the Cuban context, that those freedoms are society's best guaranties against the dogmatism and intransigence that characterize totalitarian regimes.

Autocratic Censorship, 1952-1958

On the morning of March 10, 1952, the Cuban people were informed that a military coup had overthrown the government of Carlos Prío Socarrás, whose term was almost over. Although there was general discontent at the time over the government's failure to control gangsterism and malfeasance, there was widespread hope that the coming elections would bring improvement. In the twelve years before the coup, three successive Cuban presidents had respected the people's fundamental civil rights, so there was reason to trust that change might be brought about as long as a climate of freedom existed.

It was the frustration of these hopes that caused the press to react so angrily to the military disruption of the country's political life. From the outset the press warned Batista of the need to uphold those basic rights. The day after the coup, March 11, Havana's oldest daily, *El Diario de la Marina,* carried an editorial pointing out that:

> General Fulgencio Batista will do Cuba a great service if, within the difficult framework of a de facto government, he succeeds in preserving in our homeland the glories of its social and political existence, which are its freedoms: freedom of the press, freedom of speech, freedom of assembly, freedom for political gatherings, freedom of enterprise and freedom of movement for all citizens.[1]

A few days later, the news weekly *Bohemia* protested more strongly from its editorial page, stating that as a result of the coup Cuba had joined the ranks of those Latin American countries ruled by force:

> We used to be proud that Cuba was one of the few nations of Latin America in which democracy was practiced to its fullest. From now on that pride will be replaced by a great discouragement, by a profound

anguish. Our homeland too has just become one in an ominous series of Latin American republics where governments remain in place or succeed one' another without the people's participation in the choices for power. *Bohemia* reasserts its adherence to civil and democratic principles. We believe—and we say this in all frankness and out of a sense of duty and of civic responsibility—that the coup d'etat of March 10 was a grave error which has shattered the hopes of an entire people to achieve excellence within a framework of democratic legality and mutual respect. . . . We believe that only under the rule of law and within the limits of the Constitution can the people move towards freedom, equality and brotherhood.[2]

The University of Havana soon joined the critics of the coup, and eventually it and the press were among the most powerful forces in the fight against Batista. The University Council published a manifesto calling for full reinstatement of the Constitution of 1940 and for elections. The clarity of vision for Cuba's future expressed in the manifesto can be seen in the following excerpt:

If the military coup remains triumphant, that will be the consecration of force and violence as a means of or instrument for the solution of partisan problems, and it will be a bad example for the people und a grave danger for the republic.[3]

The Cuban congress took a similar stance; the presidents of the Senate and the House of Representatives, along with the heads of the parliamentary committees, issued a document denouncing the military coup in which they held Batista individually responsible for the outcome before the nation and before history.[4]

Well-known writers and intellectuals joined in the wave of denunciations: on March 23 a *Bohemia* editorial entitled "Everyone's Responsibility and Duty"[5] stressed the illegality of the government, and an article in the same issue by Herminio Portell Vila, "Count and Recount,"[6] expressed similar views. In the magazine's next issue Francisco Ichaso's "The New Cuban Conscience and the Constitution of 1940" called on all Cubans to unite to defend the "sacred legal document which sets down those rights and aspirations which cannot be relinquished without detriment to the Republic,"[7] and Carlos Hevia's "The Reactionary Coup of March 10" condemned a piece in the *Journal of Commerce,* of New York, for stating that new prosperity could be expected as a result of Batista's takeover.[8] An article by Eduardo Suárez Rivas, "Constitutional Front," called for the creation of a new party to oppose the military dictatorship,[9] and a public letter addressed to the United Nations by Roberto Agromonte and Emilio

Ochoa, of the Orthodox party, appealed to that body to support opposition to the coup as follows:

> This is the appropriate moment for the U.N. to condemn the assault on a people preparing to hold its general elections in accordance with the law, an assault through which a group of armed self-seekers, has stripped the people of their civil rights.[10]

Batista's government paid no attention to the clamor for restoration of the Constitution of 1940. In April it issued new statutes effecting fundamental changes in former constitutional norms. Even though both texts guaranteed freedom of expression, Batista's statutes not only allowed for the suspension of that right when warranted by "State security, war or invasion, grave disturbances of public order or other circumstances which deeply disturb the tranquility of the country" but also gave the Council of Ministers the power to suspend freedom of expression with a simple decree whenever it became "necessary to combat terrorism or 'pistolerism.' "[11] This addition was, of course, meant to facilitate suppression of public protests against the dictatorship. As a result of the imposition of these statutes, Cuban students symbolically buried the Constitution. The next day civil rights were once again suspended. But, in spite of these limitations, the press did not halt its attacks against Batista.[12]

Public unrest continued. Early in 1953, during a student demonstration that the police attempted to disperse, a student, Rubén Batista, was mortally wounded. The burial became a public protest against the government. One week later *Bohemia* published an article entitled "At a Martyr's Tomb,"[13] in which the author, student leader Enrique Huertas, denounced the government. Student uprisings continued until April 14, when the University Council, which was controlled by Batista, voted to close the University of Havana. The following month, a renowned politician, Pelayo Cuervo, suggested in an article that the only way for the people to defeat Batista was through force. A short time later, on July 26, the Moncada barracks in the province of Oriente was attacked by forces led by Fidel Castro. The press had the chance to publish the news, but immediately thereafter civil rights were suspended, and *Diario de la Marina's* editorial page published this commentary:

> As a consequence of Sunday's tragic events, the government has begun to apply the Law on Public Order, which imposes censorship of the press. . . . Until now, the government of General Batista had upheld the noble Cuban tradition of freedom of the press. Without denying the gravity of the most recent events, we believe that a reconsideration of

> the measures adopted relating to press censorship would constitute an important government gesture. . . . The suspension of rights does not necessarily have to be accomplished by prior censorship. This measure has caused the greatest damage, both nationally and internationally, to the reputation of governments, and more than any other measure, it hurts the work of the press and the sensibilities of journalists, and of the public in general. . . . Faithful to an unbreakable tradition, *La Marina* will reiterate its adherence to the principle of freedom of the press and hopes that those ordinances which are enervating that freedom today will be reexamined without delay.[14]

Because of these complaints, the government did not enforce press censorship fully, and soon after the attack at Moncada, the papers published photographs of the events, clear evidence of the brutality of the authorities. As a result, on August 7 the government was forced to apply stricter censorship, and it published the names of the censors appointed for *Bohemia, Prensa Libre, El Mundo,* and *Pueblo.*

The provisions on freedom of expression and information in the Law of Public Order are particularly interesting because in fact they are very similar to provisions later included in Castro's penal code, although the punishments presented in the later code were more extreme. The Law on Public Order provided for up to two years' imprisonment for

> those who disseminate, publish or have published or transmit rumors or false or biased information contrary to the national dignity, peace, public order or trust or the stability of the Powers of State, the economy, public finances, or the reputation of the nation or the government . . . [and for] those who openly or clandestinely spread propaganda aimed at producing, or which could further the achievement of, any of the following ends: . . . subversion through violence or destruction of the political, social, economic, or judicial organization of the State, however it may be constituted . . . injury to the national dignity or to . . . the powers or organisms of the State, Constitutional law, or the actions or laws of the authorities. . . . For the purposes of this article, propaganda will be understood to mean any and all oral, written or graphic manifestation or expression which is transmitted or published through newspapers, magazines, books, pamphlets, flyers, posters, lampoons, signs posted in public places, papers, writings addressed to a group of people, or radio broadcasting, television, or films or any other means of publicity, as well as oral expression before an assembled group or crowd.

The law also provided for punishment of those who "have in their possession the publicity material indicated."[15]

After press censorship had been in effect for three months, *Bohemia's* editorial page once again denounced the abuse of power and its impact on the nation:

Censorship of the press is something that disturbs the most intimate and noble part of the Cuban conscience. Because of tradition, temperament and loyalty to the belief of our forefathers, freedom for the Cuban is a right without which life is pointless. We have shown this all throughout our history. It took half a century of fighting—of blood, sweat and tears—to win a political freedom that is worthless if it is limited by restrictions like those we have just had imposed on us. Cubans will be patient in the face of misfortune, silent through disgrace, long-suffering before adversity . . . Cubans are willing to give up many things, for no other people possesses such spirit of sacrifice. But what they are not willing to surrender for anything in this world is the right to think aloud without hypocrisy, as Martí wanted it. During three dark months of prior censorship, without a press to inform and guide us, Cuban life has been immersed in ominous sorrow. Beneath the apparent calm, a series of unhealthy rumors have been incubating, and everyone is full of rancor and resentment. Censorship has fostered what it set out to prevent. Even silence has become subversive.[16]

On the same day that editorial appeared, the renowned Cuban intellectual Jorge Mañach wrote the following on the subject in an article entitled "Yesterday, Today and Tomorrow":

Once again we can write about something other than ball games, foreign politics and culture. . . . Let's take advantage of the opportunity, then. They tell me that during this closed season on free speech that we have just been through, a friend of the regime would exclaim with repugnant euphoria to some friends, "How peaceful we are! . . . This is the way to govern!" . . . What terrible myopia and shameful abdication. This is not governing; it is simply leading and administering without referendum.

Whether they are known or suspected, abuses are certainly what most engender the irritation and resentment of a people. To be unable to judge them publicly or to urge their investigation—to be unable even to unlock the false reasoning of the official press when there is one, to deprive the citizens of breath—is to accumulate psychic dynamite.[17]

For the remainder of 1954, there was no end to press accusations against the government relating to the violation of freedom of expression. On May 2 Ernesto Montaner denounced the imprisonment of Luis Conte Agüero for having given an incorrect radio report.[18] Shortly afterward, Max Lesnik published an article entitled, "Return to Guiteras," in which he paralleled the era of the death of the revolutionary leader in 1933, during Batista's former dictatorship, with those times.[19] One of *Bohemia*'s editorials at the end of that year denounced the kidnapping of a commentator and an employee of one of the stations in Santiago de Cuba for having spoken out against Batista. It reads as follows:

We believed that these Fascist methods of repression, which were so often used in other periods too unpleasant to remember, had been abolished forever. . . . Unfortunately, these "deeds" have been repeated lately with alarming frequency. The authorities, acting in an arbitrary fashion, have brought radio hours to a close, suspended peaceful gatherings, dissolved authorized meetings, and committed other similar outrages. . . .[20]

In 1955 other important statements were made by the press against Batista. With the passage of the amnesty law midway through the year, a debate between Fidel Castro and the military leader of Oriente Province, who was responsible for the crimes at Moncada, was published. Castro published his article, "You lie, Chaviano," accusing the leader of distorting the facts to hide the military's responsibility. The article said:

When Batista spoke from the Columbia barracks the day after the events, he said that we, the attackers, had had 33 killed; by the end of the week our dead had risen to more than 80.

In what battles, in what places, in what combat did these young people die? Before Batista spoke, more than 25 prisoners had been killed; after he spoke, 50 more were killed.[21]

As disturbances erupted all over the country and the government continued to use excessive force to combat its opponents, the press had this to say: "[The police] go to cruel extremes, acting with incredible brutality, performing their duties with, we would say, almost a morbid sadism, forgetting the reserve and restraint that the authorities should always show. Nothing more disastrous can happen in a country than the confrontation of its youth with its security forces.[22]

The confrontations continued throughout 1956 between different sections of the population, principally the students against the government. The year ended with the landing, in Oriente Province, of Fidel Castro's expeditionaries. The government's initial reaction was to suspend civil rights for forty-five days. On May 17 a state of national emergency was declared, and thereafter the press was permitted to publish only the official reports from the government on the situation and activities of the revolutionaries. Two weeks after the landing on December 16, *Bohemia* protested that it had not been allowed to look into what was happening: "The government and the armed forces have hung a curtain of fire and censorship between the zone of operations and the Cuban people. No journalist has been able to pass through it. . . . The Cuban press, which has so wisely and responsibly confronted these unfortunate circumstances, does not deserve this."[23]

The initial period of censorship having ended, *Bohemia* published the following comment in an editorial of March 3, 1957:

> Once again—one of the many times since March 10, 1952—the Cuban press has had to suffer under the yoke of prior censorship.
>
> Every time the regime has trouble, which is almost always the result of its flawed inception and the mistakes that have evidenced and aggravated the flaw, it is mainly the press that pays dearly. Why this determination to have our periodicals shoulder the blame for things which in no way concern them? All things considered, what is it that the media do but simply reflect a state of things that is not secret to anyone. This is the function of the press in any country that wants to live according to civilized norms.
>
> No periodical that respects itself and its public can disregard its obligation to be truthful. Its pages are like a mirror that passes through everyday reality and gathers it faithfully on its polished surface. It is absurd to blame the mirror simply because it inexorably copies an imperfect reality.
>
> In accordance with its already well-known standards, *Bohemia* stopped publishing all editorials, criticism and commentaries on current events during the period of censorship. This inhibition signals our protest against that measure, and is also the only response it deserved. Opinions cannot be properly stated when there is no freedom to give an opinion. And if there is no freedom to express an opinion on political matters, then it stands to reason that there can be no freedom to express an opinion on social, economic or cultural matters either. Freedom is indivisible. So, in order not to surrender to fine and absurd distinctions, *Bohemia* also eliminated its "in Cuba" section, its editorials and all other columns from which all aspects of Cuban life have been independently and impartially examined.
>
> Lifting press censorship is not enough. Constitutional rights must be fully restored. Public freedoms must be respected in letter and in spirit. Politics must be set in motion.[24]

Lacking access to the Cuban press to explain their position to the people, Castro's revolutionaries decided to invite Herbert Matthews of the *New York Times* to Cuba to talk to them. Matthews succeeded in slipping an interview with the rebels through their clandestine network past Cuban censors, and the piece was published in New York. Later, on March 3, 1957 it was published in Havana.[25]

After being in the Sierra Maestra for a year without the ability to convey their thoughts and objectives to the Cuban people, the rebels established Radio Rebelde, a radio station that transmitted directly from the Sierra. As the guerrilla activities progressed, the number of rebel stations increased until by the end of the insurrection there were thirty-two stations that transmitted three hours of programs originating at the central station in the Sierra. The entire Cuban populace was taken up with these transmissions that had evaded censorship, and the people eagerly awaited the opening of the stations each evening at 7:00. Programming began with these words: "This is Radio Rebelde, the official organ of the July 26th movement and the rebel army, which form a chain of freedom with its affiliated stations . . . from the mountains of Oriente, the free territory of Cuba."

The government challenged the press over its role in the rebellion. An article by the journalist Agustín Tamargo reflects the mood of the times and the press response:

> Those who truly stir up war from their government-subsidized propaganda trenches accuse the Cuban press of inciting to rebellion and promoting disorder. . . . If the government's propagandists want to know it once and for all, here is our point of view: Yes, it grieves us that the national economy is being attacked, it grieves us that the sugar cane harvest is being delayed and that the peasant children are left without schools. But what grieves us even more are the people who are being killed and tortured every day. We know that the attacks are an abominable strategy and that the hand that places a firecracker in a movie theatre could be a criminal hand. But we also know it is equally as bad to take a man from his home in the middle of the night on mere suspicion—and because you don't like his face—and kill him with a bullet through the back of the neck. We know the country is in chaos, that the people can't leave their homes, and that every minute innocent victims fall in the streets. But we also know that all of this is not a cause, but an effect and that none of it would have occurred if the country were not in the pillory of martyrdom that it is. Violence grieves us, but injustice sickens us.[26]

One week later radio commentator José Pardo Llada made public a letter addressed to him from the Sierra by Fidel Castro. In the letter Castro stressed the importance of the press in arriving at an accord with the government, the importance of letting the people be informed of the truth before there could be talk of peace. Castro wrote:

> Since the Cuban press has the quite legitimate right to be informed about all matters of national interest, and to disclose them faithfully to the people, I write these lines to request publicly that the organs of our electronic and printed press send a delegation of journalists through whom we may express to the people of Cuba what it is in their interest to know about our position in this decisive moment that our homeland is living. . . . It is time we put an end to the unjustifiable limitation that has been imposed on the Cuban press by not permitting even one of its reporters to visit our camp of operations in fifteen months of fighting . . . They have spoken about the possibility of a solution, but nothing could work so completely against finding a solution as the confusion that is caused by the absence of direct information. . . . Our primary condition

for peace is that Cuban journalists be allowed to come to the Sierra Maestra. Peace must be preceded by the truth. The press has the right to report it and the people have a right to know it.[27]

Five days later the government once again suspended civil rights, and on May 17 declared a state of national emergency, which lasted until the fall of Batista's regime.

Totalitarian Censorship, 1958-1960

During Batista's dictatorship the government tried to control the press by bribing journalists and media management and, as we have seen, by direct censorship. Without the government "subsidies," it would have been quite difficult for so many newspapers and radio stations (more than twenty newspapers, more than thirty radio stations, and five television stations in Havana) to survive on revenues from circulation and advertising alone. Still, the number and diversity of the press outlets did operate as a guarantee of freedom of expression and access to information. Today the government's monopoly of the media has completely eradicated these freedoms; all information received by the people is cast in official terms. The principal organs of the print press are *Granma,* a morning daily of the Cuban Communist party; *Juventud Rebelde,* an afternoon daily of the Union of Young Communists; the daily published by the Cuban Federation of Labor; ten provincial newspapers controlled by the provincial delegations of the party; and four weekly magazines—*Verde Olivo,* an army publication, *Bohemia,* run by the Central Committee of the party, *Mujeres,* published by the Federation of Cuban Women, and *Con la guardia en alto,* run by the Committee for the Defense of the Revolution.

When the Batista dictatorship was overthrown, part of the mass media ceased to exist because enterprises belonging, or closely linked, to government figures were confiscated. When other newspapers began to dissent, Castro's government launched a propaganda campaign against them to intimidate merchants and industrialists whose advertising had supported the publications. Naturally, the government itself withdrew all official notices that those papers had been publishing. Another government tactic was to incite workers and associations of journalists already controlled by the government to attack the dissenting publications.

The government was fostering a simplistic distinction between revolutionaries and the counterrevolutionaries: any supporter of the government fell into the first class; and anyone who interfered with or came out against government plans fell into the second. In the midst of this *ad hoc* and arbitrary handling of the press, freedom of expression was under a cloud. To a great extent, the confusion was caused by statements like the following, made by Castro himself in April 1959:

> To persecute the Catholic because he is a Catholic, to persecute the Protestant because he is Protestant, to persecute the Mason because he is a Mason, to persecute the Rotarian because he is a Rotarian, to persecute *La Marina* because it may be a newspaper with a rightest tendency, or to persecute another because it is of a leftist tendency, one because it is radical and of the extreme right and another of the extreme left, I cannot conceive of, nor will the Revolution. . . . We are doing what is democratic: respecting all ideas. When one begins by closing a newspaper, no newspaper can feel secure; when one begins to persecute a man for his political ideas, nobody can feel secure.[28]

In one way or another, by the time that statement was made many independent newspapers had already been threatened, or had been closed, as a result of protests mounted by officials, workers' unions controlled by the government, or attacks in the official newspaper of the government, *Revolución,* or of the Communist party, *Hoy.*

Nevertheless, resistance from the uncontrolled press continued, so a form of censorship was introduced. The authorities had a good deal of influence in the Provincial Association of Journalists of Havana. On December 26, 1959, under that influence, the members of the association resolved to require all periodicals to include, in the form of clarifications or footnotes *("coletillas"),* criticisms of editorials or news items that departed from the official line. The newspapers *Información* and *Diario de la Marina* went to the Supreme Court to challenge that violation of the law, but their petition was rejected on procedural grounds. One of the magistrates, Miguel Márquez y de la Cerra, issued a private opinion that said: "In my view the measure taken . . . with respect to the editorial opinions of newspapers constitutes a moral damage . . . because it is or could be a limitation on the free expression of thought."[29] A month later, when the newspaper *Avance* refused to publish the required clarifications on the grounds that the rule violated freedom of the press, it was taken over violently by a group of employees who were sympathizers of the regime. The police made no attempt to stop the takeover and, in fact, Fidel Castro approved of it. His attacks on the director and two of the principal editors of *Avance* led them to flee the country.

The authorities closed or confiscated other publications, including *Excelsior,* basing their actions on alleged links between those papers and the Batista regime. Economic strangulation was also used to control the press; the newspaper *El País* had to close when its clients, pressured by government officials, withdrew their advertisements. Only four large newspapers were able to survive these and similar official and quasi-official campaigns: *Información, El Crisol, Prensa Libre* and *Diario de la Marina.*

A letter in support of the management of *Diario de la Marina,* signed by three hundred workers, was scheduled to appear in the paper's May 11, 1960, issue. On May 10 an armed mob occupied its offices, and the police refused to provide protection. The following day the *Diario,* then under the control of Communist and pro-Castro elements, held a celebration of the takeover. It was a symbolic burial, at the University of Havana, of a paper that in its 128 years of publication had survived numerous crises in regard to freedom of information. The deputy director of *Prensa Libre,* Humberto Medrano, dared to publish an editorial that included the following statement:

> It is painful to see the burial of freedom of thought in a center of culture. It is like seeing the burial of a code in a court of justice. Because what was buried last night on the Hill [the university] was not a single newspaper. Symbolically, the freedom to think and say what one thinks was buried. . . . A sequel to that act has been announced in a comment in the newspaper *Revolución.* The headline of the comment says it all: *"Prensa Libre* in the footsteps of the *Marina".* They do not have to say it. Everyone knows.[30]

A few days later a group of Communist workers and armed militia broke into the office of *Prensa Libre* to prevent publication of an editorial criticizing the government. When the director refused to yield to the mob's demands, he had to seek asylum in the embassy of Panama. *Bohemia,* the magazine with the largest circulation in Latin America, collapsed under similar circumstances, and its director, who had greatly distinguished himself in the struggle against the Batista dictatorship, had to take refuge in the Venezuelan embassy. The other independent periodicals were brought under government control through use of pressure by pro-Castro workers' groups, although without much public fanfare.

A similar fate befell the radio and television stations. Station CMQ, the most powerful in the country, was really blameless; the only possible basis for government criticism was that CMQ had maintained its independence. To justify taking the station over, the minister of labor cited an alleged labor dispute. Then, with the goal of "consolidating the revolution and guiding the people," an entity called the United Front of Free Broadcasting Stations (FIDEL) was created, and it brought the remaining radio and television stations under government control.

In the face of those violations of freedom of expression and information, the Inter-American Press Society, which was meeting at Montego Bay, stated on March 19, 1960: "In Cuba, where a year ago there was joy because the press had once again regained freedom after the flight of the dictator Batista, that same press is now facing seizure, confiscation and collectivization." And a few days later the president of the society stated, referring to the attitude of the Cuban government with respect to the press: "The campaign has also brought about a state of intimidation and possible danger for the personal safety of the editors, who are publicly denounced by government spokesmen as counter-revolutionaries because they express differing opinions that are not to the liking of those who govern today in Cuba."[31] The final step in seizing control was to obstruct the circulation of U.S. newspapers. The simple way to accomplish this goal was to freeze their bank accounts. In the end, Cubans had access only to a government-controlled press and publications from communist countries.

The biggest campaigns against freedom of expression were carried out by the newspapers *Hoy* and *Revolución*. Early in 1960, as has been stated above, two of the remaining independent newspapers were *Diario de la Marina* and *Prensa Libre*. A review of the attacks waged against them by *Revolución* in the days before the demise of those two papers is very instructive, for it clearly reveals the government's objective of suppressing freedom of expression.

Revolución set the tone on March 24, 1960 in the following commentary, which repeated the arbitrary, official distinction between what was revolutionary and what was counterrevolutionary, described above, and clearly threatened critics of the government:

> The newspapers and their advocates, who have made the Communist ghost the primary focus of their editorials and news reports, are only playing their assigned parts as accomplices to foreign intervention in Cuba.
>
> The struggle going on in Cuba is between the humble, the underprivileged and their exploiters; between thieves and honest men; between patriots and traitors; between those loyal to their country and those who align themselves with the enemy to brutalize and imprison it. Let each man choose; but let each one assume the responsibility for his choice.[32]

The following day (March 25) it addressed its attacks directly to *Diario de la Marina* and *Prensa Libre:*

> The North American monopolies, the international oligarchy, the war criminals, and, in their own underhanded, cowardly way, *Prensa Libre* and *Diario de la Marina* . . . brandish the anti-Communist flag with the villainous purpose of deceiving and confusing world opinion.[33]

> If *Prensa Libre* and *Diario de la Marina* and all the disgrace, misery, exploitation, servility, infamy, ignominy and shame they represent think that the Cuban people are asleep, or could be put to sleep, they are sadly mistaken.[34]

A few days later it charged that the anticommunist sentiments expressed by the two papers under attack and on the radio constituted treason: "We told the people that the sole objective of the anti-Communist campaign of *Prensa Libre,* Conte Agüero [a radio commentator], *La Marina* and the North American press was to confuse, divide, isolate and create fifth columns that aid and abet foreign aggression."[35]

In spite of such threats and attacks, *Diario de la Marina* continued to exercise its rights and to express its increasingly unorthodox opinions vis-à-vis the official government line. One need only review the headlines from the issues published on the days just before the paper was closed to understand how far the situation had deteriorated, and why the government felt the need to shut down the paper. On May 1 *Diario* published an editorial criticizing the submissiveness of cultural expression in the countries behind the Iron Curtain ("The Artist in a Communist State").[36] Since Labor Day was being celebrated on that day, another editorial was pointedly entitled "May 1 is Also Christian."[37] On May 2 the paper published an article entitled "The Truth Is Imprisoned,"[38] and the editorial for that day spoke of the "risks of negotiations with Russia."[39] Still another piece from that issue reported: "576 people are currently imprisoned, and the great majority of them are still pending trial."[40] On May 5 there was an editorial entitled "Free Work vs. Slave Work: The Backwardness of Socialist Countries,"[41] an article with the heading "The AFL/CIO States the Current Regime Endangers Peace in This Hemisphere,"[42] and still others, to discredit the system, "The Workers' Situation in Russia"[43] and "What Would Really Happen if the Communist Revolution Succeeds."[44] All these issues included anticommunist caricatures and a scorecard in a postscript that recorded the number of clarifications that newspapers were being forced to print. For example, on May 1, the scorecard read: *"Diario De La Marina,* 6; *Informacion,* 5; Prensa Libre, 6; *El Crisol,* 5; *Revolucion, La Calle, Hoy, El Mundo* and *Avance,* 0."[45] A final report to taunt the government, which appeared on May 8, 1960, was entitled

"Communist Aggression upon Sanchez Arango's Return to Cuba."
The subject, once a Communist Party member, had in later years been
a leading anti-Communist and a distinguished participant in the opposition to Batista. The article decried the abuses to which he had been
subjected by a mob of Castro's supporters.[46]

At this point, the government lost patience with that limited press
freedom and moved to force the closing of *Diario De La Marina*. On
May 11, instigated gy government officials, the workers published the
following declaration "To the Public Opinion" on the front page:

> "It is a well-known fact that the director of this newspaper, Jose
> Ignacio Rivero, has taken a clearly conspiratorial, counter-revolutionary
> position.
>
> It is Mr. José Ignacio Rivero's plan to provoke the people and, by doing
> so, to find a way to make it seem as though the newspaper has been
> targeted by the Revolution. This plan was master-minded abroad, the
> proof of which is the award given him by the SIP [Interamerican Press
> Society], which is hailed as the hero of freedom of the press; the
> agreement of the Rosa Blanca [a counterrevolutionary organization]
> with Mr. Rivero's pronouncements; and a campaign of North American
> newspapers in which this newspaper's director is cited as a participant in
> a plan to form an "underground," counterrevolutionary movement.
>
> To execute this plan, Mr. Rivero prepared a document for signature by
> certain employees of *El Diario* and then changed the wording of the
> already-signed document to make the employees and journalists of *El
> Diario* look like enemies of the Revolution.
>
> It is for this reason that a great number of the workers who do not share
> Mr. Rivero's point of view, but are, on the contrary, in agreement with
> the Revolution, have issued a manifesto defending their own viewpoint.
>
> Yesterday, Mr. Rivero refused to put out *El Diario,* so we the workers,
> have decided to take it upon ourselves to print it, without changing its
> customary status.[47]

With the bold headline "A Day with the People; 128 Years Serving
Reaction," *Diario de la Marina* came out the next day with these
statements on its front page:

> For years the employees of *El Diario de la Marina* and its public have
> had to endure the insidious press campaigns that use this paper to pit the
> company against the interests of the nation (128 years at the service of
> bad objectives), without being able freely to express our point of view
> and our disgust at those ill-aimed opinions. From the very first we
> aligned ourselves with the provincial College of Journalists of Havana
> and the National Federation of Graphic Arts, which agreed to place
> explanatory "postscripts" on every article or report that goes against
> the ideals of the Revolution, and hence, those of our homeland. In recent

months we have waged an arduous battle to explode the lies of José Ignacio Rivero and company, waylaying any attempt at aggression against Cuban ideals.

El Diario de la Marina had become the mouthpiece of the Rosa Blanca, as it had once been for the Spanish "voluntarios" [voluntary military supporters of Spain during Cuba's wars for independence] in this era of glorious Revolution, it has represented the worst interests of our nation; it represented the latifundium, the war criminals, the imperialists from abroad who try to bloody our streets; in general, anyone who opposed freedom, social justice, and the absolute and sovereign independence of the Cuban nation.[48]

Satisfied with its success, *Revolución* reported to its readers on May 12: "As of yesterday, 'the only sickness that lasted more than 100 years' along with its officers, which have hurt Cuba and its heroes and martyrs, has ceased to exist as the voice of our worst interests. It will now be dedicated to noble goals such as our popular culture.[49]

The same issue commenced attacks on *Prensa Libre* with this commentary: "*Prensa Libre's* Treasonous Voice. . . . In times like these, those who take the side of *Diario de la Marina* take the side of the counter-revolution, aggression and foreign intervention."[50] The following issue of *Revolución* (March 13, 1960) included a long editorial that paved the way for the fall of *Prensa Libre*:

Prensa Libre in the Footsteps of *La Marina*. . . . Every man has the right to choose his own path. In today's Cuba, there are only two paths: that of the Revolution and that of counterrevolution. The two paths are irreconcilable. On the path of the Revolution there are six million Cubans, the best of our breed. . . . On the path of counterrevolution are the imperialists who have exploited Latin America and Cuba for decades. . . . The latest events only serve to distinguish that much more between the paths of Revolution and counterrevolution.

Today, one is either with Cuba . . . or against her.

Whoever defends *La Marina* denigrates the memory of the martyrs of seventy-one;

Whoever defends *La Marina* denigrates the memory of Martí;

Whoever defends *La Marina* defends foreign intervention;

Whoever defends *La Marina* defends Hitler, Mussolini and Franco;

Whoever defends *La Marina* defends the counterrevolution.

For quite some time *Prensa Libre* has been beating the path of *El Diario;* the path to counteract the Revolution; the path of the SIP's rewards; the path of singing Yankee praises; the path of anti-Communism.

No one threatens, or harasses, or hounds *Prensa Libre*. . . . It will determine its own destiny; no one else will.

Anyone who opposes history will be erased from it. . . .

Anyone who opposes our homeland will be destroyed.

The words "democracy," "free press," and "independence" ring hollow when uttered from the mouth of the press of the privileged few. There is only one word here: REVOLUTION. For the first time, the people know the true meaning of democracy, freedom, independence, truth and free press—through the Revolution.

During the 57 years of the Republic, the privileged man's press never told the people the truth.

In the 16 months of the Revolution, all of the truths have been told in Cuba; all the liars, charlatans and false apostles have been unmasked.[51]

As described above, *Prensa Libre* replied defiantly to this challenge, but it ultimately fell in the government's drive to consolidate its monopoly over "free journalism." *Prensa Libre*'s buildings, presses and officers were taken over by *Revolución* on July 4, 1960, and eleven days later, *Revolución*'s old shop was given to the newspaper *Hoy*.

On July 21 came the news that *Bohemia,* too, had fallen under government control. The item appeared on the front page of *Revolución* as follows:

This Friday, as usual, *Bohemia* will take to the streets in a public display of enthusiasm and struggle. Now published under the direction of Enrique Delahoza by the employees of that work center of journalists and artists, *Bohemia* is initiating with this issue a newly productive stage, in which much more editorial and informative emphasis will be placed on the defense of our national interests, which are irrevocably tied to the Revolution.[52]

Thus did freedom of information come to an end in Cuba. The school of journalism changed its name and personnel[53] as it shifted to a new goal of training for indoctrination; the function of the press in this new era was to be to change the Cuban people's way of thinking.[54] Journalism, like all cultural expressions, was to become an instrument of the Communist party, "an engineer of souls." In fact, the people were now seeing the results of the attitude that the journalist Agustín Tamargo had ingeniously described months before when Castro accused him of being a reactionary because he did not agree with Castro. In response, Tamargo wrote in *Avance:* "Commandant Castro: I will no longer be a journalist, because you don't want journalists, you want phonograph records."[55]

The Platform of the First Congress of the Cuban Communist Party of 1975 is something of a summary of the Cuban phenomenon beginning in 1959. The preamble of the platform stated that it would be "the guiding document for all the work of the Party . . . , its principal ideological instrument and its battle flag," and that it was going to "serve as a basis for the work of the Central Committee." Part 101, "Tasks of the Ideological Struggle," stated:

> The Party considers as the principal tasks for the Communist education of our people and internal and external ideological confrontation:
>
> The defense of Marxist-Leninist purity; the struggle against the concepts and theories of the bourgeoisie, imperialism and its servants, pointing to the crisis in which they find themselves; opposition to and confrontation with all manifestations of ideological diversionism through the study of the scientific ideology of the working class and knowledge of the laws of universal development;
>
> Disclosure of the lies in the insidious anti-Soviet campaigns, through clarification of the role of the USSR in the world struggle for social progress and in the creation of more favorable conditions for the struggle of nations for their definitive liberation;
>
> Opposition to the ideas held by the revisionists of the right who deny the class struggle and the leading role of the working class in the Socialist revolution, and proof that they are shameless defenders of the bourgeoisie order;
>
> The consequent combat against the political and ideological positions of the revisionists of the left, as well as dogmatism and sectarianism, identifying the anti-Soviet leftist pseudorevolutionaries as actual servants of imperialism and enemies of humanity.[56]

Of course, in the hands of the state, the press had turned into the best weapon for that "ideological struggle." In dealing with the mass media, part 105 of the platform states:

> The Party shall provide systematic orientation for and attention to the instruments of the mass media and shall promote the enthusiastic and creative participation of all workers who base their opinions on the Communists and on the activity of the labor union movement of journalists and writers, so as to succeed in having the radio, television, written press and films carry out more and more effectively their role in the political, ideological, cultural, technical-scientific and aesthetic education of the population.[57]

As a summary of the First Congress of the Communist Party, Fidel Castro read a "report" in which he said the following about radio and television:

> As a vehicle for spreading the ideas of the bourgeois society in the capitalist stage, the radio had the role of an agent selling commercial

products. The dramatized serials, with their deforming content, were used indiscriminately, and their mark of vulgarity and poor taste fostered superstition and a low cultural level. . . . Television, which came after, adopted the formulas that had proved successful in radio. It used what was fashionable and sold more, and in order to make its imitation of the American television model more complete, it included religious conversations, which had had great success in the United States.

With the triumph of the Revolution, the stations involved with the tyranny were seized, and the Independent Front of Free Broadcasters was formed. The nationalization process of the radio and television was completed later, and in May of 1962 the Cuban Radio Broadcasting Institute was created and charged with centralizing these media in order to serve the interests of the Revolution.[58]

The following year, in 1976, Cuba's socialist Constitution went into effect; chapter IV is "Fundamental Rights, Obligations and Guarantees." With respect to freedom of information and expression, article 52 states:

> Freedom of speech and the press is recognized for citizens in accordance with the goals of Socialist society. The material conditions for their exercise are guaranteed by the fact that the press, the radio, television, movies and other mass media are state or social property and cannot be the object, in any case, of private property, which ensures their use in the exclusive service of the working people and the interest of society.[59]

Because article 5 of the Constitution provides that the party is the "vanguard of the working class and the leading force of society and the state,"[60] article 52 in effect means that freedom of information and expression can only be used for the "exclusive service" of the Communist party.

Conclusion

On the basis of the foregoing account, one might conclude that censorship of the kind practiced by autocracies is not only tolerable but even defensible in certain circumstances, for autocratic regimes can be relatively sensitive to press reaction and moderate or uninterfering in many aspects of life. If we freeze time and compare that kind of censorship with the other, totalitarian brand, no doubt the first is preferable. The case of Cuba seems to show at least that an autocratic regime can be toppled, but there seems no exit from the grip of a totalitarian rule. The mistake, however, lies in thinking that we can freeze a segment of a process. Seen in history's dynamics, the autocratic regime cannot be excused, if for no other reason than that it may actually lead to another, more repressive government. Under the autocracy the people become accustomed or inured to force in power, and then, to overthrow it, they seem to justify even worse abuse.

Other countries have extricated themselves from unjust governments without falling under totalitarian rule. To date, El Salvador is an example. Its people have chosen a democratic path in their efforts to free themselves from continued violations of human rights and oligarchies that drained the national wealth. The example offers hope to other countries in Latin America. Cuba was not as lucky, nor was Iran nor Nicaragua, and we must learn from these sad experiences if we want to avoid the same mistakes.

Every person, institution, and government with any influence over a dictatorial regime should use that influence to demand that its rulers respect freedom of the press, freedom of expression, and freedom of information. The other rights that democracies hold so dear should not be forgotten, but only through those guaranties of thought can the dangers of totalitarianism be averted.

Moderator: Mr. George Volsky, *New York Times*

There are three underlying themes or issues throughout this discussion. The first is the degree to which media newsmen play a historical role; can a historical dynamic be reversed or changed or is it irreversible? The second is to which degree are media used by leaders, charismatic or less so, and how do newsmen view themselves in their historical role? The last issue goes to how newsmen and editors see themselves; are newsmen advocates first or do they adopt a priori an "I-am-the-camera" attitude or both?

Respondent: Mr. James Nelson Goodsell, *Christian Science Monitor*

In the United States one thinks of freedom of the press in general terms. It is a precious commodity that we need to understand better. The press has tremendous power when allowed to operate freely.

There were strong practitioners of freedom of the press in the Batista years and the early Castro years—gutsy newsmen and editors. The press gradually undermined the Batista dictatorship by denouncing its illegal claim to power and its abuses.

Batista's reaction when Castro landed was to suspend civil rights for forty five days and thereafter the press was permitted to publish only the official government reports on the situation and the activities of the revolutionaries.

There are journalists throughout the world doing a great job imperfectly—because journalism is an inexact science—to bring the news to their audience, and I pay tribute to the Cuban journalists who printed the truth during the Batista regime and the early Castro years.

I wonder if Cuba would be without Castro today if Batista had shown greater respect for the press. In this country we are beginning to see the distinction between an autocratic and a totalitarian regime and beginning to appreciate the differences. When we have an autocratic rule, the cure may be worse than the illness itself. In a totalitarian government the press is eliminated as an effective alternative voice to that of the government and that is certainly true in Cuba.

There's a strong indictment of Castro here and of his view of the press. When Castro speaks of supporting freedom of the press, but very cynically tries to repress this freedom, it is an eloquent example of the Castro government's duplicity in dealing with the press.

The situation in Cuba is a warning of what could happen in other countries if there isn't greater care taken by the citizens and the government and the press to protect the freedom of expression.

Respondent: Dr. Luis Aguilar, Georgetown University

Castro's duplicity is long-standing. Castro always maintained that there wasn't a cult of personality, yet an organized cult of personality began on January 1, 1959 (the day that Castro took over). The use of government slogans was pervasive, intrusive: "Gracias, Fidel," "Fidel, this is your house," "Fidel, this is your country." I'll always remember the announcer's voice coming on the radio in between the news saying, "Esto que la patria no sea un cuartel, esto tiene un nombre, se llama Fidel." (Translation: The country is not a fortress because of Fidel.) There were music, songs and countless announcements to encourage the personality cult of Fidel.

The media also tried to encourage mass hysteria or paranoia among Cuba's people. Radio, television, and the newspapers would repeatedly broadcast or publish shrill and urgent warnings about counterrevolutionaries and enemies of the people, trying to create an atmosphere of impending disaster and threat to the national security. It has a very strong impact when you hear it so often.

One of the most insidious instruments of the totalitarian regime is its use of the "undefined crime." When the government says that "any rumor that can endanger the stability of the state is counterrevolution-ary" and subject a rumor monger to punishment, then the government can make a criminal out of anyone.

I could comment one morning, "It's raining too much in Cuba." The government could argue, "You mean to say that the rain is endangering the sugar crops which are vital to our economy and that therefore our economy is going to collapse. You're spreading rumors against the state and you are therefore a counterrevolutionary."

An innocent comment becomes a massive conspiracy to undermine the revolution. Castro was a master at using this strategy to control others and get rid of those who threatened him in one way or another.

Discussion Summary

In Central America we must distinguish between the written and the broadcast press. In Nicaragua the Sandinistas are allowing the newspa-per *La Prensa* to be published with only some censorship, yet you have to remember that 60 percent of the population is illiterate. The San-dinistas allow a newspaper to be published because it will reach a minority, but the radio and television are totally controlled by them.

There is a department within the Central Committee of the Commu-nist Party of Cuba that controls all media. Some stories are totally suppressed. For example, Cuban media have never covered the breakup of relations with Somalia.

Castro was personally involved in the repression of freedom of the press. There are witnesses that Castro personally supervised and dictated coverage and copy for newspapers, radio, etc.

In Cuba, *Granma* is called the golden standard. If it is published in *Granma,* then the provincial papers and the other media can use it; if not, then whatever is published is suspect.

There is a linkage in the thinking of autocratic regimes that leads to worse abuses under a totalitarian regime. People become accustomed to the idea that the press can be censored under an autocrat, then freedom of the press is totally lost under a totalitarian regime that replaces the autocrat.

The totalitarian press does not meet its objective of getting everyone to think the same way, to say the same things. Many of the Cubans who came over via Mariel had been subjected to the Cuban press all their lives, yet the degree of indoctrination was not great, considering the effort. Under the veneer, the totalitarian press is perceived as propa-ganda by many among its intended audience and found to be deficient.

Notes

I wish to thank Felix Martin, a postgraduate student of the Department of Political Science at Columbia University, for his generous help in doing basic research for this study.

1. "El cambio de gobierno; Cuba no debe retroceder en su historia de libertades y democracia," *Diario de la Marina,* March 11, 1952, p. 1.
2. "Ante el hecho consumado," *Bohemia,* March 16, 1952, p. 51.
3. "Pronúnciase el Consejo Universitario en torno a la situación política," *Diario de la Marina,* March 23, 1952, p. 1.
4. "Documentos para la historia; República de Cuba; Poder legislativo; A la nación," *Bohemia,* March 23, 1952, p. 28.
5. Ibid., p. 59.
6. Ibid., p. 56.
7. Ibid., April 6, 1952, p. 35.
8. Ibid., p. 108.
9. Ibid. p. 67.
10. "La Ortodoxia se dirige a la O.N.U.," ibid., p. 72.
11. *Constituciones Cubanas,* ed. L. A. de la Cuesta (New York, 1974).
12. On October 15, *Diario de la Marina* published a document ("Exhortación Patriótica") by Bloque Cubano de Prensa, signed by José Ignacio Rivero (*Diario de la Marina*), Ramón Vasconcelos (*Alerta*), Julio C. González Rebull (*El Crisol*), Joaquín Claret (*Información*), Luis Botifoll (*El Mundo*), Clara Park de Pessino (*The Havana Post*), José López Vilaboy (*Mañana*), Miguel A. Quevedo (*Bohemia*), Alfredo T. Quilez (*Carteles*), Josefina Mosquera (*Vanidades*), Jorge Zayas (*Avance*), Humberto Medrano (*Prensa Libre*), Francisco González (*Ellas*), Cristóbal Díaz (*El País & Excelsior*), *Diario de la Marina,* p. 1.
13. *Bohemia,* February 22, 1953, p. 71.
14. *Diario de la Marina,* July 28, p. 1.
15. "Sanciona la Ley de Orden Público falsas noticias y rumores; Modifica artículos del Código de Defensa Social sobre el desacato a las autoridades y los delitos contra el honor, difamación, injuria y calumnia; Penalidad a la propaganda ilícita," *Diario de la Marina,* August 7, 1953, pp. 1, 2.
16. "Nuestra Palabra," *Bohemia,* November 1, 1953, p. 69.
17. Ibid., p. 66.
18. "Hermanos contra hermanos," ibid., May 2, 1954, p. 58.
19. Ibid., May 9, 1954, p. 69.
20. "Vuelen los métodos fascistas," ibid., May 1, 1953, p. 73.
21. Ibid., May 29, 1955, p. 94.
22. "Editorial," ibid., December 11, 1955, p. 79.
23. "Fotos de las operaciones; Lo que nos han dejado ver," ibid., December 16, 1956, p. 106.
24. "Nuestra invariable actitud," ibid. (Supp.), March 3, 1957.
25. "En la Sierra Maestra; Famoso corresponsal americano entrevista a Fidel Castro; Herbert L. Matthews, del *New York Times,*" ibid., p. 2.
26. *Bohemia,* March 2, 1958, p. 64.
27. "Un documento sensacional de Fidel Castro a Pardo Llada," ibid., March 9, 1958, pp. 76-77.

28. Leovigildo Ruiz, *Diario de una traición, Cuba, 1959* (Miami, 1965), p. 75.
29. Adolfo G. Merino, *Nacimiento de un estado vasallo* (Mexico, 1966), pp. 201-2.
30. Humberto Medrano, *Sin patria, pero sin amo* (Miami, 1963), p. 450.
31. Merino, *Nacimiento de un estado vasallo*, p. 209.
32. "La cortina de humo del anticomunismo," *Revolución*, March 24, 1960, p. 2.
33. "Zona Rebelde; *Prensa Libre* y el fantasma del comunismo," ibid., March 25, 1960.
34. Ibid., p. 2.
35. "Zona Rebelde; La careta de la conjura," ibid., March 30, 1960, p. 1.
36. *Diario de la Marina*, May 1, 1960, p. 1.
37. Ibid., p. 4-A.
38. Ibid., May 2, 1960, p. 1.
39. Ibid., p. 4-A.
40. Ibid., p. 10-A.
41. Ibid., May 5, 1960, p. 1.
42. Ibid.
43. Ibid., p. 4-A.
44. Ibid.
45. Ibid., May 1, 1960, p. 16-B.
46. Ibid., May 8, 1960, p. 1.
47. Ibid., May 11, 1960, p. 1.
48. Ibid., May 12, 1960, p. 1.
49. *"Diario de la Marina* a imprenta Nacional," *Revolución*, May 12, 1960, p. 1.
50. "La voz traidora de *Prensa Libre*," Ibid., p. 19.
51. *"Prensa Libre* en el camino de la *Marina*," Ibid., May 13, 1960, p. 1.
52. Ibid., July 21, 1960, p. 1.
53. "Inauguran el día 25 Curso Periodístico; será convertida la Escuela Márquez Sterling en Centro Superior de Periodismo. Asistirá el Ministro de Educación A. Hart al acto," ibid., May 23, 1960, p. 1.
54. "Expulsa el Colegio a trece periodistas; mantuvieron nexos con la derrocada tiranía y ahora realizan labor contra su patria en el extranjero. Denuncia; elecciones," ibid., June 14, 1960, p. 3.
55. *El Avance Criollo*, September 29, 1959, p. 4.
56. "Tesis número 6. Proyecto de Plataforma Programática del Partido Comunista de Cuba," *Bohemia*, October 26, 1975, p. 26.
57. Ibid., p. 28.
58. *First Congress of the Communist Party of Cuba; Central Report* (Havana, 1978), p. 151.
59. "Constitución de la República de Cuba," *Revista Cubana de Derecho 7*, (January-June 1976): 151.
60. Ibid., p. 137.

4

Covering Cuba

Vivian W. Dudro

A compilation of recommendations and observations on the potential pitfalls and the dynamics of covering Cuba as a journalist. The paper is based on interviews with eleven journalists who have covered Cuba for a variety of media. The paper discusses the preparations necessary for getting to Cuba, the restrictions that a journalist can expect to find during a stay there, and the possible steps that a reporter can take to circumvent the interference and potential bias that can arise from excessive Cuban government involvement in his or her activites.

"The underlying criterion that the Cuban government uses in permitting journalists to come to the island is that the coverage will expectedly advance the cause of the revolution or, at the very least, that the coverage won't hurt the cause. American notions of freedom of the press, ready access to information and journalistic objectivity simply do not apply in Cuba."

—Antonio Guernica

Introduction

The author of this paper has never been to Cuba. Consequently, the information herein is based largely on telephone interviews with eleven journalists who have visited Cuba since the revolution. Nine of the journalists were from the United States—two from a wire service, four from major metropolitan newspapers, one from a major television network, one from a religious magazine, and one from a nationally circulated newspaper who also has reported on Cuba for public and private television. Also interviewed were a Cuban-born U.S. citizen

109

who filmed a program in Cuba for public television and a correspondent from a foreign television station.

Five of the journalists had been to Cuba only once, one had been twice, the other five had been six to fifteen times. Most of the visits were between 1974 and 1984. Only one of the journalists had visited Cuba prior to 1974.

Several of those interviewed requested they not be identified; therefore, for the sake of consistency, none of them will be named. One of the journalists said he did not want to be named because his comments could provoke the Cuban government to restrict his future trips to the country.

Though the information in this paper is secondhand, it nevertheless paints a picture of Cuba useful to the journalist preparing to visit the country for the first time. In addition, the insights and advice offered by those interviewed could be helpful to any journalist in assessing the challenges of working in Cuba.

Getting to Cuba

The first step in covering Cuba is getting there. Access to Cuba is restricted by the Cuban government, and travel to Cuba by U.S. citizens is restricted by the U.S. government. Hence, getting to Cuba sometimes can be problematic, especially for journalists in a hurry, as they often are when trying to cover a timely event and/or meet a deadline. Journalists should be forewarned that obtaining a visa, preparing oneself adequately, and booking a flight take time and effort.

Visas

Though all the journalists interviewed said the majority of their visa requests were granted routinely, they pointed out several aspects of Cuban government procedure that could frustrate an inexperienced reporter.

Visa requests are made to the Cuban Interests Section in Washington, D.C., and must be cleared by the government in Havana. The process can take from two days to two months, depending on the individual and the nature of the project. The government is somewhat unpredictable and may not notify a reporter whether or not he or she may come until the last minute before the scheduled departure. The uncertainty over when and how Havana will respond can be "a pain in the neck," one reporter said. In case of a last-minute response, a reporter should be prepared either to leave for Cuba on a moment's notice or to take up an alternative project.

The foreign television correspondent said that after he did not receive a visa in time, he went to Cuba anyway, hoping he could get one there. When he arrived, the authorities sent him back to Miami and told him to wait there until further notice. The next day he was permitted to return to Havana. Though he got into the country faster this way, taking such a risk may not always produce favorable results.

The Cuban government requires extensive information before granting a visa, especially if the reporter has never been to Cuba before. If the journalist wants to cover a specific press conference or news event, visas are relatively easy to obtain. "When the Cubans decide they have something to say and want an audience for it, there is no problem getting visas," one reporter said. In fact, the government has quickly accommodated reporters who respond to its own short-notice invitations by giving them visas at the Cuban airport.

For a journalist seeking permission for an extended visit to work on an in-depth research piece, the visa process is more time consuming and complex. For example, in preparing for its coverage of the twenty-fifth anniversary of the revolution, one newspaper sent visa requests for five reporters and two photographers along with a broad outline of the project to the Cuban Interests Section three months in advance. A couple of weeks later, a reporter from the paper in Cuba on another assignment followed up on the request by meeting with Cuban officials. Next, the newspaper sent more detailed information about the stories it was after and the people it wanted to interview. This initiated a series of communications between an editor and the Cuban government, which ultimately resulted in an agreement.

For a variety of reasons, the Cuban government does not grant all requests for visas. The reporters who said they on occasion had been denied entry into Cuba were not always given an explanation. A reason cited by two reporters was government displeasure with stories they had written about Cuba. One said the Cuban Interests Section told him he could assume his story about the release of U.S. prisoners from Cuban jails "had something to do" with his subsequent visa request's being turned down. In that story some of the former prisoners were quoted harshly criticizing their conditions and their treatment while in prison. A few years later, the government allowed the reporter to reenter Cuba. Another reporter was forbidden to return to Cuba two weeks after he had written about the 1980 emigrations from Port Mariel. The Cuban Communist party newspaper criticized him for writing that a violent attack on Cubans trying to leave the country had been instigated by the government. "They [Cuban officials] were quite angry at me," he said. But, he added, the government's reaction should be seen in the context of the "mass emotional trauma" in Cuba during that time. Two years later he was again not permitted to visit Cuba; however, the government relented after his editor explained that another reporter would not be sent in his place. "There was an argument in the foreign ministry about this that was resolved in my favor," he said. "Whether the threat [from the editor] was influential, I don't know."

One newspaper reporter said the Cubans will restrict a journalist whose purpose, they think, is to discredit the revolution. "Sometimes it's hard to figure out what would give them that idea," she said. "It's hard to assess what criteria they use." Another newspaper reporter said the criteria are factual inaccuracy, unsubstantiated judgments, or anti-Cuba bias. The government "will restrict you in a minute," he said, if it believes a reporter is guilty of any of these. It will restrict reporters whose stories are a priori suspected of such flaws. The government, he added, assumes Cuban exiles are incapable of objective reporting about Cuba.

Many of the journalists speculated that internal reasons were behind some refusals of entry. A wire service reporter, who went to Cuba on short notice to cover the Soviet brigade "discovered" by the Carter administration, was not given a visa when he arrived in Havana as were the other journalists. Instead, he was sent back to Miami because the authorities had expected a different reporter from his agency. "It was a bureaucratic mix-up," he said, "not an expression of hostility." A newspaper reporter was denied a visa one time because he wrote a story about Cuba for a magazine. Apparently the Cubans did not appreciate being surprised by the unexpected article. Another newspaper reporter said he has been denied access to Cuba a number of times without explanation, though the government gives him visas "with some regularity." Perhaps the government "finds it too difficult to cope with so many journalists" and limits the number of foreign reporters in the country at any one time, he said.

Preparation

According to all the journalists interviewed, a reporter planning a trip to Cuba should become as thoroughly educated about the country as possible. All of them recognized that time is the limiting factor. Many had little time to prepare themselves adequately before their own first or first several trips. This was especially true for those who went to Cuba just once or only a few times for some specific event.

One of the most important things to know is the language. Reporters who do not speak Spanish are at a serious disadvantage; they have to be accompanied by a government translator, "whose job," according to one reporter, "is to see to it you get their point of view." Even at press conferences with Fidel Castro or other officials who also speak English, Spanish is spoken and translated into English by an interpreter.

In addition to the language, Cuban history is valuable to know, according to one of the newspaper reporters. Some facts are particularly vital, he said. For example, before the revolution, Cuba had a long and important relationship with the United States and was quite an advanced country. It would be inaccurate for a journalist to assume that prerevolutionary Cuba was like any other Latin American or Third World country, he added.

If Cuba is the journalist's first communist country, he or she had better do a lot of reading on communist ideology and strategy, including works by Marx and Lenin, according to several correspondents. It is nearly impossible to understand Cuba without understanding communism in general and Cuban communism in particular. "You have to understand the system," said a newspaper reporter. "Ideologues set up the system. The system has a life of its own." This reporter also recommended reading about the Cuban revolution itself because the people who took power in 1959 still run the country.

One journalist advised reading Castro's speeches. Although they are uncritical of the regime, they do mention certain problems facing the country that could be good starting points for questions. A reporter also can glean from them the "ideological drift" of the country, he said. For the same reasons reporters should read *Granma,* the daily newspaper of the Cuban Communist party.

Several journalists recommended reading Hugh Thomas's book *Cuba: The Pursuit of Freedom* (New York: Harper & Row, 1971), which they said was ideologically neutral. And many advised talking to scholars, dipomats, and Cuban exiles in the United States, who may be able to provide current information about Cuba, as well as names of contacts inside the country.

Reporters need to learn not only about Cuba but also about the particular events they intend to cover. Background research must be done before arriving in Cuba, a reporter said, because while in the country, "you're only going to get the [Cuban] government's side."

Transportation to Cuba

One reporter made the comment that it was almost easier to get a visa than to get a flight from the United States to Cuba. Although this was an exaggeration, Miami is the only U.S. city that has regular flights to Havana, of which there are only a couple each day. Flights are limited because the U.S. government forbids travel to Cuba except by academics, diplomats, journalists, and those with close relatives there. Both Canada and Mexico, however, schedule regular flights to Cuba.

A few of the journalists mentioned that it is sometimes possible to be welcomed aboard a chartered flight with an empty seat and travel for free.

Government Arrangements and Restrictions inside Cuba

As one reporter said, getting to Cuba is the hard part; once the journalist is inside the country the Cuban government takes care of everything. According to all the journalists interviewed, the government arranges a great deal of a reporter's itinerary, in order to watch and control as much of his or her activity as possible. However, depending on the reporter and the assignment, the degree of government involvement and scrutiny varies considerably.

Hotels

After the government gives a journalist a visa, it makes an official reservation at one of the government-run hotels. A foreign visitor is not permitted to stay in Havana without such a reservation. All the journalists said that during their stays in the capital, they were assigned to either the Riviera or the Habana Libre hotels on a special floor for foreigners. One reporter assumed the government keeps foreign visitors together so it "can keep an eye on them," and because there are not many places equipped to handle them. The hotels in Cuba are similar to those in the Soviet Union, China, and Saudi Arabia, she added.

All of the journalists assumed their rooms had been bugged and their phones had been tapped, though most had seen no evidence of such. One of the wire service reporters, however, was sure his phone conversation with a dissident had been monitored. In a subsequent interview, a Cuban official told him "something that could only have been obtained from someone who had listened to that call," he said.

Guides

The Cuban Ministry for External Relations assigns to each journalist or group of journalists at least one guide—someone to assist and accompany reporters as they go about collecting information for their stories. The guide also serves as a translator and, as mentioned earlier, is a necessity for those who do not speak Spanish. Some of the journalists said they were not allowed to go anywhere without their guide(s). This was the case for most when they traveled outside Havana and/or had filming or photographic equipment. Many of the print journalists said they were able to roam the streets of Havana alone; a few had been able to leave the city unescorted.

The reporter from a nationally circulated newspaper, who has been to Cuba many times during the past twenty-five years, said he has received both kinds of treatment. "When I go to Cuba, each visit is different. Sometimes the foreign ministry is very involved because it wants to be or because I have needed it. Sometimes I have been able to wander on my own. . . . Other times I am met at the airport and dogged the whole time." Since the mid 1970s, he added, he has been accompanied by a guide during most of his visits.

One of the reporters who has traveled inside Cuba on her own said one method the guides use to stick with a journalist is to say they are supposed to go along and will "get in trouble" if they do not. She said the system has a built-in incentive for journalists to make use of the guide—at many places the authorities will either not let an unescorted person in or will at least cause him or her a lot of extra trouble. There is "monumental confusion" when a journalist arrives for an interview with a public official without a guide, she said.

Wherever the Cuban-born journalist showed up with his taping equipment, the first question asked was, "Has this been cleared?" Without the guides, he said, "would we have been able to go to my former school and shoot [film]? No, we wouldn't have been let in the front door."

There was one occasion during his trip that this same journalist was permitted to tape without the presence of guides but accompanied by his cousin and his cousin's son, both of whom are Cuban nationals. The group went to visit a shoemaker, a friend of his cousin's. A crowd gathered out of curiosity over the camera, and shortly thereafter the police arrived. He and his film crew were detained until his guides, who were only a block and a half away, were fetched by his cousin's son and explained to the police that the visit has been authorized.

Transportation

Though reporters sometimes manage to roam about without their guides, unless they travel on foot, they will find themselves accompanied by yet another government employee—the cab or rental car driver. For a fee, the government arranges all transportation to appointments it has authorized. If the reporter prefers to wander about on his or her own, there are government-operated cabs, rental cars, buses, and trains. Journalists can travel throughout Havana and to areas not too far from the city by taking a cab. However, travel in the interior is not so easy. "Theoretically, you can go wherever you want," a reporter said. "Control doesn't come by saying you can't go here or there. The problem is no transportation." She explained that a journalist may be able to take a cab from Havana to another village, but may not be able to find a cab there that is allowed to drive back to Havana. If a journalist attempted to leave Havana on a public bus, he or she would "stand in line three days and make everybody nervous." Another reporter added, "If you want to get out of the city [Havana], it's a lot of red tape." Every journalist agreed that one of the major obstacles to investigative reporting in Cuba is the tightly controlled transportation system.

Interviews

In addition to accommodations and transportation, the government either directly or indirectly controls most of a journalist's interviews. Clearance for interviews is necessary "in a centrally planned, Marxist-Leninist state, where anything of importance—factories, newspapers, farms, etc.—is run by the government," a reporter explained.

One institution in which interviews are not arranged by the government is the church. The journalist who wants to interview a minister or priest, some of the reporters said, simply enters a church and finds one. "Few talk frankly," a reporter said. "But they will talk to you." One journalist discovered that this approach does not always work. He tried to interview a Catholic priest, but the priest refused without permission from his bishop, who was out of town and could not be reached.

In seeking permission to cover the twenty-fifth anniversary of the revolution, newspapers were required to submit a list of the people they wanted to interview. The government chose from the list and made the appointments. The Cuban-born journalist followed this same procedure, but in order to interview the people he requested, the government required he also interview some public officials not on his list.

Certain interview requests are turned down consistently by the government—military officials, Soviet personnel, political prisoners, and so on—the journalists said.

According to all of the journalists, it is fairly easy to get interviews with qualified, middle-level Cuban officials. One of the reporters from a wire service said it was easier to arrange these types of interviews in

Cuba than in Iran. "Brazil is infinitely worse [than Cuba] as far as interviews go," said a newspaper reporter. Nevertheless, the journalists warned that unless appointments are arranged prior to arrival in Cuba, it takes a long time to set them up. Consequently, "bunching up interviews toward the end of a visit happens a lot," one journalist explained.

Appointments with high-level officials are rarely granted to journalists, unless they have a long-standing relationship with important members of the Cuban government, as does one of the journalists interviewed, who has been able to interview Fidel Castro. "Everybody is on the list [to interview Castro]," another reporter said. Castro grants only a few interviews a year.

When it comes to "man-in-the-street" interviews, most of the journalists said they were allowed to walk through the streets of Havana and talk to people. Two exceptions were the Cuban American and a reporter who covered the twenty-fifth anniversary of the revolution. The latter said that on other occasions he had been allowed to approach people in the streets. "Ordinarily, this doesn't make the Cubans upset. Because this was such an extensive project, they were desiring more control."

Even when journalists are allowed this freedom, government control, albeit indirect, is evident. "You can talk to anyone you see on the street, if they will talk to you," explained a newspaper reporter. But many people, he said, will not be interviewed without permission from their local Committee for the Defense of the Revolution (CDR). Each block has a CDR, which reports to the authorities any unusual or counterrevolutionary activity. This reporter was in Cuba shortly after the U.S. invasion of Grenada and tried to interview a man who had returned from there. The man refused unless a CDR member authorized it. "I couldn't find anyone who would get involved, so that was the end of that," he said. Later, while questioning people in a crowd listening to a speech about Grenada by Castro, a CDR member told him he was not permitted to interview the bystanders. "People are leery [about talking to reporters]," he said. "I think they think it's a good way to get in trouble." Cubans are nervous about being "fingered" by their CDR said another reporter who had difficulty finding someone willing to discuss Angola. Therefore, "everyone wants to plug you into the [CDR] structure."

Official Tours

It goes without saying that when the Cuban government arranges an interview it also arranges where the interview takes place. In doing so, the government asserts some control over what a journalist sees and perhaps over his or her impression of Cuba. Another way the government attempts to influence a journalist's opinion of Cuba is with an official tour.

Most of the journalists had been taken on an official tour of one or more of the following locations: Ramón Castro's dairy farm, the Isle of Youth, the Lenin Vocational School, the Alamar housing project, and the psychiatric hospital in Havana. Many journalists said they also were taken to a sugar cooperative and/or refinery outside Havana, but it was not clear if they all had been taken to the same ones. One reporter explained the government's inclination to take journalists on tours by saying, "There are things they want to show you to demonstrate their success."

The government often tries to schedule these tours into a journalist's "free time." But for reporters covering a trip to Cuba by diplomats or other dignitaries, such tours may absorb their entire visit. All of the journalists said they were free not to participate in side trips, and one who has been to Cuba many times during the last five years said he has never been urged to go on one. However, an unsuspecting journalist could be taken on an official tour without realizing it. One journalist was taken to Ramón Castro's farm when he asked a cab driver to take him to a farm.

Many of the journalists advised reporters to avoid such trips when possible. One called them "charades" and another said they were "a waste of time." For this reason, reporters need to know in advance what they want to do and where they want to go. "You have to be creative with requests so you're not just stuck," a newspaper reporter said." [Otherwise] they will fill up your time." "Some things they will never let you do," she continued. For years, she added, she has tried unsuccessfully to see a guerrilla training base.

Cameras

All the journalists said the government never attempted to control their notetaking or writing. However, the government does restrict the use of cameras. For example, it forbids the photographing of police and anything having to do with the military, including soldiers, Soviet ships, and certain government buildings. The reporter who covered the twenty-fifth anniversary of the revolution said the government tightened its control over photographers from his newspaper. In addition to the above-mentioned restrictions, they were not allowed to photograph poor people or statues in Havana.

Filming at many locations requires authorization from the central government. Because obtaining such permission takes time, many journalists prearrange their filming, as they do their interviews, before arriving in Cuba.

The foreign television correspondent did not prearrange his filming with the government and met with mixed results. When he tried to film an elementary school, he was told he needed authorization from the Ministry of Education, which would take two days. At Ramón Castro's farm, he was not allowed to film. At another dairy farm a person in authority there let him shoot. When he followed a film crew from a U.S. television station to Port Mariel, he was left behind at the gate. The other crew was let in because it did have official permission.

A television journalist from a major U.S. network said he cooperated with the government's restrictions on his filming. "We didn't act stupid and try to photograph what we were forbidden or we would've risked confiscation of everything," he said. None of the journalists interviewed ever had film confiscated.

Filing Centers

When journalists visit Cuba to cover a government-sponsored event, the Cubans establish a press filing center where reporters can send stories to their editors over the telephone. Despite the special arrangements, telephone connections take a long time to establish, though not as long as usual. The Cuban government currently charges $4.00 cash per minute for phone calls to the United States. Traveler's checks are accepted, but credit cards are not.

Stories sent from Cuba by telephone are monitored. According to the U.S. television journalist, a guide told a reporter in his group that the story the reporter had sent contained false information—this before it had been published.

Because telephoning is costly and requires long waits, one reporter recommended the use of Telex. There is a Telex office in the Habana Libre. It accepted credit cards, and "the service is excellent," he said.

Getting Around the System

The government's arrangements and restrictions constitute a system of controlling the foreign media in Cuba. Though there are limits set by the regime that journalists will never get beyond, good reporting skills can be adapted to the Cuban environment.

Journalists sometimes manage to circumvent the system and capture in print or on film an aspect of Cuban life not disclosed to them by the authorities, but they must have modest expectations of such an opportunity. They must accept patiently the limitations imposed on them by the government "or go crazy," a reporter said. "Cuba is a terribly frustrating place to work. Be ambitious, be vigorous, but don't set your sights too high."

Contacts

Journalists sometimes can sidestep the need for the government to arrange all their interviews by having contacts in Cuba. There usually is no rule against calling a government official or a local citizen on the telephone to make an appointment.

As was mentioned earlier, scholars, diplomats and Cuban exiles in the United States can be good sources for names of contacts in Cuba. The reporter from a religious magazine acquired the name of a Cuban Jew from someone in the Jewish community in the United States. The young man proved to be a great help to the reporter. He took her all over Havana, including to people's homes, their synagogues, and to a Seventh-Day Adventist service.

Reporters who cover Cuba regularly can build contacts in the country the way they do anyplace else. "If you haven't been there a lot, it's difficult to get around the system" a newspaper reporter said. "[But] the more you go, the more contacts you make. . . . Take the trouble to find out people who know things without being the typical official voices." Middle-level officials are accessible by telephone, he said; upper level officials are not. The Ministry for External Relations is the liaison between journalists and the higher ranks of the government, but good contacts are helpful in obtaining these interviews also. A reporter who has interviewed Castro and several cabinet officers attributed his success to the contacts he has built over the years. "The better the liaison [at the foreign ministry], the better the relationship, the better the interviews," he said. He added he had met certain Cuban officials as early at the 1960s outside Cuba and maintained contact with them ever since.

Having friends in Cuba as well as contacts can be advantageous. One reporter said she avoids the hassles of the transportation system by borrowing a friend's car.

Though helpful, making friends and building contacts in Cuba can undermine a reporter's objectivity, a journalist warned. "It's easy to get too close to this or that official," he said. Warming up to Cuban officials to gain favors or certain advantages may weaken a reporter's will to ask tough questions or to uncover and reveal discrediting information.

Diplomacy

Most of the journalists noted the need to exercise the art of diplomacy while working in Cuba. Though the assertion of one's rights in the United States knocks down unlawful barriers to the press, such an approach in Cuba, where the press has no rights, provokes further restrictions. Journalists cautioned against being confrontational with guides or government officials. "Don't ever get mad" when prohibited in any way, warned a reporter. Artful persuasion, on the other hand, sometimes paves the way past an obstacle. For example, if a guide forbids a photographer to take a particular picture, he or she should ask the reason it is not permitted and explain the importance of the shot. If the photographer cannot change the guide's mind, he or she can appeal to a higher authority. This approach worked for a television journalist who visited a Cuban oil refinery.

Another journalist said if the person in authority seems uncertain about the action in question, he or she can sometimes be convinced that no harm will be done by it. If the person, however, is certain a particular action is forbidden, no attempts at persuasion will succeed.

Diplomacy is also valuable when interviewing Cubans. Asking tough questions is the job of a reporter, but appearing antagonistic is unproductive. The object of interviewing should be the facts, not antigovernment quotes. "I'm an adversary as far as the Cubans go but not an unfriendly one," a journalist said. Cubans are hesitant to talk to reporters who bait them to criticize the government, said another.

One tactic useful in disarming lower-level authorities and ordinary people is to act ignorant and ask simple questions, a journalist explained. "We found it useful to pretend to be more ignorant than we were," he said. "Asking real basic questions can provide good insights." Such questions, he added, must be asked "in a very innocent way." For example, in an interview with a CDR member, he asked about the purpose of the CDR. When the woman explained her job is to report counterrevolutionary activity, he asked her what she would consider counterrevolutionary. An unfamiliar car parked in the street, she said.

Off the Beaten Trail

All of the journalists recommended going off the beaten trail as much as possible. Instead of going on official tours, journalists should scout areas and spend time with ordinary people, whether or not their story requires doing so. The reporter from the religious magazine, for example, took the initiative to attend worship services not on her itinerary. By doing so, she was able to get a better glimpse of religion in Cuba than some of the other journalists in her group.

Talking with and listening to people going about their daily lives broadens a reporter's understanding of Cuba, the journalists said. "Don't wait in your hotel room for a phone call from some government official," a newspaper reporter declared; rather, visit local stores, restaurants, and bars. Entering conversations or simply overhearing them can give "a feel for what's going on." Realizing that activities are watched, this journalist never tries to hide from the government where he goes. Being evasive only arouses government suspicion, which could lead to tighter controls.

"Go to CDR meetings," another journalist advised. "It's a good way to meet people. Granted, they're gung-ho about the revolution." Though CDR meetings are uncritical of the government, they are forums for expressing grievances about local problems. A reporter may be able to learn from them more about daily life in Cuba.

Dissent

Going off the beaten trail may lead a journalist to someone critical of the government. "You won't be able to find any dissidents," one journalist said. "They are either quiet or behind bars. But [unhappy] people may try to communicate with you." On his visit in 1974, this television newsman had met a critic of the regime at a CDR block party. A teenage boy standing back to back with him whispered, "All is not what it appears to be." The journalist inferred that those at the party were coerced into attending. When asked, the boy agreed to an interview. When they met again, the teenager gave "the party line," the journalist said, so he concluded the interview early. "We knew someone had gotten to him," he said. As the crew was packing the film equipment, the boy was picked up by the police. The crew turned the cameras back on and filmed him being taken away in a car. Later the journalist was told by U.S. intelligence officials that the boy had been shot.

Because criticism of the Cuban government is punished severely, journalists need to protect their leads, a reporter said. In his stories, he does not name those who make critical remarks and he fabricates facts about them "to get the scent off."

Sometimes dissent is communicated to reporters "on the sly," a journalist said. Therefore, journalists must "keep their eyes open, look through the obvious" and be ready to record the more subtle forms of protest.

Opportunism

All the journalists noted that to get a good story in Cuba, one must have an opportunistic streak. Reporters "must know how to squeeze into things in a daring way but not in a confrontational way," a television correspondent said. An example of seizing an opportunity was described by the television correspondent from the United States. At a party for foreign guests, the journalist approached Fidel Castro and began talking to him in English about baseball. Castro, an avid baseball fan, responded in English. The subsequent conversation, which the journalist described as "most unusual," was filmed.

When the police showed up at the interview with the shoemaker, mentioned above, the cameraman continued to film in an inconspicuous manner. "He held the camera at his side as if he was simply carrying it. They weren't aware that they were being filmed at that point." Had the police realized the camera was on, he continued, they would have told them to stop and could have confiscated the film. When taking advantage of such an opportunity, a journalist must be aware of the risk, he said. "At any time things could be brought to a halt."

There is a distinction between getting around the system and defying it. Disobeying Cuban procedure is dangerous. Two French journalists visited Cuba in 1983 with tourist visas, though the intent of the trip was to interview a Cuban dissident. After an interview with the man, the two reporters were arrested, interrogated, and detained for ten days. Their release was won by the intervention of the French Embassy."[7]

Balancing the Story

The ability to write or produce a balanced report is the mark of a professional journalist. The journalists interviewed offered advice on how to balance stories about Cuba.

Certain Assumptions

Gathering balanced, accurate information is difficult in a country like Cuba, where the regime exerts both direct and indirect control over the activities of the foreign press. Many of the places and people encountered by journalists are arranged by the government in order to impress upon them a certain image of Cuba. In analyzing their experiences in Cuba, journalists should keep in mind several facts.

Cuban authorities show and tell reporters only that which advances a favorable impression of the revolution. As was mentioned earlier, official tours are conducted at places groomed for visits by foreigners. Because such tours do not honestly represent Cuban life, most journalists interviewed said to avoid them. The other places journalists are allowed to see must be evaluated with suspicion. "Unless a prison visit is beneficial to the government, you won't go on one," a reporter said. Journalists also must be skeptical of the information given them by the government. "You won't get any scoops unless they decide to give them to you," the reporter continued. "You can hang around there forever trying to find out which Soviets are where. And there's a 99 percent chance you won't get anywhere." Another journalist warned that the high-ranking officials are masters of media manipulation. "It's easy to get snowballed by any one of them."

Those who criticize the Cuban government will suffer for it. Because the Cubans are not free to express themselves, just about every journalist interviewed advised reporters to weigh carefully what they hear. "Conformity [to the party line] is not only a virtue but also a necessity," a reporter said. He noted that recently a man was sentenced to four years in prison for saying "Viva, Reagan!" "If someone is unhappy, he is not going to say so," he added. Another reporter explained social advancement in Cuba is based on loyalty. The best jobs, and houses, he said, go to those who are most enthusiastic about the revolution. And, he added, some are better off because of the revolution. This reality makes responses from people difficult to interpret, another journalist said. "Is it a case of conviction . . . or a case of convenience . . . or a case of fear? [Not knowing for sure] makes it so difficult." Any outsiders, including reporters, are looked on with suspicion, he continued, because even they have some degree of government sanction. Journalists can expect no deviation from the party line among government officials. "A Cuban official has to support the ideology," a reporter said. "He can't deviate from that."

Public events are sometimes staged for the media. A journalist who covered Jesse Jackson's campaign visit said she witnessed special events planned for Jackson's trip. One such event was a church service, which Fidel Castro attended. Castro's presence was "weird," she said; one must be an atheist to belong to the Cuban Communist party. The church was filled with people, she added, but the journalists were not given the time to talk to any of them.

During the emigrations from Port Mariel, a journalist witnessed a progovernment demonstration, which "many well-dressed" people attended. Those he questioned said participation was voluntary, but he learned that the CDRs take note of which people come to such events and which do not.

Bias

Neither naiveté nor an anti-Cuba bias helps a reporter. A reporter must understand the Cuban system and the ideology behind the system; this knowledge may compel a journalist from the United States to form a negative opinion about Cuba. However, the purpose of professional news reporting is never to advance an opinion. While it is not easy to divorce opinion from fact, this is the task of reporting.

The journalists interviewed also recognized that reporters can form opinions sympathetic to the revolution. Realizing the possibility for journalists to be either hot or cold and the effect it can have on their reporting one newspaperman said a reporter with strong opinions about Cuba should not cover news there. Another journalist voiced a less extreme position. "I don't think any press is unbiased. On the other hand, you can write accurately without letting biases predominate," he said. Reporters need to look at everything with a critical, but not a cynical eye. "A journalist is part alley cat; they have got to dig up the dirt."

The journalists gave suggestions on how to ensure a story is unbiased. One was the balancing paragraph. When quoting Cuban criticisms of the United States, for example, a reporter should always include a paragraph explaining the U.S. position. When covering a speech by Castro, a reporter should focus on the substance of the speech and not the strictly ideological content. Another suggestion was to check all statistics provided by the Cuban government against those from other sources.

The journalists stressed there are two sides to the revolution. Some people have gained by it, and others have lost. A story should include those facts that indicate the regime's successes and failures.

Conclusion

Covering Cuba is no easy assignment. First, there are Cuban government restrictions that journalists must accept and others they must learn to circumvent. Second, because the Cuban communist system rewards loyalty and punishes dissent, responses from people may not always be sincere. Finally, the Cuban government is eager to do as much for foreign journalists as they will allow. Ironically, the convenience of government arrangements makes the reporter's task more difficult. As one reporter explained, the government's hospitality can lull journalists into "complacency. They make things so comfortable for foreigners," she said, "you can think you're someplace you're not." Taking the easy route is a temptation in every occupation, and mediocrity is usually the result.

For journalists in Cuba, the easiest road is to let the government do all but write their stories for them. However, it is the responsibility of the good journalist to look for the story behind the version officially sanctioned by the Cuban government, to probe beyond the superficial image staged by that regime for the benefit of the Western press.

Respondent: Ms. Joanne Omang, *Washington Post*

The Cuban guides, cum guards, keep an eye on what you're doing, stand very close to you and try to listen to your conversations. It is the duty of any responsible journalist to try to escape from these people and talk to others.

It is very important that you speak Spanish in Cuba because if you don't, you are at the mercy of the guides or of interpreters whose origin you don't know.

Foreign diplomats, who may or may not be friendly to Cuba, are a good source of news for journalists in Cuba. Some defend the revolution, others criticize it, but they provide perspective. Talking with church people is also a good way to gain perspective; they are already in trouble with the government.

A journalist will get an average person in trouble if he or she gets them to say something bad about the system, yet I doubt that a person would be shot just for talking to a journalist.

Many of the points made in the paper are true when reporting on any government. The goal of any government or movement is to have a cheering section in the press. This is contrary to the goal of the press itself, which is "to comfort the afflicted and afflict the comfortable."

The salient factor in press coverage in Cuba is the presence of the guides. You have to resort to subterfuge and dodge them in one way or another.

Covering a right-wing dictatorship is just as difficult, if not worse, than covering a left-wing dictatorship such as Cuba. A good journalist is out to get everybody, no matter whose side that happens to hurt— the right or the left. Our goal in life is to find out what's going on. You listen to all sides but don't believe anyone totally. Everybody has a piece of the truth but no one has the whole thing. No one can give you the whole picture. You as a journalist try to piece it together.

The biggest problem is probably arrogance. If you think that you understand, if you think that you know, you're probably wrong.

Respondent: Mr. Antonio Guernica, Independent Producer

Providing objective coverage in Cuba is extremely difficult. The whole thrust of any official involvement with a reporter is to direct the coverage so that it will reflect well on the government—from facilitating journalistic activity to restricting movement. If the government decides that you have been critical of it, it is likely that you will not be allowed in the country again.

There will be restrictions imposed by the Cuban government, and it is the responsibility of the journalist to inform his or her audience of what they are. It's a disagreeable admission to make but it should be made. If your ability to provide objective coverage is compromised, you should inform your audience.

Journalists will find that there is no "factual" objectivity in Cuba per se. Objectivity is what the Cuban government says it is. A reporter should always keep that in mind when relying on the Cuban government as a news source, be it in the form of an official tour, an interview, a report, or sets of figures.

Given these circumstances, there's little value in sending a journalist to Cuba who does not speak Spanish. There's a debilitating arrogance in the attitude that a journalist can adequately cover events in a country where he or she doesn't speak the native language and the only sources of information are those chosen by a government that actively suppresses divergent points of view. Arriving at a true representation of events is difficult enough for those who do speak Spanish and who are familiar with Cuban history and its political system.

The Cuban government's assertion that Cuban exiles cannot be objective about conditions and events in Cuba is based largely on the fact that Cuban exiles have direct personal and historical experience with Cuba; they have a frame of reference and a perspective that is independent from that of the Cuban government.

As a journalist, you should likely assume that you will be under more or less constant surveillance while in Cuba; at least we found evidence of that to be true in our case. You should take steps to try to break and confuse that surveillance.

Journalists should also take steps to try to protect their sources. Criticism of the government is a punishable offense against the state.

Don't expect the Cuban people to be eager to criticize the government. The degree of government control in Cuba is such that your mere presence in the country is interpreted by the Cuban people as a sign that you are likely in sympathy with the government, whether or not that is the case. As a journalist in Cuba, you are held suspect not only by the government but also by those who may disagree with government policies. Criticizing the Cuban government in an interview with a journalist would place the person in serious risk.

Lastly, go beyond the image. The reality behind the facade is much more newsworthy and of greater consequence than the staging put on by the government.

Discussion Summary

Another dimension of the challenges faced by journalists in Cuba is the practice, which has been documented, of blackmail or attempted blackmail of the press by Cuban intelligence. Cuban agents have tried to entrap members of the Western press through male and female prostitutes, drugs, and so on.

Cuba, however, is not the only country to use intimidation to influence press coverage. While the military junta ruled in Argentina, files were kept on journalists, and attempts were made to entrap them, as they are made by other repressive governments.

Given the difficult circumstances regarding press access to Cuba, journalists who intend to return to Cuba for coverage may have to measure their words very carefully in criticizing the regime or risk losing access in the future. This is an implicit condition when covering Cuba, and another example of the government's attempts to compromise coverage.

Newspapers with large resources, such as the *Washington Post* and the *New York Times,* and media such as the three television networks can afford to send a variety of people if one or more of their reporters are rejected. Most newspapers and other media do not have that luxury. Reporters who are believed to be unsympathetic to the ruling government receive special attention and vigilance in other repressive countries as well.

The Cuban government uses a formidable apparatus to control, artfully and deliberately, the foreign press. The government's duplicity in its handling of the press makes it particularly difficult to reach individuals in Cuba who represent a truly dissident view.

Note

1. Jacquelin De Linares, The Desperate Act of Cuba's Dissident: Ricardo Bofill, *Le Matin de Paris,* October 7, 1983. Reprinted in *Of Human Rights* 1983-1984 (Washington, D.C.: Georgetown University).

5

Fidel Castro and the United States Press

John P. Wallach

A look at Fidel Castro's image in the U.S. press and some reasons that he has generally received such sympathetic coverage. The paper examines Castro's ability to manipulate the press, citing examples and outlining strategies that he has used repeatedly. The paper also discusses the self-interest of the journalist as an incentive for providing sympathetic coverage of Castro and the Cuban revolution.

> *One remarkable thing about Castro is how durable his image has been. It is amazing the extent to which American journalists have succeeded in divorcing the political and economic realities from the image. No matter how many refugees come out, how many political prisoners tell the horror stories, Castro's image is untarnished. It is even more incredible that Castro's image is maintained and promulgated by supposedly hard-nosed probing reporters.*
>
> —Dr. Paul Hollander
> University of Massachusetts

Introduction

When Fidel Castro graduated at seventeen from high school, not an ordinary public school but a private Catholic seminary called Belén, the legend under his photo in the graduation class yearbook concluded: "The ham in him will not be lacking."

There are few modern political heroes on the world stage who have been more successful in manipulating the media coverage of themselves than this bearded, aging revolutionary. One only has to recall the titles of interviews. Frank Mankiewicz and Kirby Jones, who filmed more than thirteen hours of interviews with Castro in June and

129

July 1974, called the book drawn from their experience simply *With Fidel*. The subtitle was *A Portrait of Castro and Cuba*.

Castro and indeed Cuba were secondary. The notion that was paramount was the fact that these two quasi-journalists (Mankiewicz had been a Peace Corps director and later Robert Kennedy's campaign manager; Kirby similarly was a Peace Corps director in Ecuador and then George McGovern's press secretary) had been permitted to peek behind the tightly controlled curtain of censorship that Castro had established by denying to give many previous interviews. Kirby and Mankiewicz were on a first-name basis with Fidel; consequently, the title.

The point is almost too obvious to mention. But consider the title of Barbara Walters's interview as broadcast in a full hour almost three years later. The June 9, 1977, ABC special was called "Fidel Speaks: An Interview with Barbara Walters." This was not to be the mountain coming to Mohammed, but Mohammed coming to the mountain.

How can I forget my own excitement when I was able to get a visa to travel to Cuba in 1972. It was an exotic land, off-limits to almost all of my colleagues. Naturally, the visa I was granted was to report on the July 26 commemoration of the nineteenth anniversary of the unsuccessful 1953 attack on the Moncada barracks that is celebrated as the start of the Cuban revolution.

Indeed I began my very first story, dispatched from Havana on July 25, 1972, with these words:

> "We want you to see Cuba when the people are happy," a Cuban diplomat explained before leaving Mexico City. So this American correspondent, tightly gripping the immigration documents that will get him back into Mexico sometime next month, boarded Cubana Airlines Flight 465, a Soviet Illyushin-18 propjet, for the three-hour trip from Mexico City.

The point is that the trip into Cuba was as important as almost any story that I would write once there.

> The four-engine plane is crowded with Castro supporters coming to this once-a-year, quasi-religious rite. On board, among others, is an Indian diplomat, a group of French tourists, a Japanese newsman, several British engineers, two American leftists sporting "Victory to the Revolution" buttons and a Soviet embassy courier jealously guarding his nation's padlocked diplomatic pouch.

Even the in-flight service was deemed worthy of comment:

As the Cubana flight is airborne, attractive mini-skirted stewardesses (those were the days of the mini-skirt) offer the passengers hard candies, soon followed by Cuban rum mixed with ginger or cola and subsequently followed by a delicious lunch of chicken fricassee, rice, peas, cake, sweet dark coffee and beer on the rocks.

I went on to describe the newspapers—*Granma* offered in Spanish and English, and full photographs of Castro embracing African and East European leaders.

When I returned from the three-week trip, I was an instant celebrity. Mildred Hilson, one of New York City's most prominent hostesses, a widow who was then in her early seventies and had been one of Mamie Eisenhower's closest friends, threw a dinner party in my honor at her thirty-sixth-floor suite in the Waldorf Towers. The guest list was impressive, particularly for a twenty-nine-year-old reporter. My dinner partners that night included Governor and Mrs. Nelson Rockefeller; Mr. and Mrs. Walter Cronkite; Robert Gray, who had been Dwight Eisenhower's appointments secretary; Mayor and Mrs. John Lindsay; Barbara Walters; and Jackie Onassis. The evening would have been a triumph but for one fact: Mrs. Hilson insisted I show the slides of my trip after dinner and accompany them with a short narration. Within minutes of the beginning of the slide show, every one of the distinguished guests excused themselves one after another, until only Barbara Walters, Mildred Hilson, and I were left.

Castro's Superhuman Image

Fidel Castro has always been bigger than life, the most fashionable revolutionary the modern world has known. Frank Mankiewicz to this day is impressed with Castro's apparel. "He wears those fatigues but they're designer fatigues . . . I mean they're not the kind of fatigues you'd expect to get if you entered the Army," he told me. "They're very light weight, well cut—I wouldn't be surprised if they were Oscar de la Renta." But it's not Castro's outward appearance that has made him so fashionable. It is the fact that he fits to a glove the image of a revolutionary that we have in our own minds. It is trite to say that if Castro did not exist, we would have to invent him. The fact, however, is that we have invented him.

Castro is more interesting because of what he tells us about ourselves than any other legendary or even fictional history book character. He epitomizes all those characteristics admired most by Western intellectuals. He was born the son of a poor, pick-and-shovel laborer for the United Fruit Company, whose sugar plantations were on the northern shores of Oriente Province. His father became a wealthy landowner—the very epitome of a capitalist success—sending his children to the best schools and leaving them a sizeable inheritance, only to have his eldest son, Fidel, after graduating from law school, turn his back on the family fortune and become an underground (and underdog) guerrilla fighter.

We were always ready to give Castro the benefit of the doubt because of our puritanical revulsion for Latin "dictatorships" in the Batista model. "I suppose that what you are saying," Mankiewicz suggested to Castro at one point during their interview, "is that in a certain form, the socialist government of Cuba involves itself in the ordinary life of the Cuban in a more or less easygoing way—a less demanding way than other Communist governments, right?"

The idea that Castro, as the romantic embodiment of our own liberal traditions, could establish a humane, caring society where a cruel dictatorship had existed—becoming the world's first "good" Communist—is nowhere more cryptically expressed than in this sentence from Herbert Matthews's February 1957 interview with him in the Sierra Maestra: "It is a revolutionary movement that calls itself socialistic. The program is vague and couched in generalities, but it amounts to a new deal for Cuba, radical, democratic and therefore anti-Communist." Indeed, Castro's idealism reminded Julian Bond of nothing so much as the "connection between socialism and Christianity."

Just listen for a moment to the disappointment in the voice of Andrew St. George shortly before he returned to Cuba in July 1960, fearful that his "warm wartime friendship with Fidel" would be a thing of the past. "My phone functioned fitfully, requiring peculiar repairs and wiring," the journalist wrote of his last visit following the triumph of the revolution. "Overnight I became an 'imperialist agent', instead of an honored hero of the revolution. Today, newsmen from the *other* side—Russians, Czechs, Bulgarians, Red Chinese—are inaugurating a new cycle as the 'Heroic Correspondents of Our Anti-Imperialist Struggle'." Surely Castro could not have forgotten that "the only magazine article he ever wrote" appeared in *Coronet,* which was St. George's principal employer.

This sense of personal betrayal led St. George to conclude: "Tragically, Castro probably does have the timbre of a great new Latin leader—the irresistible personality, the instinct for timely social reform, the sure touch with the masses. But as a result of his mistakes, Fidel Castro does not even rule Cuba today." He went on to bemoan the fact that Castro had to share power with his brother Raúl and "El Che," Che Guevara. "If Fidel recognizes his mistakes before it's too late, he and his country may still have a great future," St. George concluded.

Not only did we in those early days want Castro to be charismatic, a reformer with a social conscience, a revolutionary, a guerrilla fighter, and the personification of the noble "masses," but we wanted him to be all-powerful as well. In a world of McCarthyism, of dull, imperfect, and even corrupt politicians, Castro was the romantic hero of our bedside novels. "It was as if," Norman Mailer wrote in 1959, "the ghost of Cortez had appeared in our century riding Zapata's white horse. You were the first and greatest hero to appear in the world since the Second War . . . the answer to the argument of Commissars and Statesmen that revolutions cannot last, that they turn corrupt or total or eat their own."

Castro, in short, had completed the same voyage as Homer's odyssey through Iliad and had been crowned king of the Western intellectuals. To a question of what it meant to be a professional revolutionary, Castro was quoted as replying: "I can't stand injustice." Jean-Paul Sartre even noted, during a visit to the Sierra Maestra hideout, that long after midnight, "Castro is the most wide awake . . . Castro can eat the most and fast the longest. [They] . . . exercise a veritable dictatorship over their own needs [and] roll back the limits of the possible."

Castro's Manipulation of Media Images

The projection of superhuman and at the same time profoundly human attributes onto Castro is something he has been aware of, and able to manipulate brilliantly from his first day in power. That should not come as a complete surprise because he was a journalist of sorts himself, interestingly a sports reporter for a magazine called *La Calle* and then for a Cuban newspaper. Hero worship was nothing new to Castro. He was almost signed by the Washington Senators as a relief pitcher. In the late 1940s he wrote for a time under the pseudonym Alejandro, was coeditor of *La Acción,* the strongly anti-Batista newspaper at the University of Havana Law School, and contributed articles to *Bohemia,* the most respected periodical in Cuba. As a self-styled intellectual, Castro had a strong sense of the importance and power of words."

Castro's three trips to the United States—on his honeymoon in late 1948, when he returned on a fund-raising drive in 1955, and his triumphant visit to Washington in 1959—must have made him keenly aware of the power of a free press. "He clearly understood that the United States was the media market of the world and that this is where you had to make your impact," British-born Peter Bourne, the closest thing to a real intellectual in the Carter administration, told me. Anyone who doubts Castro's ability to bend words to his own use should read a transcript of his appearance on "Meet the Press" on April 19, 1959. "There is no doubt for me between democracy and communism," he said. "Not only democracy as a word. That is why we call our ideas humanism, because we not only want to give freedoms to the people, but to give them a way of getting their life: to eat, to live—not only theoretically."

Even in those early days of Castro's rule, when he was vehemently denying that he was a communist, he had the traditional Marxist perception of the role of information in a socialist state, namely that all power flows from the top unless you happen to be in a capitalist country like the United States. Then you conveniently ignore the elected government for the much more revolutionary "public opinion" of the people. "That is our way of doing things," Castro told the nationwide television audience. "We go first to the public opinion, and when public opinion supports our cause, it will be easier that the government support and understand our cause." Making no bones whatsoever about to whom he was appealing, Castro added confidently: "It is a matter of public opinion because this country is a country of public opinion." He never tried very hard to hide his contempt for the idea of a free press.

"We do not have your same perceptions," he told Walters in 1977. "Our concept of freedom of the press is not yours. I say this very honestly. I have nothing to hide. If you ask if a newspaper can appear against socialism, I can say very honestly, no, it cannot. In that sense, we do not have the freedom of the press that you possess in the United States, and we are very satisfied about that."

Castro's attraction for communism was easy to understand. It offered him an institutionalized structure to get hold of power, supreme and absolute power. No other system would allow him to do that without being accused of being just another Latin American dictator. But Castro was smart enough to know that he had to rationalize this shortcoming, even for the most liberal believers in the U.S. media. To do away with one of the most precious rights enjoyed by the greatest democracy in the world, Castro knew he had to come up with a vision of himself and particularly his own place in history that would transcend such petty things as ideology and human rights. Now more than ever he needed the right words and the media to communicate them to the American people. When asked whether he was a communist or believed in Marxist ideology, Castro replied with comments such as, "I'm committed to a theory of humanitarian socialism." He was so adept at using words that Sol Landau, who filmed an interview with him for public television in 1967, declared him "a man who has been steeped in democracy."

Again projecting what we most wanted Castro to become—not what he was—Leo Huberman and Paul Sweezy wrote: "First and foremost, Fidel is a passionate humanitarian . . . in the meaningful sense that he feels compassion for human suffering, hates injustice because it causes unnecessary suffering, and is totally committed to building in Cuba a society in which the poor and the underprivileged shall be able to hold up their heads."

Castro told the "Meet the Press" panel: "Democracy is my ideal" and "I am not a Communist." The phrase he preferred was "a revolutionary idealist." He also pledged that there would be free and open elections in Cuba "as soon as possible" and with absolute certainty within the next four years. Bourne believes this adroit use of the media—and particularly democratic-sounding reassurances—was a very calculated effort to buy time so as to prevent the United States from intervening in Cuba's internal affairs.

When we examine how Castro sees himself, it is above all as one of the great figures in history. "One would have to say he is unbelievably egotistical," Bourne admits. But also a genuine intellectual, or so he would have us believe. Bourne obtained a receipt from a bookstore in Mexico City where Castro purchased many books during his period in exile. The books included the story of Hannibal's victorious military campaign to defeat the Romans; Rommel's memoirs; *The Life and Times of Disraeli; The Works of Lenin* and Hitler's *Mein Kampf.* David Caute wrote that while imprisoned, Castro spent all of his time reading works by St. Thomas Aquinas, John of Salisbury, Luther, Knox, Milton, Rousseau, and Thomas Paine.

"[Castro] views himself in the same category as Julius Caesar and Napoleon. He regards himself as being in their company," Bourne told me. That, in turn, allows Castro the luxury of believing that he is beyond ideology. I mean people do not ask: "Was Napoleon a communist?" Bourne believes that Castro genuinely sees himself as someone who is neither anti-American nor pro-Soviet. "He regards himself as being among the great thinkers of history for whom the ideological things are purely small-time tactical issues. Even with Lenin," Bourne suggests, "he was much more interested in Lenin as a person who created a successful revolution than he was in whether Marxism was a valid theoretical basis on which to run a country."

The historical figure that Castro seems most fond of comparing himself to is an American: Abraham Lincoln. He etched for Mankiewicz and Jones in one paragraph the epitaph that he probably envisions for himself:

> If you ask me for an American that I deeply admire, I would say Lincoln. I believe he was one of the most moving characters in history— especially how he worked in the fields and cut down trees; how he was so poor and lived under such difficult conditions; how he had to go through so many hardships in order to learn to read and write, to study; how he picked up the banner of justice during his time and so bravely and wisely struggled against all these difficulties; how he became the President of the United States; how he had to carry on a war, when he so loved peace. It must have been a real struggle for such a peaceful man to find himself involved in a civil war. And then for his life to have ended so dramatically, so unfairly.

Whether he genuinely fears for his life or not, Castro has turned the assassination of Lincoln and the CIA efforts to do away with him into the single most important *modus vivendi* of his existence. Everything revolves around the mystique of his constantly evading plots to assassinate him, even to the point where he is able successfully to use the real assassinations of the Kennedy brothers—"Robert and John" as he calls them—to bolster the belief that he remains the number-one target on the CIA "hit list."

It is hardly accidental that almost all the interviews Castro has given to network correspondents took place at night, often well after midnight. Mankiewicz ascribes this simply to Castro's being "basically a night person." But the other element that runs through almost everyone's experience in interviewing him is the element of surprise: his showing up unexpectedly, often at inconvenient hours.

What left the most lasting impression was Castro's apparent lack of fear among his own people. After two nights of interviewing, Castro suggested to Mankiewicz and Jones that "we go out tomorrow morning and I'll show you some of the countryside." At about ten or eleven o'clock, Castro showed up and "we climbed into his jeep, Kirby Jones, me, Saul Landau and a cameraman. Castro drove. And now began really the most astonishing part of the whole trip."

"It was amazing," Mankiewicz said. "Open jeep, cars would pull up alongside, they'd see him, they'd wave, 'Hello Fidel.' I mean, for a dictator, it was a pretty astonishing performance. Plus the fact, of course, that everyone in Cuba is armed. The government has given everyone a gun." The drama is an essential part of keeping the myth alive. Mankiewicz fondly recalls the night of Labor Day in September 1974 when he returned with Dan Rather to film an interview with Castro for "CBS Reports," the program Edward R. Murrow had immortalized. It was to become a vehicle for Rather, who had been relieved of his White House assignment after dozens of CBS affiliate stations complained that he was too antagonistic toward Richard Nixon.

When Nixon was forced to resign in August 1974, CBS brought Rather to New York. "They had to find something for him to do, quickly, as a face-saver," Mankiewicz said. That fit the plans of Mankiewicz and Jones because none of the networks were interested in the thirteen hours of interviews they had brought back, particularly because much was instantly dated in the wake of Nixon's resignation. "Well, now they needed something to get on the air in a hurry for the first program. So they said," Makiewicz recalls, "All right, if Castro will allow you to go back with Dan Rather, and talk a little bit about Ford and maybe some other things, then we'll buy your material, and we'll use a blend of the two as the first program in the new series." But much to their horror, they discovered that New York's senior Republican senator, Jacob Javits (who was trying to head off a liberal Democratic challenge from Ramsey Clark), and Rhode Island's Senator Claiborne Pell were visiting Cuba at the same time with a press contingent of about a hundred television and newspaper reporters. "Gordon Manning [vice-president of CBS News] let it be known that if anybody got an interview with Castro on the air, we were done—that we had to have the first one," Mankiewicz said.

The press people accompanying the two senators were waiting for the meeting with Castro to break up, anxious to snare what they hoped would be a question-and-answer session with the Cuban leader. Rather had left the Riviera Hotel to cover the expected news conference as well. "I'm sitting in my hotel room, sweating it out, shaving. And there's a knock on my door," Mankiewicz recalls. "I go to the door, and my God, there is Fidel Castro. I'm in my underwear, and I'm wearing a back brace because my back is giving me trouble, and my face is covered with shaving cream, and here is the *líder máximo.*"

"He said, 'May I come in?' and I said, 'Sure, come in.' And I quickly got the stuff off my face, and pulled on my pants. And he said to me, 'I want some advice. I've never been in an American election campaign before. I don't want to appear to be helping one man [Javits] as against the other [Clark], but on the other hand I want to be courteous. I don't want to hurt Mr. Javits, who is a reasonable man. Tell me what you think I should do.''

An obviously excited Mankiewicz replied: ''Well, let me tell you first of all it's your country, and I know our financial success has no bearing on you, but I must tell you that if you give anybody an interview over there, we will be, and I used the Spanish word, 'aruinados' which means, as you might gather, ruined.'' Castro was said to have paused, and then said quietly. ''Ah, well, all right.'' He went to the Habana Libre, the former Hilton Hotel, where the meeting with Javits and Pell was to take place, and announced that there would be a photo opportunity but he would not answer questions.

There was pandemonium. ''Why won't you answer our questions?'' a reporter shouted. ''Because,'' Castro replied, ''I have promised an exclusive interview to another group.'' ''Is that the Mankiewicz group?'' the reporter asked. ''Yes, it is,'' Castro replied. ''I'm going to give them an exclusive or they will be *'aruinados'.* '' ''But,'' the reporter protested, ''they're amateurs and we're professionals.'' To which Castro replied: ''Yes, I know, but they got the interview, didn't they?'' An interesting footnote, perhaps, is the fact that in the final CBS product forty-eight minutes of Rather's questions to Castro were used, representing almost one-half of the two hours Rather spent with the Cuban leader. Only three to four minutes of the thirteen hours that Mankiewicz and Jones had filmed were used in the Rather program because CBS refused to air an interview that had been produced independently.

The flair for the dramatic is a boon to correspondents who want to write about him. Such a one-on-one relationship with any world leader is what reporters dream of. But if the ''friendship'' is important to the writing press, the ''ham in him'' virtually guarantees high ratings for television correspondents for whom visuals are as important as what is said. The opening of the Barbara Walters 1977 interview is particularly noteworthy. Water literally splashes across the bow of a speeding Cuban patrol boat as Walters asks her first question: ''Is it true that we are the first Americans to cross the Bay of Pigs in 16 years?'' Castro responds, ''As I remember, it's the first time.'' And then he jokes, ''You didn't come here to invade the coast, did you?''

In fact, a visit to the Bay of Pigs or Playa Girón is practically obligatory for all foreign journalists during the first week of their stay in Cuba. I doubt that Castro could even remember the number of newsmen who were escorted to the museum built there to commemorate the abortive 1961 invasion. His deft use of the words ''As I remember,'' however, covers the lie and allows Walters and ABC to begin their interview with precisely the visual image required to get across the message that "we are now entering forbidden waters."

The most effective use of visual imagery occurs during the interview when the camera pans shots of Castro picking up small, adoring children on the beach and cradling them in his arms. In the next shot, he is delivering a salute to passing crowds that seems almost patriarchal, a cross between a blessing a pope might render to his flock and Hitler's smart return of a Nazi salute from the admiring masses. Those two back-to-back images are used to cover this line of narration: "He says he dislikes the cult of personality and blames China's Mao Tsetung for making himself a god."

Walters inadvertently puts her finger on one of the secrets of Castro's success when she says to him, "You are a man of big mystery to us. First of all, why the mystery? You come from nowhere. You seem to disappear. We hear you have no one home. You seem to be a man of secrecy and mystery." To which he replies: "So then we could say we are facing the theory of mystery. So then I'm the first to ask myself: Where is the mystery? And who are the ones who invent the mystery?"

He then deftly turns everything around to underscore the perception that he wants us to have: that since the Bay of Pigs, he is obsessed with nothing so much as the effort to stay alive. "Why should I tell the CIA and the tourists that we are going to make a trip?" he says to Walters. And she falls, hook, line and sinker for the bait. "One would say he seemed obsessed with the CIA, until he tells you that he knows of at least twenty assassination attempts against his life," she announces with a serious, dramatic tone of candor.

The CIA becomes the whipping dog for everything, the excuse that enables Castro to explain away all that he promised in the earlier days of his regime. When pressed on the absence of a free press in Cuba, he responds: "As long as hostility against Cuba exists, and as long as there is counterrevolutionary activity supported by the United States, we will not allow any paper that goes against the revolution, simply like that." He pauses for dramatic effect. "Besides, who pays for it: the CIA?" Concludes Walters: "He feels that the CIA has trained so many terrorists, not only Cuban exiles but also terrorists around the world, that even if the United States has stopped direct attacks against him, the CIA and this group have a life of their own, and that life continues to threaten his." Without being fully conscious of it, perhaps, she has tacitly legitimized his fears and concerns by underscoring them for him.

Castro even pokes fun at the CIA to deflect questions that he does not want to answer. When Walters persists in asking him how many paramilitary Cuban advisers there are in Ethiopia, he responds: "Why do you make so many detailed questions on these matters? I cannot work free of charge for the CIA." And he adds, in case anyone missed the point, "I will not work even being paid, or for a salary, much less for free." It is an "inside" joke that provokes a good round of on-camera laughter.

But he can't afford to joke about the one thing that has successfully shielded him from criticism by liberals in the Western media: the genuine murder plots that have been hatched against him. Indeed, it is hard to imagine Fidel would have been able to consolidate power as successfully as he has without the existence of a credible and personal "threat" against his own life.

Castro is deadly serious, even when he summons up the chutzpah (as he often does) to suggest that the United States itself will one day become a socialist nation. "But if one day the people of the United States decide they want socialism, I ask myself: Will the CIA agree? Will the Pentagon agree?"

We project a great deal onto the figures we cover. If they are astute, as Castro is, they can easily take advantage of our own hunger for distinction. Thus, Mankiewicz is struck, above all, by three traits: Castro's height, his spontaneity, and the "softness" of his hands. What does he remember about the last time Castro surprised him, arriving at his hotel room an hour or so before midnight and staying up until four a.m. to talk about the energy crisis? "He called room service to get some margaritas sent up and maybe a sandwich," said the astonished Mankiewicz.

What is the great intellectual most interested in discussing and learning from a visiting American?

> He talked to us at great length about American automobiles . . . whether the heater was an extra element and the air conditioner . . . how in extremes of climate automobiles are built. He talked to us about municipal taxes, about how New York, for example, pays for those bridges. People from New Jersey come to New York. How do you get people from one jurisdiction to pay for the support of government in another jurisdiction? We talked about baseball. And movies. He liked "The Godfather." "Godfather II," the one [that takes place] in Havana. We talked about cigarette smoking and the public health hazards, and capital punishment.

Hardly the grist of intellectual discourse he would like us to believe is his stock and trade.

"[Castro's] hands are very soft," Mankiewicz noted with similar amazement. If Castro were a concert pianist, one would think nothing of his having soft hands, but the hands of a guerrilla leader are supposed to be hard and dirty.

Our unthinking capacity to project onto Castro what we want him to be—for our purposes as much as his—is beautifully capsulized in Walter's introduction of her guest: "He is 6 [feet] 2 [inches], a massive man, and this adds to his image. Add, too, a keen sense of humor, an apparent warmth for the people he likes, and a gallantry with strangers. . . . He enjoys driving, but rarely drives himself these days, although with us he took the wheel of his Russian-made jeep, with his rifle across the dashboard, and then. . . ." Guess what comes next? "He drives, talks and smokes all at the same time. Except when driving he wears a .45 caliber automatic on a belt around his hip." And guess what? "He is surprisingly soft-spoken almost as if he knows it will be a surprise." The drama is in the fact that a guerrilla leader is supposed to be loud and gruff, not articulate and soft-spoken.

Most reassuring perhaps to our own image of what a self-styled revolutionary should be is the perception of Castro as the embodiment of power and good. American liberals do not like to use power. Its use is somehow immoral. It was no accident that Jimmy Carter delayed for so long in ordering an Iran rescue mission, and then when he did order it, instructed the commandos to check back with him at every stage of the operation. It probably was doomed from the start because Carter did not like to wield power. Although clearly well-intentioned, his human rights policies also were a convenient excuse for avoiding the use of U.S. power in support of less-than-100-percent-pure democratic leaders in the Philippines, Iran, South Korea, Argentina, and elsewhere. Carter, in short, was a power-hater.

In contrast, Castro somehow came to embody morality and power at one and the same time. Thus, we excuse the fact that he is a dictator. That is hardly relevant in the context of a reformer who is in direct touch with his people. "Many people in this country," reported Walters, "feel that Cuba is Fidel and Fidel is Cuba. Some people," she added, "even think he is a dictator." The "even" is intended to imply that such an outrageous thought is not shared very widely. Castro himself told Mankiewicz and Jones: "Today, each Cuban citizen can say as Louis XIV said, 'L'Etat—c'est moi' [I am the State]. And this identification between the citizen and the power is decisive, for without it the Revolution could not have maintained itself."

The Willing Suspension of Disbelief by the Press

It is we who make the leap, who engage in what English teachers call "the willing suspension of disbelief." Angela Davis reported, for example, that Castro was indeed human. "He made mistakes, human errors, and people loved him" for it. "Fidel was their leader, but most important he was also their brother in the largest sense of the word." Here, then, is an intellectual who is also a doer, not a dreamer; whom Paul Hollander described as "the man who at last bridged the gap between word and deed: . . . with great skill he cultivated important Western intellectuals, at any rate during the beginning stages of the new regime." In short, he is a courageous man who is unafraid to use power and uses it for the common good. The fact that in three decades of power no one, not a single Cuban, ever was consulted at the ballot box is dismissed as irrelevant when matters of such historic consequence are at stake.

"So there we were driving around," recalls Mankiewicz. "He took us by some housing developments, and then we drove out to the beach, Santa Rosa, I think. And there we got out and started walking along the beach, and . . . then this amazing thing happened. Someone saw him from the ocean, and then suddenly everybody comes out of the water, it's like a reverse lemming drive, and they all stand around and talk for a while on the beach." What does Mankiewicz conclude from this? "On the way back to the car, on the beach, I said to him, 'It's just like an American politician going to Coney Island during an election campaign.' " To which Castro replied: "Yes, but the difference is that I come back after the election."

What impresses us, because we have to come up with a rationale for subjugating the importance of things such as free elections, freedom of speech, and freedom of the press, is Castro's almost unbelievable ability to spout off all kinds of figures; in short, his instant recall. His impressive ability to provide statistics becomes a substitute for asking the people what they think of him. Again, through the personal relationship he permits a hand-picked group of correspondents to have with him, we project onto him the totally untested assumption that Castro is popular with the Cuban people.

"I went there to talk to him about health care and he knew off the top of his head all the infant mortality rates of every province in Cuba. He knew all the latest World Health Organization plans in terms of their world health policies," gushes Peter Bourne. He admits that "part of it is that he's been there [in power] for 30 years so obviously he's had a chance to learn a lot whereas somebody who's President for only four years might not because it's such a transient situation."

Part of Castro's undeniable charm, says Bourne, is that he appears to be so forthcoming. "He has a tendency to talk voluminously," he says, "so that he controls the situation. With journalists I think he does very, very well because he controls the interview, but at the same time he's so forthcoming that they really feel they're getting a lot out of him. You know, people don't go away disappointed but they haven't then necessarily gotten what they ought to have gotten from him."

The spontaneity Castro demonstrated when he turned up unexpectedly in Mankiewicz's hotel room is even more evident in the show he puts on for other visiting newsmen. In my case, I was promised I would meet the *líder máximo* once I had fulfilled the obligatory part of the bargain: visiting health care centers, mental hospitals, vocational schools, sugar plantations, housing projects, cattle ranches, farms, and fertilizer factories for the necessary indoctrination. I was told that if an interview occurred, Fidel probably would appear, almost magically, without advance warning, at some farm or factory we were in the course of visiting. "Like the kings and princes of folktales, he would suddenly and unexpectedly materialize in different parts of his realm and minister to the needs of the poor," writes Hollander.

When Walters asked why he prohibited visits by the International Red Cross to inspect conditions inside Cuban prisons, Castro replied: "Actually, we do not allow it. We are very allergic to all forms of investigation and interference in our internal affairs." It was the first time in the interview he used the royal "we." Fidel could just as easily have said, "L'Etat—c'est moi."

When he speaks, wrote the *Nation*'s Elizabeth Sutherland, "it is as if his own dedication and energy were being directly transfused into his listeners with an almost physical force."

This is how I described his electrifying performance on July 26, 1972:

> Jabbing one, two or three fingers into the air to underscore a point, shaking his torso vigorously, or delicately fingering one of five gooseneck microphones, Castro remains an incredibly effective political orator. It was an unusual scene—a prime minister in drab army olive fatigues, unbuckling his gun belt, stowing his firearms beneath the lectern and occasionally resting a hand on his full beard.

I used these quotes: "We represent a moral position. We are a banner." And I referred to Castro's prediction that all of Latin America would prove "our fatherland of the future." We marvel at this phenomenon when we probably should recoil in horror. It never occurred to me that the last political figure who spoke of a "fatherland" was a twentieth-century German leader who also claimed to have psychic powers to communicate with his people.

"In many ways he is real softie," says Bourne. "Time after time he has done things out of compassion. That shows a susceptibility to emotional appeal which is quite contrary to his public image." Bourne admits that the "cynics" say this is a reflection of Castro's "absolute power," which resembles nothing so closely as that of Emperor Julius Caesar. "But the people in Cuba say, 'If only I could speak to Fidel he would solve my problem.' " The record shows numerous examples of mothers and fathers who have made personal appeals to Castro to free their sons from prison. "That is absolutely true," confides Bourne. "I have story after story of people who, you know, the husband was sentenced to 30 years for trying to overthrow Fidel and finally the mother and children got to Fidel and gave him a sob story and Fidel had the person released."

Thus, we endow the emperor with the power of forgiveness, rendering him human after all. As evidence that Castro is not the "repressive, repulsive harshness of the cartoon tyrant he is often made out to be," St. George also recounts this story of the dispensation of royal mercy: "When, not long ago, someone pleaded with Castro for a fellow revolutionary whom he had sent to prison for seven-and-a-half years, Castro began to count on his fingers worriedly: 'How much time has he already spent in jail? Three months? Well, if he was given seven and a half years, he must spend at least six or seven months in jail before we can think of letting him go'."

This picture of royal mercy is often contradicted by such human rights watchdogs as Amnesty International, which pointed out in its 1984 report that it was "concerned about the government's practice of not releasing long-term political prisoners who had completed their sentences."

René Dumont, a French agronomist, noted that "travelling with Castro I sometimes had the impression that I was visiting Cuba with its owner, who was showing off its fields and pastures, its cows if not its men." Waving his magic wand, Castro discovers a bridge in bad shape and orders it immediately repaired. Fifty miles further along the same road, his jeep gets stuck in the mud. "See to it that a good asphalt road is built here," Castro orders. Driving through a region that has experienced a recent drought, he orders, "I want an agricultural school here."

Mankiewicz boasts that Castro knew the annual construction rate of schools, housing, factories, and hospitals. "He knows the number built and being built, their scheduled dates for conclusion, and the building plans projected for the next five to ten years." Also, he knows how many students will graduate in the next five years; the monthly water temperature at fishing ports; the stress levels of concrete and "he knows, almost hourly, sugar's price on the world market," says Mankiewicz. These or comparable figures could be cited by many communist leaders throughout the world. But when Romanian president Nicolae Ceausescu demonstrates an equally impressive facility, we dismiss it as the ravings of someone who rules a virtual police state. When Castro displays his dexterity with figures, his instant recall is transformed into an almost paternal beneficence.

Wrote David Caute: "Castro is like a loving, intelligent and autocratic father who, when he has decided what is best for his children, sits them on his lap and asks them gently to express their own wishes . . . when they are finished he 'persuades' them precisely why they really want to do what he wants them to do."

But Castro's concept of himself as a father figure is not entirely innocent. "I have a very different vision of the world," he told Walters. "My family is very large. I have nine and a half million brothers. My family is not only Cuba. My family is Angola. My family is the liberation movement in southern Africa. My family is made up of all the progressive, revolutionary peoples of the world." If we were to ask Castro today, undoubtedly his arms have extended even further: to Nicaragua, to the guerrillas of El Salvador, and to other corners of the world.

When asked about the export of revolution, the response generally is a variant of the same answer he gave Mankiewicz and Jones in 1974: "I can assure you that Cuba is above all an exporter of sugar. It is an absurd assumption that revolutions can be exported, because they either spring from the people of the nation or else no one can carry them out for them."

Castro has never hidden his zeal to become a worldwide revolutionary. "The United States will have to face the fact that, in the future, Cuba will not be the only revolutionary country in this hemisphere. In the future," he told Mankiewicz and Jones, "the United States will have to deal with one, two, ten socialist countries in this hemisphere, and maybe even with a union of these peoples."

As far as any "right" the United States may have to resist this inevitable, preordained historical tide, Castro serves notice that is simply out of the question. "The United States has to learn to live in peace with the rest of the world because peace interests all of us. Nothing would please us more than to know that the United States is going to follow with regard to Latin America a policy of respect and a policy of nonintervention." In other words, what's mine is mine and what's yours is mine. This is traditional communist claptrap meant to cleverly disguise the use of Cuba as a Soviet surrogate to change social and political systems by force.

Perhaps it was inadvertent, but visual images televised during the Walters interview also lend credence to Castro's presumed right to send his military forces to other continents. At one point she actually discusses the physical similarities between Cuba's terrain and that of much of Africa: "The barren, rocky, tropical terrain of Cuba seems to provide Castro with a natural, tactical understanding of other underdeveloped countries. These sites that he showed us in southeastern Cuba, near the mountains, are not unlike those to be seen in Africa." An interesting leap of faith is made: the viewer is asked to assume that because Cuba may resemble Africa in climate and terrain, the physical resemblance may somehow endow Castro with a "natural" right to intervene in the internal affairs of underdeveloped nations.

Castro versus Nixon

It probably is due to the fact that Richard Nixon was one of the few U.S. politicians to remain unimpressed with Castro that led to Castro's almost pathological hatred for him. "Nixon is the only person I know who has met with Castro and come away with a negative impression," says Bourne.

The two men met in March of 1959 chiefly because President Eisenhower deliberately arranged to fly to Augusta to play golf so that he could avoid meeting with Castro. Although still classified, the memo Nixon sent to the State Department after the meeting reportedly called Castro "a very dangerous man" and instructed John Foster Dulles to begin preparing an anti-Cuban strategy that would one day restore democracy.

Much has been written about the vicious twist of the "x"—replacing it with a Nazi swastika—every time Nixon's name appeared in the Cuban press. When I visited Cuba in 1972, Castro went out of his way to make clear that he could talk with George McGovern, who was challenging Nixon for the presidency, but never with the Republican standard-bearer. "Whoever told this gentleman that he can play around with the Cuban revolution?" Castro asked thousands of wildly cheering Cubans in the emotional high point of his July 26 speech. With bitter invective, he added: "We simply say that the doors of Cuba have been closed totally to the maneuvers of Nixon."

To make clear that he was indeed siding with McGovern, Castro referred to "one of the candidates who is in favor of ceasing the blockage [trade embargo]" against Cuba. "With that government we might talk," he said, but never so long as the U.S. demanded that Cuba give up its military ties to Moscow. Castro was referring to the 1972 Democratic party platform, which stipulated that Cuba could not become a Soviet base for exporting revolution. "We would like to tell those gentlemen, for a starter, that in our territory, we do as we damn please!" Castro declared. And he served notice that "whenever the United States wants to hold discussions with us, the subject will not be Cuba. It will be Latin America."

It is not the purpose of this paper to probe the depths of the animosity between Castro and Nixon. It is worth noting, however, that Castro was so knowledgeable about U.S. politics and so adept at manipulating the media that he seldom missed an opportunity to vent his hatred for the Republican politician.

In her interview, Walters quotes Castro saying that "I am certain that if there were CIA plans to assassinate me, Richard Nixon did not change them." She also makes clear that the Cuban leader blames Nixon and not Kennedy for formulating the plans for the CIA-sponsored invasion at the Bay of Pigs. "John Kennedy, he insists, only inherited the plan. His fault, Castro says, was in carrying it out," Walters explains.

Watergate, of course, was a godsend to Castro. Mankiewicz recalled an anecdote that amply illustrated how obsessed Castro was with Nixon during the summer of 1974, specifically about two months before he was forced to resign. After completing the second full day of filming at the Presidential Palace, in late June 1974, Castro dropped the two reporters back at the Habana Libre but asked that the crew remain behind for another few weeks to film his delivery of the annual July 26 speech.

"Now July 26th was pretty late for Nixon," Mankiewicz said. "I remember Castro had read my book on Nixon and argued with me about whether Nixon would be impeached. I said I thought he would be." Castro disagreed but "finally by the time we were about to leave, he said, 'You know, I agree with you. I think he will be.' " Mankiewicz and Jones returned to Washington but left the crew and producer Saul Landau behind.

Castro apparently wanted to play a bit part in the Watergate hearings. "He obviously knew that there was a good chance he was going to be on American television," Mankiewicz said. So he had a separate platform erected for the Mankiewicz crew, just to the right of his podium and a few feet away from the other cameras that were filming his speech for networks throughout the rest of the world. "He came to a certain point in the speech, and he sort of nodded to Saul Landau . . . turned toward the platform where our camera was, and looking right at the camera said: 'They hired Ex-Cubans to try to overthrow the government of Cuba, and all they succeeded in doing was overthrowing the government of the United States.' And then he turned back to the audience.''

Mankiewicz was in Cuba in June 1974, when Nixon was holding his climactic summit meeting in Moscow with Leonid Brezhnev. "Well, what do you do when Nixon, the man with the swastika, is the honored guest at the head of the socialist fatherland?" Mankiewicz said. Castro decided simply to omit any mention of Nixon's name "and it's hard to write major news stories every day and not use the President's name if he's in Moscow." Instead, he was referred to in a number of ways: as leader of the Western alliance; as president of the United States; as head; as chief, even as the chief magistrate but never as Richard Nixon or President Nixon.

The Journalist's Desire for Distinction

Parallels can be drawn among all the interviews Castro has granted to the elite press. For example, the timing of the interviews frequently coincides with the delivery of his impassioned and inflammatory July 26 speech commemorating the 1953 attack on the Moncada barracks. There also is continuity from one interview to another; Mankiewicz deliberately asked Landau to be his and Jones's producer because he knew Landau had previously interviewed Castro and Castro liked the results. Dan Rather likewise latched onto Mankiewicz, who also was well liked by Fidel. Also, it is unusual to obtain the prized interview without the reporter's having served an internship of several weeks, which provides the Cubans with a chance to imbue the visitor with Cuban-style, anti-American patriotism. Once admitted into the forbidden kingdom, reporters are surprised to have Castro visit them in their hotel rooms or to happen upon him in the fields, the country preacher ministering to his flock.

Mankiewicz, from what he saw of Castro, concluded: "I think he could be the leading elected politician in any free country. He has enormous charisma. And he knows how to manipulate the media." Bourne recalls Castro's asking for a copy of *The Powers That Be,* David Halberstam's prize-winning epic about the media elite. Castro learned his lessons well.

Castro also is adept at flattering reporters' egos. He made sure Mankiewicz knew he had read his latest book. He asked Bourne to get him a copy of *The Powers That Be*. Such attention to detail is evident in his carrying aboard the jeep that took Walters around Cuba, "perhaps for our benefit," she notes, a volume of *The Selected Works of Ernest Hemingway*. With both Mankiewicz and Bourne, he asked them to become valuable intermediaries, setting up back channels to Henry Kissinger and Jimmy Carter. K. S. Karol wrote of the praise lavished on C. Wright Mills: "One day, Fidel Castro had looked him up in his hotel, telling him straight out that his *Power Elite* had been a bedside book of most of the guerrilleros in the Sierra Maestra." Ditto for Sartre, McGovern, Mailer, and dozens of other intellectuals courted by Castro.

Castro began to "use" the media when he conceived the idea of inviting Herbert Matthews to interview him in his Sierra Maestra hideout. Because of censorship imposed by the Batista government, Castro could not reach ordinary Cubans even to communicate the fact that he was alive. Matthews often is credited with trying to create sympathetic public opinion for Castro throughout much of the world. Castro probably regarded him in far more parochial terms, as the only way he could reach the Cubans at home. He said as much during his February 1957 interview with Matthews: "The Cuban people hear on the radio all about Algeria, but they never hear a word about us or read a word, thanks to the censorship." He told Matthews, "You will be the first to tell them."

It was a marriage made in journalism's heaven. The fact is that Matthews needed Castro as much as the Cuban guerilla leader needed him. The *New York Times* correspondent was nearing sixty and the end of his career. He believed, according to colleagues, that he never got the credit he deserved. Here was the chance to get the scoop of a lifetime. The front-page headline read: "Cuban Rebel Is Visited in Hideout"; the subhead: "Castro Is Still Alive and Still Fighting in Mountains." When Batista denounced the story as a lie, the *New York Times* got "fired up" and ran a photograph of Matthews and Castro. It was not a very clear picture, which the *Times* apologized for. Its quality "is poor because of lack of light," the legend said. But it got enormous play—three columns wide by four columns high—to underscore the point that its reporter had indeed gotten an exclusive.

So adroit had Castro been in exploiting the opportunity that even today, almost thirty years after the interview, jokes still make the rounds in Havana about how Fidel put one over on Matthews. "Castro only had about fifteen men with him in the Sierra Maestra. And while the interview was going on," Bourne said Castro had boasted to him, "Raúl would march in a group of ten men, and then they would be marched off stage, they would change hats, and be marched on stage again." Castro was so successful that Matthews's three lengthy articles were laced full of references to "Castro, with about three hundred troops," and to "our other camp where the rest of our troops are."

Conclusion

It is worth ending this study where we began—with a look at those ideals that we projected onto Castro and that reflect more of our own values than any actually possessed by the undeniably charismatic Cuban leader. "His is a political mind rather than a military one," wrote Matthews. "He has strong ideas of liberty, democracy, social justice, the need to restore the Constitution, to hold elections." In the McCarthy era, when almost anyone with those aspirations would have been suspect, the idea that a new leader could emerge who was noncommunist and also a devout believer in democracy was balm for the romanticist's vision of the United States.

To a nation looking to restore its own belief in the values that were part of its birth, here was a revolution that like our own was easy to identify with, it even had a leader who freely quoted our founding fathers. If the United States was experiencing moral decay, here was what Saul Landau called "the first purposeful society that we have had in the Western Hemisphere for many years . . . the first society where human beings are treated as human beings, where men have a certain dignity, and where this is guaranteed to them."

The litmus test was none other than Castro himself. "The personality of the man is overpowering," Matthews wrote. "It was easy to see that his men adored him. Taking him as one would at first, by physique and personality, this was quite a man—a powerful six-footer, olive skinned, full-faced, with a straggly beard."

Here, too, then was a genuine dark-skinned Third Worlder who fit the bill we had drawn up for the true revolutionary. Endowed with spontaneity, humor, a familiarity with literature and political thought, and above all with suffering, we could accept Castro as the virtual George Washington of the underdeveloped world. In embracing him, we could put all our guilt complexes behind us. Here was a symbol of the need to do away with repressive dictatorships, world hunger, overpopulation, and disease all wrapped into one. So intense was our fascination that Matthews, in 1957, described the details of his facial movements. "His brown eyes flash; his intense face is pushed close to the listener and the whispering voice, as in a stage play, lends a vivid sense of drama." Twenty years later, Kirby Jones was just as hypnotized by his aura. "What is your formula for being successful? What would you advise someone to do if they wanted to lead a revolution?" Jones asked Castro.

"Well, it helps to be taller than anyone else in the country," Castro replied. "You have to be very healthy but it helps if you are big." Noted Mankiewicz (in full candor), "This is not something people talk about very much, but it's true. And you can see it standing there on the beach. He's a full head taller than most Cubans!"

I am hard pressed to think of a better phrase than "the willing suspension of disbelief." It is almost incredible that anyone would judge the success of a revolution, or indeed the humanity of it, on the basis of the height of its leader. This is yet another illustration of how Castro has mesmerized the U.S. media.

I recall a "documentary" I was shown in Havana in 1972. In it a machine gunner pops out of a giant wedding cake. The wedding is that of Luci Baines Johnson, Lyndon Johnson's daughter, and it is taking place at the White House. The disguised guerrilla proceeds to mow down all the guests in a rapid flurry of fire. The next image is one of Nazi firing squads punctuating every phrase of Martin Luther King's "I Have a Dream" speech with a rapid volley of rifle shots. The documentary, titled "LBJ," was made by Santiago Alvarez, at the time one of Cuba's most skillful filmmakers and political propagandists. The film alleges that the assassinations of the two Kennedys were part of a sinister conspiracy spearheaded by Johnson. In a clever pastiche, LBJ is even shown toying with a rifle at his Texas ranch immediately following newsreel shots of each assassination and the funeral procession.

The brief footage underscores several things. First of all, the film is about hate—pure, unadulterated hate. It espouses that hate is justified because there are, as Communist dogma states, "good" and "bad" Americans. The Kennedys and Martin Luther King were good Americans; LBJ and Nixon were not. But more important, what this documentary showed is something far more dangerous: the deliberate corruption of American ideals. It is as if Castro, casting himself in the role of a founding father, takes everything valuable to us and through a cruel parody turns the same value system against us.

Alvarez made another "documentary" that depicted Mickey Mouse being machine-gunned in Vietnam. There could hardly be a more cryptic example of what is at the basis of Castro's use of the media. It is a perverse effort to turn us against ourselves.

As long ago as 1959, Castro said this on "Meet the Press": "I read this morning at the Lincoln Memorial and the Jefferson Memorial that declaration that appears in the Constitution of the United States, that all men are born with some rights—self-evident rights: to justice, freedom and life. And I want to ask, what would you do with those who abolish that right? What to do with those who abolish that right? That is the question I put to the public opinion of the United States."

Abraham Lincoln was a great American because he respected those freedoms that Castro despises. Castro is right in asserting that Lincoln rose from humble stock; that he worked in the fields and cut down trees; that he overcame personal hardships to run for Congress and triumphed over injustice by leading a divided nation in a war against itself. But Lincoln's triumph was the triumph of the individual and the triumph of personal freedom. It is the antithesis of everything that Castro stands for: power centralized in one man whose own charisma is the only glue that holds the nation together. That is anticonstitutional, antidemocratic, antilibertian, and anti-American.

Perhaps Castro was writing his own epitaph when he said of Lincoln: "It must have been a real struggle for such a peaceful man to find himself involved in a civil war. And then for his life to have ended so dramatically, so unfairly." His appeal is to our emotions. And that, finally, is the last place where we must judge Fidel Castro, regardless of his unquestioned success in conveying what he wants us to see and hear of him in the media.

Moderator: Dr. John R. Silber, President, Boston University

The influence of the media on the perception of public figures has never been greater. If the role of the journalist is "to get everybody," as has been advanced, then there has been a singular lack of interest in "getting" Mr. Castro. In fact, the media have allowed themselves to be manipulated in Castro's case.

It has been said that a right-wing dictatorship is as bad as a left-wing dictatorship. In referring to the historical record, we find that Franco's dictatorship in Spain, Salazar's in Portugal, and the military's in Argentina have ended and we find the restoration of freedom in these countries to a spectacular extent.

We look back in vain to find a left-wing dictatorship giving way to freedom or even to a right-wing dictatorship. We do find in Nicaragua, the right-wing dictatorship of Somoza giving way to the left-wing dictatorship of the Sandinistas.

I don't know why we don't have more journalistic evenhandedness in the coverage of right- and left-wing dictatorships. If the media were right to say "Down with the Somoza dictatorship," and they were, then they are also right to say, "Down with the Sandinista dictatorship," and they don't.

Respondent: Dr. Paul Hollander, University of Massachusetts, Amherst

The reason that Castro has been seen so curiously misjudged falls within the larger phenomenon of why socialist leaders are so badly misperceived. Castro is misperceived in part because some journalists are favorably predisposed toward the society he represents. There is also the desire to find the "authentic" socialist state. For those in the Western press who are not friendly to the United States, there is also the adage of "the enemy of my enemies is my friend," which is connected to perceiving Cuba as a victim of the United States.

Castro's case is not unique. There have been similar, if not more incredible, misperceptions of leaders of totalitarian societies such as Hitler, Mussolini, Stalin, Mao Tse-tung, and Ho Chi Minh. The personal charisma that Castro shares with them, similarly, is largely a wishful projection by Western journalists.

Castro's is a case of political hero worship, and he is viewed as a combination political James Bond and Renaissance man. Within the routine life of the Western journalist or intellectual, Castro offers an excellent outlet for vicarious gratification. Castro offers excitement, the use of violence for noble ends, and the union of thinker and doer.

In the view of some journalists, Castro brings together egalitarianism and elitism. He claims to uplift the masses but does so from an unquestionably elitist position. In practice, all Marxist systems very soon have become elitist and the role of the masses has become totally negligent. A cult of personality centering on one man, a projected "superman," has quickly developed in differing degrees. The importance of the masses has not been very significant except in the wishful imagination of Western journalists. The close and paternalistic ties between the leader and the masses also is a fabrication.

Americans resonate to the sins of our society. We are quick to feel guilt for our imperfections and injustices. Castro's aim is to turn us against ourselves through the deliberate corruption of American values. The perception of Castro by U.S. journalists has much to do with this.

The perception of Castro by Western journalists in general is full of wishful thinking. The readiness to be impressed by this manipulative and clever dictator by people who are ostensibly committed to democracy is a puzzle, but one that can be understood by studying these underlying forces.

Respondent: Dr. Daniel James, Author and Journalist

There has been a suspension of disbelief by the press in its willingness to forgive Castro any lie, cruelty, or indiscretion. Going far beyond even this, Herbert Matthews of the *New York Times* helped to cover up Castro's dictatorship and gave it the credibility of his great newspaper.

Some journalists seem to forget how to be journalists once they get to Cuba. A reporter from the *Wall Street Journal* went to Cuba and wrote that there was no mayhem, no cruelty by the government. He substantiated his assertions by saying that he had talked to hundreds of Cubans who told him that life in Cuba was wonderful. All interviews were conducted through an interpreter. There are over 10,000 political prisoners in Cuban jails for the crime of disagreeing with the Cuban dictator, but no mention is made of this.

Today in Cuba there is no room for creativity, only total submission to the regime is tolerated. A study issued by Georgetown University's Center for Strategic and International Studies entitled "The Cuban Revolution 24 Years Later" states that "the Cuban revolution cannot offer a single notable novelist, a famous poet, a penetrating essayist or even a fresh contribution to Marxist analysis."

There has been a drop in illiteracy but the end purpose has been to turn out dedicated Marxist-Leninists, not youngsters who think for themselves.

Marielitos are a great source of information on life inside Cuba, yet it seems that journalists don't see them as a source. There is little evidence in the press of Castro's personal dictatorship in Cuba, or indeed that he is a Marxist-Leninist. It's almost kept a secret. The press refers to Pinochet and others of that ilk as "an authoritarian ruler" yet Castro miraculously escapes this type of reference. Castro is treated with kid gloves ideologically and personally; he comes under a protective cloak.

There is also the myth in the press that the United States pushed Castro into the arms of the USSR because it refused to support him economically. This is not true, but has been encouraged by Castro and used as rationalization for excesses and failures and used as a motivational tool with the Cuban people.

In the press Castro purports himself to be the champion of the downtrodden in the fight against their main enemy, the United States. In fact, Castro is the leader of the comfortable inside Cuba, the new government class that defines the privileged elite on the island.

References

The following sources were used in compiling this paper:

Bourne, Peter. Personal interview with the author.

Hollander, Paul. *Political Pilgrims: Travels of Western Intellectuals to the Soviet Union, China, and Cuba, 1928-1978.* New York: Oxford University Press, 1981.

Mankiewicz, Frank. Personal interview with the author.

Mankiewicz, Frank, and Kirby Jones. *With Fidel: A Portrait of Castro and Cuba.* Chicago: Playboy Press, 1975.

Matthews, Herbert. "Cuban Rebel Is Visited in Hideout." *New York Times,* February 24, 1957, p. 1.

"Meet the Press." Interview with Fidel Castro, April 19, 1959. Produced by Lawrence E. Spivak.

St. George, Andrew. "A Revolution Gone Wrong." *Coronet,* July 1960.

Walters, Barbara. "Fidel Speaks," an ABC special report, June 9, 1977.

6

Castro's Fickle Friends: The Verdict of the European Press on the Cuban Revolution

Daniel Johnson

An extensive content analysis of the European press coverage of Castro and Cuba during 1983-84. The paper focuses on coverage provided by newspapers in the United Kingdom, West Germany, and to a lesser extent, France. The thematic focus is on the mythology of the Cuban revolution, Castro, social reforms, the economy and political repression. Some of the underlying reasons for the general timber of coverage by the European press are also examined.

The catastrophe of the Cuban revolution generally is recognized by the European press, lamented by many, deplored by a few. The majority of the press in Europe know Fidel Castro rather well. The focus is now on Central America and many recognize who is behind the unrest.

—Dr. Joachim Maitre
Boston University

Introduction

For the last quarter of a century the face of Cuba has worn a beard and a green cap. Castro, the friend of countless hijackers, has succeeded in hijacking not only a country but—perhaps even more extraordinary—its reputation. The picture of Cuba in the minds of Europeans before Castro was, to a degree almost inconceivable today,

157

unpolitical. In those days, the name Cuba conjured sugar cane, cigars, Casablanca. The world of Graham Greene was beginning to encroach upon a history that the less cynical could call "the pursuit of freedom," but few Europeans had heard of Batista, and nobody saw in him a mystic symbol of his nation.

All that changed with Castro's eruption into world politics. Instead of the solid exports that had made Cuba prosperous and respected, even if corrupt, there now came cooked statistics, promises, sabre rattling, and—for insurgent groups everywhere—guns. It was no longer fashionable, comfortable, or even possible to be a tourist in Cuba. Instead you coud be a pilgrim or a crusader of revolution, in the safety of the Left Bank or the Free University in Berlin.

Just as in the Middle Ages the pious began to substitute reenactments of the stages of the Cross and replicas of the Holy Sepulchre for the physical journey into the Holy Land, so the Europeans of the 1960s preferred to rehearse the campaigns of "Fidel" and "Che" without physical confrontation of the reality that these men were creating. The entire radical chic of Western Europe knew Castro and Guevara by their first names; and, partly to cater to the newly intensified guilt feelings toward developing countries of such people, Castro began to purvey an image of Cuba as a leader of the "nonaligned" states, a "Third World" country. Yet, before his policies had stifled free enterprise, few would have considered Cuba poor enough to be thus designated.

In the United States the same views of Cuba's romantic revolution were, naturally, common enough, but there they were tempered by growing acquaintance with the sufferings of the mounting number of exiles. It simply became impossible to dehumanize these hundreds of thousands of ordinary, hard-working people as "counterrevolutionaries" and "parasites." This acquaintance was largely lacking in Europe, and the moderate degree of sobriety induced by the proximity of Cuba in the minds of U.S. intellectuals was also absent among their European counterparts, for whom Cuba was a distant, exotic place about which they could believe what they liked.

The romanticism of the Cuban revolutionary regime for the New Left in Western Europe was, of course, in large part a function of changes in attitudes toward the United States and the Soviet Union in the same circles. The rising tide of anti-Americanism among the young, who were ignorant of the liberation and reconstruction of Europe, brought with it a flourishing of conspiracy theories and an extraordinary narrowing of focus: the United States, though more accessible than ever before and the source of so many movements approved by the European New Left and its students, was whittled down into the CIA, the multinational companies, and very little else.

On the other hand, there was a paradoxical consequence of the thaw inaugurated by Khrushchev, which later developed into *détente*. Though the USSR became respectable again among liberals and social democrats, as it had not been since 1945, just because of this, the New Left also lost interest in Soviet affairs, leaving a legacy of willful ignorance from which the present "Peace Movement" still suffers. Communist heroes now came exclusively from outside the USSR or its satellites, and the less obvious the control it exercised over these heroes, the better the predominantly Trotskyist, Sartrian, Marcusian, or Gramscian radical chic liked it. Ho Chi Minh, Allende, the Cultural Revolution, the urban terrorists, and the PLO—these were the kind of leaders who would leaven their Marxism with an aggressive national- ism that young Europeans could indulge in only vicariously; who could satisfy the nihilistic cult of violence; who could still outrageously flout conventions—the more trivial, the better.

In this canon Castro and Che Guevara occupied high places. The thrust of their propaganda was entirely directed against the CIA and the multinational corporations, yet they could claim to have preserved on ideological and strategical distance from the USSR until the mid-1970s, however implausible such claims may have seemed after the 1962 missile crisis to any objective observer.

The myth of the Cuban revolution thus overlaps and implies numer- ous other myths. It would be as mistaken to attempt to explain the Castro phenomenon solely in terms of the Cuban propaganda machine as to deny the importance of a consciously projected personality cult surrounding the "telluric totalitarian" (as Cynthia Grenier recently dubbed Castro) and the footloose failure Guevara (posthumous and leaning heavily on the predilection of Western youth for those unequal to their responsibilities).

The structure of self-deception among sophisticated and undogmatic European minds concerning the meaning of the Cuban experience could be very complex. It is therefore worth examining a specific case, which was influential in its day and also not untypical of the percep- tions of Cuba among those in Western Europe who prided themselves on being rigorous but independent of parties, on the Left but attached to bourgeois culture, squeamishly revolutionary but impeccably anti- American.

Hans Magnus Enzensberger's *The Hearings of Havana*[1] appeared in 1970. Enzensberger is probably the most famous living poet in the Federal Republic; he is certainly the most fashionable one. Germany is also a place in which the political opinions of literati have always mattered much more to the general public than in Britain or the United States. As one might expect, Enzensberger's interest in Cuban affairs, and in the Bay of Pigs episode in particular, is primarily aesthetic. His book consists of a long essay, "A Self-Portrait of the Counterrevolution"; a selective translation of ten interrogations before a tribunal of journalists of captured members of Brigade 2504; and a series of appendices, including a transcript of Castro's own questioning of the prisoners, potted (and highly tendentious) biographies of *dramatis personae,* photographs, and the judgment of the court (a tirade against "North American imperialism"). The interrogations are preceded by scene-setting directions, and the re-creation of the trial on stage or television is discussed. Each interrogation is given an ironical title, such as "The Saviour of Free Elections," "The Landowner as Philosopher," or "The Revolution of Shareholders."

The didactic purpose of *The Hearings of Havana* is to construct a psychological archetype of a "ruling class" and, by repeated performance, to learn to recognize the same characteristics everywhere. The interrogation is, declares Enzensberger, "a case of heuristic serendipity" unparalleled in Europe because only as defeated counterrevolutionaries does the bourgeoisie reveal its true colors. But the prisoners are interchangeable; the same types are to be found in every West German, Swedish, or Argentine city.

Despite the zest with which Enzensberger informs the reader that gunfire from mopping-up operations was audible in the background during these hearings, the atmosphere he succeeds in lending them by his selection and presentation is utterly unreal. This is deliberate. Any reader encountering these transcripts without the benefit of this stylization would surely conclude that these wretched prisoners had nothing more in common than a—by then extinguished—quixotic bravery, and the desire to earn lenient treatment by being cooperative. The purposes of the inquisitors were equally uncomplicated: to pour scorn on the defeated, and to use them as pawns in the denigration of the United States. But Enzensberger wants us to see the sequence of interrogations as a repulsive yet compelling process of secular revelation. That which is revealed is not in any ordinary sense of the world "human": the fact that these counterrevolutionaries appear as individuals, which might normally arouse at least some sympathy, is turned against them, for individual characteristics and above all Cuban nationality are mere psychological defenses against reality.

What is the reality that a European intellectual like Enzensberger sees in the browbeating of the losing side in a Cuban skirmish? Unlike his own experience, this reality may be black and white; which is why it must be adversarial. "The task of the interrogation is, to be sure, contrary to that of bourgeois parliamentary procedure: the former exposes what the latter is there to obscure."[2] This higher reality must also be violent in the extreme, if only abstractly; though only one of the prisoners is a Batista thug, this demonstrates the ubiquitously uniform nature of counterrevolution—for the West German chancellor Kurt Georg Kiesinger, though once a member of the Nazi party, had similarly not been acquainted with the *Kommandant* of Auschwitz. Useless for a Cuban to object to this comparison: Enzensberger presses on to resolve all who opposed what Castro made of the revolution into the semimythical figure of Calvino the Murderer: "He restores the totality which all the others seek to dissolve. He alone exposes the logic of the system to which they owe their rule and which they serve. With the murderer, the hidden truth of the whole steps onto the stage."[3]

This baroque vision evidently tells us more about the private confrontation of the generations in the Federal Republic than it does about Cuba, but fifteen years later, and twenty-five years since the revolution, such narcissistic interpretations of it are still common in Europe. This example seemed worth dwelling on because it shows so clearly how the quite uncritical attitude toward official Cuban sources, and the ability to gloss over such facts as the arrest of over 100,000 potential opponents by Castro within days of the bombing before the Bay of Pigs attack are only symptoms of the desire of many Europeans to force Cuban history into a generalized schema, while yet denying Cubans the decisive capacity that they have shared with Europe and the United States, the love of liberty.

The Hearings of Havana, however, represents only one end of the spectrum of assessments of the Cuban revolution that were prompted by the tenth anniversary in January 1969. At that time the obsession with Vietnam had diverted attention in Europe away from Cuba, but the Latin American specialist Gordon Connell-Smith suggested in a sober and objective article in *The World Today*[4] that relations between Cuba and the United States remained critical.

In "Fidel Castro's Challenge: Ten Years On," Connell-Smith argued that Castro's detachment of Cuba from the rest of Latin America had breached the Monroe Doctrine "at a time when the United States had never been more powerful, and when the Doctrine, in practice, had been extended to Western Europe and other parts of the world." He predicted that a withdrawal from Vietnam by the new Nixon administration would be followed by renewed pressure on Cuba, though he would have preferred to see relations eased. In Connell-Smith's view, Castro's challenge had succeeded in calling into question the identification of Latin America as a whole with "the West," as opposed to the Third World.

It is, perhaps, significant that this British academic should have skeptically placed *the West* in quotation marks, whereas the notion of the Third World apparently engendered no such doubts. Characteristic, too, of the heyday of détente was the endorsement, in a reputable journal published by the Royal Institute of International Affairs, of the view that Castro was not, even ten years after the revolution, a Soviet puppet.

Shortly after this tenth anniversary, any excuse either for ignorance of the historical background of the Castro regime or for faith in its propaganda and statistics was removed by the publication of Hugh Thomas's exhaustive and readable history, *Cuba: The Pursuit of Freedom*. To set the record straight, Thomas was obliged to devote an inordinate amount of space in this monumental work to the years immediately before and after 1959. If Castro's European admirers have troubled to consult this first objective account of the country under his rule at all, the idea of the dictator as the father of his people, as the man who first put Cuba on the map, should not have persisted. Yet, even at the least sophisticated level, a politicized, post-1959 portrait of Cuba seems to have been indelibly engraved upon the public mind.

In Britain a massive advertising campaign in 1984—for which the Cuban government paid not a peso, though it must have earned a good many pounds sterling—offered Havana cigars "at revolutionary prices" in duty-free shops. Cuba's lush tropical colors blended well with Castro's instantly recognizable features in the glossy color supplement to one of the Sunday newspapers in Britain at the turn of 1984. A sordid dispute about the ownership of Che Guevara's diaries, which were to have been auctioned in London, can still arouse the interest of the media, even if posters of the hero no longer excite young people and have mostly been relegated to the offices of social workers and Citizens' Advice Bureaus.

The visits to Europe by prominent Cuban dissidents now provide television and radio with the best possible opportunity to overcome their inherent disadvantages by comparison with the newspaper correspondent in reporting on closed societies. Yet, the visits to England by Huber Matos and Jorge Valls, both of whom had spent two decades in prison, passed almost unnoticed. The only important television documentary about Cuba on the British network in 1984, ITV's "Cuba—25 Years of Revolution," unfortunately began its six weekly parts, at peak evening time, too late to be considered in this paper. But two newspaper reports on July 26 suggest that the general tendency will prove to be all too familiar:

> A quarter of a century of Communism under Fidel Castro has brought this Caribbean island, just 90 miles across the sea from Florida, outstanding health care and a 96 percent literacy rate even if what there is to read is strictly controlled. The economy is underpinned by the Russians and of the population of 10 million, six millions comprise their fighting force [London *Guardian*].

> The massive steel gates that swing open to admit a thousand or so highly excited Cubans in the opening seconds of Central Television's new documentary series also must admit the film's title. It is an impressive device. On the evidence of the first episode, it is not possible to determine whether a comparable amount of effort has gone into providing a balanced picture of what has been afoot in the Caribbean island during the past quarter of a century. Fidel Castro will have little cause to complain about the amount of screen time that he and his anti-American speechifying are given. And although Frank Hayes's opening film duly notes that there is no free press in Cuba, no voice of dissent, severely limited exit facilities, and rationing that allows only one pair of knickers every six months, it concludes that most Cubans are happy with their lot . . . [London *Times*].

On the other hand, it should be said that Cuba does not preoccupy Europeans very much in 1983-84: many major newspapers passed over the opportunities offered by the anniversaries of Castro's attack upon the Moncada barracks (26 July 1983) and his assumption of power (1 January 1984) to reassess the record of his regime. The leading West German weekly paper, *Die Zeit,* for example, which provides the fullest possible foreign news stories and features (and which is associated with such influential figures as former Chancellor Schmidt), chose to print only the most perfunctory report of Castro's celebrations in the issue of 2 to 6 January 1984 (p. 8). The British, French, and West German weekly papers and magazines in general appear largely to have ignored Cuban affairs, perhaps because hardly any have Havana correspondents.

A similar indifference is usually shown by television and radio, at least in Britain, by comparison with the treatment of Eastern Europe, Afghanistan, or Nicaragua. Apart from books and articles in academic periodicals by more or less reliable experts, West Europeans must rely on the testimonies of exiles, regular correspondents of the national daily papers, and occasional pieces in the latter by nonspecialists who visit Cuba for some particular purpose and who record their impressions.

The fact that the West European press now treats Cuba so patchily means that the margin of error that will pass muster, both with editors and with the public, is considerable. The East German reader of the main state organ, *Neus Deutschland,* would, by comparison with a West German counterpart, be familiar with much more material about Cuba, even if much of it were trivial and still more of it lies. It has not been possible to compare the West European press with the main daily papers of the United States in their coverage of Cuba, but the *International Herald Tribune,* though it prints features rarely if ever on this subject, certainly offers more news items than any of the British, French, West German, Swiss, Irish, or Austrian papers. One example must suffice: President Reagan's important broadcast to the Cuban people, reported at length in the *Herald Tribune* on 7–8 January 1984, went unreported in the main Western European papers. Was the reason for this the illusion that Cuba is an unimportant Third World country, or was it the president's message? "We have to wonder," he said, "what would Cuba's economy be like today if those people [the exiles] had been allowed to use their great talent, drive and energy to help you create prosperity on your island?" Though men like Enzensberger may have changed their view both of Castro and the exiled Cuban-American community, the causal connection that Reagan makes is still unpalatable to many Europeans.

Review of European Press Treatment of Cuba, 1983-84

This survey will concentrate chiefly, though not entirely, on the following themes: the mythology of the revolution; Castro and his associates; the social reforms since 1959; the economy; and political oppression. A conclusion will then attempt to explain some of the variations in accuracy and fairness of comment—though there are, of course, limits to the explanation of acute gullibility and willful myopia. As the editor of *Encounter,* Melvin Lasky, wrote about a story in the London *Times* on Castro's welfare state:

> For a moment we could have been caught up in some journalistic time machine and transported into other lands and other enviable achievements. . . . In each case there was, subsequently, a rude awakening—a sad one, for no one takes pleasure in the sickly spectacle of an ill-fare state . . . most of all there was shock at the wide-eyed naivety of the innocents or the cynical propaganda of the manipulators who get away with the same canard once (or twice) in every generation.[5]

The Mythology of the Revolution

If the reality of the long civil war, of which the Moncada fiasco and the anticlimax of Batista's flight were the highlights, was anything but romantic, the revolution was nevertheless by far the most glamorous episode in Castro's career. It was also the one least closely associated with the Soviet Union, and so might have been expected to occupy a large part of the coverage of the anniversaries of 26 July 1953 and 1 January 1959 by those European journalists wishing to present the Cuban regime in a favorable light. In fact, interest in the revolution seems to have been slight, and evocations of it in the press were scanty.

In the reports of Castro's speech, "Cuba Cannot Export Revolution, nor Can the United States Prevent It," which was given at Santiago de Cuba on 1 January 1984, none of the Western European journalists mentioned an important and unusually frank remark about the early opponents of Batista (so many of whom were imprisoned later by Castro): "No mention was made then of the Marxist-Leninist Party, of socialism and internationalism; capitalism was not even mentioned by name. Indeed, very few would have understood its true meaning at the time."[6]

The only substantial article devoted exclusively to the narrative of the revolution was that by Marcel Niedergang in *Le Monde* of 1 February 1984, entitled: "Il y a vingt-cinq ans. Les 'barbudos' entrent a La Havane." This was a conscientious and intelligent piece, which grasped the point that Castro was still, in 1959, in the tradition of Bolívar rather than that of Lenin, or at least was believed to be so. Once in power Castro quickly abandoned this tradition, but he evidently does not mind still being associated with it in spite of occasional gestures toward the Spanish, as Richard Williams in the London Times did: "If it is his destiny to become a second Bolívar, then the Cuban people will probably have to tighten their belts yet again."[7]

Marcel Niedergang's article emphasised the moral purpose behind the overthrow of Batista, though the contrast with what followed is only implicit:

> In the United States, Fidel became a generous, idealistic and disinterested hero, who wanted to overthrow a regime supported by the United States, but manifestly corrupt and unjust. This "image" of Fidel remains valid for the majority of American opinion until 1959. . . . Havana, "the brothel of America," "seethes with its casinos, its gigantic balls, its seedy clubs, fiefs of gangster rings authorized by Batista. "Morality" is still, in 1959, the primary motivation of the Fidelistas.[8]

This stereotype of prerevolutionary Havana was also used, but to different effect, in one of the most rhapsodic articles to emerge from the journalistic invasion of Cuba that followed the expulsion of the Cubans from Grenada: "An Island with a Sense of History" by John Rettie, in the London *Guardian*. This is a fair sample:

> And even today, largely isolated though Cuba is, the sense of being in the greatest Caribbean city of all is still as strong as ever. And the Cubans know it—don't they just know it. This passionate, sensuous tropical city throbs with a lifestyle envied by all Spanish speakers in the area. . . . Of course much has changed in Cubans' lifestyle since the revolution. The gross prostitution, the gambling, the violence and the scandalous distance between rich and poor have gone. Instead, everyone has enough to eat, virtually everyone can read and write, and Cuba's health problems are now those of rich countries. . . .[9]

One wonders how many "Spanish speakers" this correspondent consulted in order to arrive at this opinion, but he wisely leaves to the reader's imagination what the throbbing lifestyle actually consists of, and what precisely the methods were that have brought about a moral regeneration of which Dr. Goebbels or Mme. Mao might have been proud.

But the character of the new morality was described more prosaically by the former revolutionary Armando Valladares, who spent over twenty years in one of Castro's dungeons, in an interview with Richard Paseyro in *Politique Internationale:* "Our 'child pioneers' are educated in the cult of these 'heroes of the Soviet Pioneers,' who had denounced their fathers and their grandfathers."[10] These children were described by the *Guardian*'s Rettie as "the Pioneers, an organization roughly comparable to the Boy Scouts and Girl Guides."[11] The story has been recounted by the actor Sir Alec Guinness that, while filming Graham Greene's *Our Man in Havana* on location, he was invited from his café to shake hands with Castro in the thronging square. Impressed by the Cuban leader's courage in appearing amidst a large crowd, he was astonished to discover when he reached Castro that the latter was surrounded by diminutive but fierce child pioneers armed with knives, invisible at a distance but admitting only selected people to approach their master.

The *Guardian* was, therefore, right to quote Castro at a "Children's Day" speech shortly before the thirtieth anniversary of Moncada (even if the terrible meaning of his remark was not in keeping with the reporter's sympathetic portrayal of the scene): "Fidel went on to say he was sure that any enemy attack on Cuba would come up sooner or later against Cuba's children."[12] This is taken from a long appreciation of the significance of Moncada, entitled "Cuba Keeps Calm as Castro Celebrates Disaster," with which the *Guardian* marked the anniversary. The paper sent one of its leading writers, the author of several books on the Soviet bloc, Jonathan Steele. Three long features appeared, each more enthusiastic than the last; it is a tribute to the Cuban regime's gift for organizing festivities that such an experienced analyst of Eastern Europe could be entirely taken in.

Steele recounts the whole saga, from the "piffling accusations" of the Cuban Communist party against Castro after Moncada, the return to Cuba in the *Granma,* to final victory. Alongside an account of events in Chile and Nicaragua hostile to the role of the United States, long discussions of the latter's possible invasion plans against Cuba (based apparently, on sources like the Cuban deputy foreign minister Alarcón) and the vigilance of Cuban defenses, we find the following mythological paragraph:

> But for Fidel the assault on the Moncada still has the symbolic and historical primacy. This was the moment when the armed struggle first sparked into life, opening a new era in Latin America. How many times had Yankee imperialism used force—and would do so again—to get its way in Latin America and the Caribbean, in Nicaragua over and over again, in Guatemala in 1954, in the Dominican Republic in 1965. At Moncada in 1953 the fight back began, for the first time since the 1930s.[13]

At least the first sentence of this paragraph was true.

In both the news stories that Steele wrote on the Moncada celebrations in addition to his features, the parallel between Maurice Bishop's coup in Grenada in 1979—"a successful Moncada," as Castro himself put it—and Moncada was given prominence. "An especially affectionate hand was given to Mr. Maurice Bishop, the leader of Grenada, who stood next to Dr. Castro's brother Raúl."[14] When Bishop presented Castro with a rifle captured in the overthrow of Gairy,

> to cheers from the crowd, Dr. Castro drew back the breach [sic] and aimed the rifle into the air before embracing the Grenadan leader. Wiping his eyes, Dr. Castro said that the rifle would be kept in a special place in perfect condition so that "it will definitely be used against the imperialists if they ever come here."[15]

in the same speech Castro showed that he had more than an inkling of what might befall this "personal friend and ally"[16] when he mentioned the airport that his men were building for Bishop: "The only problem might be if the airport was used by a band of mercenaries or counter-revolutionaries coming in to overthrow Grenada's Socialist Government, he said, raising laughter from a crowd of 2,000 factory workers."[17]

The precise role of Castro in the murder of Bishop a few months later is unclear, but the undoubted fact that he ordered his military personnel to fight to the death for the regime of Bernard Coard and other assassins of Bishop must surely place this emotional scene in Cuba in a new light, and with it the credibility of the sympathetic *Guardian* writer.

Castro and His Associates

"Castro has been the beneficiary outside his island of more credulity than any other leader of his time."[18] the *Times* of London, in a cool leading article assessing quarter of a century of his rule, ventured this bold aside in spite of the paper's own occasional flirtations with this "great survivor." While conceding that Castro was entitled to claim some successes in foreign policy to compensate for the failures at home, and that "his spell is still potent," the *Times* nevertheless stated with admirable bluntness that "he was the first Latin American to discover Marxism-Leninism to be an unbeatable justification for staying in power, and to install with it the Soviet apparatus that supports the justification."[19] *Times* leaders are not famous for unequivocal, forthright language or sentiments, but in this case the paper offers a partial explanation of the change in climate that has again made strong criticism of figures like Castro permissible; "Cuba will take tourists with dollars, but no longer welcomes the fellow traveller."[20] It is surely true that Castro takes less trouble than he did once to woo the Left in Europe and the United States, whether because he considers the Right to be in the ascendant, or because he no longer needs fellow travellers.

But the critic of Castro must still, on both sides of the Atlantic, risk the accusation of cold warmongering. Not one of the writers reviewed here dared to accept this with the panache of Irving Kristol:

> And there is still a sense, I suppose, in which I can fairly be called a cold warrior. What I mean is: I believe in individual liberty and representative democracy; I prefer a modified form of capitalism to any other proposed economic system; I am certain Castro is no good model for Latin American progress; I consider Maoism as detestable as fascism and not easily distinguishable from it; I do not see that the underdeveloped countries of the Third World represent any kind of wave of the future, and Che Guevara is not my idea of Robin Hood.[21]

Not only does Kristol believe these words now, he first published them in 1968.

There seems to be general agreement among European observers, whether hostile or friendly to Castro, that he is irreplaceable. In the interview published in *Politique Internationale,* Armando Valladares was sure of that much, though he refused to be drawn on the implications:

His disappearance would allow the domestic disputes, the hatreds and personal ambitions that have accumulated over quarter of a century to explode. The consequences of these antagonisms seem to be incalculable today.[22]

This should be compared with Steele's treatment of the problem of the success in "Doctor's Orders Find Favour with the Patients."[23] This is characteristic of the romantic view of Castro: the article was accompanied by a flattering photograph of the dictator aiming a rifle and the caption "Still on target." Though Castro's *machismo* is emphasized, the mention of his aging adds a "human touch." The "informal political style" is considered "more relevant" than the fact that Castro has never tolerated serious opposition, and indeed it is more relevant to the priorities of Western Europe's new radical chic.

Finally, a woman who evidently owes her job to Castro is quoted by Steele as if her loyalty were surprising:

> More relevant is the question how far Cuba's informal political style is due to Fidel, or whether it has become a traditional and natural enough part of the system to survive his eventual departure.
>
> The first flecks of grey have begun to appear on the 56-year-old Cuban leader's beard, but as Magali García More, the editor of the trade union newspaper and the first woman to edit a daily newspaper in Cuba, put it, "we still have the privilege of Fidel."[24]

However, it is no longer quite so easy for journalists to indulge in panegyrics of Castro with impunity. The leading London Sunday paper, the *Observer,* was severely chastised by Melvin Lasky in *Encounter* for the fifteen pages of its color supplement devoted to the anniversary of the revolution on 22 January 1984. In particular, the *Observer's* main Havana correspondent, Hugh O'Shaughnessy, received a drubbing:

> In the last analysis, the whole *Observer* feature is a bromidic exercise in Western hero-worship, extolling a despotism and what once used to be notoriously known as the *"Fuhrerprinzip."* Here is the Cuban coda rising to a crescendo:
>
> Breeding cattle and directing the operations of the firemen at a particularly nasty blaze in Havana, a proud father who has no time for family life, Castro is constantly achieving, active, never resting. He is the Moses to his people, leading them away from the captivity of their enemies toward a Promised Land that he himself will never live to enjoy. . . ."
>
> Poor chap, he will have to content himself with merely enjoying the passing pleasures of absolute political power over a 25-year-reign which

is already twice as long as Hitler's and roughly equivalent to Franco's and Stalin's. One hopes that these statistics nicely balance flattery and distress.[25]

It cannot, however, be left out of consideration that for every reader of Lasky's critique, there were a hundred readers of the original feature. The depiction of Castro as both a frank, humorous, humane man of simple tastes and as a national partiarch is too common to provoke angry denials as a rule. If such portrayals appear inconsistent with the aggressive, swashbuckling challenges to the United States, it is suggested that Castro's natural goodwill would immediately manifest itself if only the West appreciated him better. Here is Steele again, in an article entitled "The Popularity Isn't Just a Front":

> If Washington lifted the pressure on Cuba, one feels that Castro's tough Marxist-Leninist colleagues, and his Russian allies that he needs to survive, would find themselves losing influence. And Fidel himself could indulge his great passion, and go to a baseball match in the United States.[26]

It will be shown below how, in practice, the "tough Marxist-Leninist colleagues" from whom this author is clearly anxious to detach Castro, are treated by the European press. What is striking is the willingness of a Castro sympathizer to suggest that this leader, who has demanded so many sacrifices from his people in the name of his principles, might be ready to change his tune if the United States conceded enough.

The thesis that Castro is, as Steele put it, "a man of immense charisma . . . still universally seen in Cuba as a great historic figure to be trusted and followed,"[27] seems necessary to some commentators in order to explain the acquiescence of the majority in dogmatic politics. In this form the idea is plausible, though it requires empirical proof. But some write as though Castro's hypothetical popularity were also the justification for his deeds, which his own cooked statistics have denied him and his sympathizers.

This populist image is certainly not unwelcome to Castro himself; he constantly presents his opponents as "terrorists," and Richard Williams, in the *Times,* argued that he would refrain from revenging himself for the Grenadan humiliation by increasing support for Salvadoran or Bolivian leftist guerrillas, or for the "M-19" in Colombia, in order not to place his "responsible" image in jeopardy: "Although, after 25 years, true revolutionary ardour has abated in many Cuban breasts, what one western diplomat here called 'the patriotic nerve' is still strong enough to act as a surrogate."[28]

The claim that Castro has become respectable does not, however, bear even the slightest examination. To refer to Reagan as a "total liar,"[29] and to the United States as "those Nazi-Fascist barbarians, like their Hitlerian predecessors," suggests that, as Lionel Martin of the *Guardian* put it in his report of the Santiago speech somewhat flatteringly, "Danton's dictum of 'audacity, audacity and more audacity' is still Dr. Castro's guiding star."[30]

It is odd that the otherwise excellent report of this speech by Reginald Dale in the *Financial Times* referred to it as "essentially defensive," though in the context of "widespread fears that a U.S. invasion of Cuba itself could be imminent," with the anniversary celebrated "in a manner so subdued as to have surprised many long-term observers of the local scene."[31] Dale was no doubt right to interpret the belligerent rhetoric at Santiago as intended mainly for home consumption.

But the patriotic interpretation of Castro can shade into sycophancy, as in Rettie's piece "Castro Still the Spirit of Cuba" in the *Guardian:*

> He is to Cuba what Churchill was to Britain in the second world war—and perhaps more. Confidence and trust in him is overwhelming. He has, after all, made the Cuban revolution and then kept it alive and well, against incredible odds. He even destroyed the old, traditional Communist Party when it tried to gain control of the government in the early years of the revolution.
>
> Then he allied himself with the Soviet Union to ensure his survival; espoused a Cuban version of Marxism-Leninism on his own terms, and set up a new Communist Party which he controlled. . . . No wonder they trust a man of such political skill, and with such a dominating personality.[32]

Imagination and identification with another "island people" have here obscured the fact that democracies often reject leaders whom they revere on account of their policies, and that genuinely popular statesmen like Churchill or de Gaulle accepted such defeats with good grace. Castro's equivalent of elections is—as another *Guardian* writer, Steele, politely put it—to "rid the country of malcontents"[33] by means of periodic purges. It was certainly not Churchill from whom he learned this device.

If the charisma of Castro be considered as mitigating evidence in defense of those journalists who seem insufficiently skeptical of his pretensions, the same does not apply to their treatment of members of his government. *Le Monde,* in particular, makes no distinction in its interviews between Castro himself and his henchmen; in both cases propaganda designed for a European audience is allowed to pass unchallenged. In his interview with Tad Szulc, for example, Castro was full of admiration for Kennedy, and it may be added that the following month saw the *Daily Telegraph* carry a story about a "peacenote" that Castro claimed he had received from the president on the day he was assassinated (24 April 1984). He assured Szulc that "it isn't us who declare the United States to be enemies. It is the United States which makes enemies in advance of revolutionary countries."[34] Castro even added that he had been "irritated" by the failure of the Soviet Union to consult him about the withdrawal of nuclear missiles in 1962.

The interviewer of the left-of-center *Le Monde,* which is critical of both the United States and the USSR, failed to confront Castro with his own words about the United States in the Santiago speech. An equally lax attitude was adopted by Marcel Niedergang in his interview with Armando Hart in *Le Monde*. "Reagan's policy in Central America threatens to turn into a situation of the 'Vietnamese type,' the Cuban Minister of Culture told us."[35] And so on, quite predictably.

No less passive was the attitude of the *Guardian's* Rettie in dealing with another party boss:

> A strong emphasis on egalitarianism marks Cuba out from most of its socialist allies. Raúl León, the president of Cuba's national bank, sits in a splendid office beyond a hall of marble columns. On the wall is a combination of mural and collage showing Che Guevara on one side and a sewer outlet called the United States on the other. The sight of revolutionary art in such surroundings of opulence invites cynical disbelief at first, but Raúl León still speaks the language of equality.[36]

That apparently is sufficient to convince Rettie, who accepts without demur León's claim that to license even small shopkeepers would promote inequality. The system of distributing the pitiably small number of consumer goods by "elections" is described with only very slight criticisms. Of course, León may be right. If so, it is evidence of how far liberty must be sacrificed to maintain absolute equality.

The Social Reforms since 1959

Health and the welfare state were the categories that enjoyed the fullest coverage in the surveys of Cuba since the revolution that appeared in January 1984. In no other field is success such a relative notion, and statistics are nowhere more deceptive. But journalists are especially ill-equipped to judge for themselves whether social "reforms" are what they claim to be; whatever they see in a closed society like Cuba is unlikely to be typical unless they have found it for themselves. Neither of the authors of the two main articles considered here, Francis Pisani of *Le Monde* and the anonymous Reuters reporter in the *Times,* seems to have grasped the last point. They both describe in admiring detail the same showpiece hospital in Havana (Pisani calls it "Frères Ameijeiras"; Reuters, "Hermanos Ameijeiras"; but it is evidently the same building, and no doubt the same guided tour for foreigners), but neither has managed to find out whether any other Cuban hospitals have any comparable equipment from abroad, nor even whether all inhabitants of Havana enjoy equal access to this hospital. We learn only that the casualties of Castro's foreign embroilments, such as Grenada, are treated there.

Similarly, the Reuters correspondent describes a school at length: "The Salvador Allende primary school in Alamar, east of here, is used as a showpiece for foreigners to tour but is not untypical of schools that have sprouted up in the past 25 years." How does he know?

Francis Pisani's long study of "the Cuban health system as a model and training ground for the Third World" appeared under the title "Cuba Dans le Cabinet du Dr. Castro," and adorned with a large drawing of a cigar-smoking Cuban soldier wearing belts of syringes instead of bullets. Pisani begins by comparing health statistics before 1959 with those provided by Castro, whose personal responsibility for the priority given to health is stressed throughout, in a speech of 1980. Castro's figures show that Cuba not only has achieved vast improvements since the revolution but has left behind its Latin American neighbors. After describing the Ameijeiras hospital, a much less exemplary "polyclinic" in Alamar, where the ambulance has broken down, is sketched. Pisani then briefly mentions the "collaborateurs bénévoles" of the Committees for the Defense of the Revolution (CDRs)—without a trace of irony, which is noteworthy, given the normal role of the CDRs as informers and the connotations in French of *collaborateurs*—and the Federation of Cuban Women. Criticism of the bureaucratic nature of the service is then discussed, and Pisani remarks upon the "presence of psychologists at every level." No political significance is attached to this because, after all, "90 percent to 95 percent of Cubans are satisfied with the quality of health," according to one Dr. García. Finally, the "socialist character" of the Cuban system is considered as an explanation of its success, and the new "code of medical ethics" is examined. The article concludes thus:

> Some are seduced by the results, others are repulsed by the political dimension of the enterprise. But, for most countries of the Third World, it is undoubtedly a matter, not of judgement, let alone of imitation, but of knowing that such a thing exists.[37]

A good deal of Pisani's article is taken up with statistics, and he asserts that "statisticians are ubiquitous, and the Ministry of Health has the best information system in the country at its disposal." Yet, it is clear that the figures have all been accepted on trust, even where alternative sources were available; and even wild assertions about the relative stagnation of health in other "Third World" countries are repeated without qualification. In his article in *Encounter* of March 1984, "A Look at Castro's Statistics," Professor Norman Luxenburg showed that Castro's claims, repeated uncritically over several years by publications like the *Wall Street Journal*, the *New York Times*, *Newsweek*, *Time*, and the West German *Stern*, did not bear scrutiny, even if his boasts for the years since 1976, the last year for which the United Nations *Statistical Yearbook* listed figures for Cuba, were accepted. For example, the rate of increase in the number of physicians relative to population has slowed down since 1959, even if Castro is telling the truth when he claims that the number of medical doctors has doubled since 1976. Pisani accepts the figure of 17,000 and quotes Castro: "I believe that there can never be too many doctors."

The question, though, is not what Castro believes, but what is the case; and a country that in 1959 had a lower infant mortality rate than Spain, Italy, or Germany (it now, according to Luxenburg, has a higher one) cannot, for health purposes, be treated as a "model for the Third World."

What might have been the most interesting part of Pisani's article, the examination of the "code of medical ethics," is unfortunately too superficial. "It is expressly stipulated," he writes, "that the 'socialist character' of Cuban medicine implies 'ethical principles radically opposed to those of bourgeois medicine'."[38] Nothing that follows, however, suggests any departure from the Hippocratic tradition—unless the defense of the Socialist party, to which Cuban health workers must pledge themselves (using arms as well as medical knowledge), were to take precedence over the commitment to preserve life at all costs. In Nazi Germany such political priorities made possible the euthanasia campaign and later the experiments in the death camps. The prevalence of "psychologists" in Cuba also has a sinister ring since their activities in the USSR became known. Pisani makes no attempt to allay the reader's doubts.

Turning to the *Times* article, "How Castro Has Created a Welfare State to Be Envied," one sees that Castro's apologists have not even agreed to repeat the same lies. Pisani states that infant mortality before Castro was 40 per thousand (the true figure is 32 per thousand); the Reuters reporter gives 60 per thousand. The latter has no scruples to claim that "official statistics, backed by United Nations specialists working here, illustrate the transformation that has taken place,"[39] even though the UN, however sympathetic to Cuba in general, has certainly not given its approval to these figures. After a rapturous but not very precise account of the "cradle-to-grave social benefits," the author passes on to an unintentionally disturbing description of a school:

> Patriotic and Communist teaching play a large part in the daily routine beneath revolutionary slogans and pictures of such "martyrs" as Ernesto "Che" Guevara, the dead guerilla leader. The sports facilities are modern but much of the teaching would appear old-fashioned to visitors. They are often struck by the parrot-like responses of the children instilled with the notion of collective, rather than individual, mentality. . . .[40]

What happens to these children when they leave such "old-fashioned" pedagogy behind? Do they enjoy the same kind of higher education, if they are able, that Castro himself and so many revolutionaries did?

> "The old idea that the pursuit of academic excellence releases you from your obligations to help the economy . . . has to be forgotten," an Education Ministry official said. The concept of patriotic duty is fundamental to schooling and the 200,000 students in higher education are obliged to "repay" the state through work in isolated regions or abroad.[41]

The proper commentary on this interpretation of "patriotic duty" was provided in an article by Robert Held in the *Frankfurter Allgemeine Zeitung,* entitled "Angola-Kuba-Salvador":

> These days the inflated world-political role of Cuba is, for those who care to look, luridly illuminated. . . . Whether in the African bush or in the jungles by the volcanoes of Salvador, nothing happens without the involvement of the Cubans.[42]

It is, of course, part of the Cuban emphasis on social policy to express pride in achievements by exporting them, in spite of suffering, according to Armando Valladares. Greater casualties have resulted in proportion to population than the United States suffered in Vietnam, mostly inflicted by people who reject these policies. As Rettie wrote somewhat mildly in the *Guardian:*

> They are even happy to share [their achievements] with other countries by sending doctors, teachers and technicians to other countries like

Grenada, Nicaragua, and even Angola and Ethiopia. But the revolutionary equivalent of the white man's burden is not always an easy one.[43]

Indeed not. It is, however, rendered less difficult by articles such as the feature in the *Guardian's Third World Review* entitled "Cuba's Island in a Class of Its Own," and subtitled "Victoria Brittain Visits the Island of Youth, where the Children of Africa Get the Chance of an Education All Too Rare at Home." All the children on this island off the Cuban coast were, apparently, orphans of South African massacres or "the common desperate African war against economic and social decay produced by economic dependence on the West."[44] No matter that the Left in Britain is now fiercely critical of the British and U.S. governments for their acceptance of boat people from Indo-China. The products of the Island of Children will all be sent back to African countries like "Swapo": "For these African countries," she concludes, "this Cuban contribution to their education and the country's long-term development prospects is worth many times over the entire educational aid of the West not just in cash terms, but in effectiveness."[45]

The brazenness of Brittain's assertion surpasses the Reuters reporter in the *Times* article mentioned above, who spoke only of 14,000 foreign students in Cuba in courses "which, the Government emphasizes, are to train them in technical skills useful to their own countries and not guerilla subversion, as is alleged by many Western governments."[46] Unlike this journalist, Mark Fazlollah of London's other daily quality newspaper, the *Daily Telegraph,* had taken the trouble to investigate what actually happens to many of the foreigners who come to Cuba as "students." In an article by which Fazlollah must have placed his status as a correspondent in Havana at risk, he described a trip to the secret Guanabo base for guerrillas: "They will never give you any information, but everyone knows that the foreigners have trained there,' said a Guanabo taxi driver."[47]

The Economy

For one of the two main Austrian newspapers, the Cuban economy was the principal subject of the substantial coverage (including a cartoon of Castro and Reagan and a photograph of "74-year-old Teobaldo Hernandez" reading *Granma*) given the twenty-fifth anniversary celebrations. The *Wiener Zeitung* headed its report: "In Cuba Jeans and Coca Cola-Substitutes Are the Summit of 'Consumerism.' " The report emphasized the simple nature of Cuban life, especially for young people with leisure, who find even a single room hard to acquire.

Fazlollah in the *Daily Telegraph* even reported that "when boy meets girl in Cuba, courtship frequently takes place in pay-by-the-hour rooms in Government hotels" (quoted in *Encounter,* March 1984). The *Wiener Zeitung* pointed out that rents were a fixed 10 percent of income. No attempt is made to display goods attractively in the shops because they are rationed. Although several other articles asserted that the rations were at least sufficient, the *Wiener Zeitung* at least offered some quantities and quoted one man in a queue as dissatisfied. It is hard to imagine that many people would not grumble about 2kg of rice a month and less than ½ kg of meat every nine days—and only four cigars a month in Havana! The article includes a careful description of the state-run "parallel market," in which goods can be bought without ration cards—but at highly inflated prices.

Private trade was abolished in 1968, and the author amusingly describes the anxious functionaries' evocation of the bloated shop-keeper, and the appreciation of the woman journalist for Bulgarian apples imported specially for the anniversary, after denouncing the economic decline of the West. The author concludes:

> That which today expresses itself in renunciation of consumption, self-denial and community spirit is born of necessity, rather than the ideal of the "noble" revolutionary—an image linked to the dead Che Guevara. His splendid ethos has become somewhat ordinary in everyday life.[48]

Most of the reports in the European press that deal with the Cuban economy are devoted either to debt crises or, if they include firsthand material, the standard of living in Havana. Among the articles surveyed here, only Fazlollah's piece, "Small Farms Dying in Cuba," written from San Antonio, was based on interviews with the remnants of the 150,000 small farmers who had still existed in the early 1960s. Though there had been no coercion, life was made so difficult for them that the "private owner is becoming a dying breed."[49]

The rescheduling of Western debts of $1.3 billion, which was reported in the *Financial Times* and *Guardian* on 6 January 1983, naturally received no explicit mention in the survey of Cuban economic planning in the East German *Neues Deutschland* on 3 January 1983, but the crisis was made apparent by the attack upon "sinking sugar prices and high interest rates manipulated by imperialism." Hugh O'Shaughnessy in the *Financial Times* ("Cuba Puts a Brave Face on Debt") stated unequivocally: "In one important area, the Soviets have left the Cubans floundering. Moscow has made it very clear that it is not going to advance the islands the money they need to pay their overdue debts for foreign banks."[50] The same journalist followed this story with a more sensational one, "Castro's Secret Promise," in the London *Observer*. He revealed that a memorandum had been sent to Western banks offering a consumer squeeze in exchange for a stay of execution. The Cuban government apparently used as one argument the fact that Cuba was the only country in the Third World to receive weapons free of charge: "The document makes clear that Cuba's position is desperate. Its debts to the West are more than $12 billion, and it has not been paying interest on them since last September."[51]

A less gloomy view of Cuba's economic record was taken by *Le Monde's* Francis Pisani in a piece published on 16 August 1983 and headed "Cuba Still Depends on Sugar and the USSR." Although conceding that hopes of coastal oil were flimsy, that much of the growth was artificial, and that the weight of bureaucracy on the economy was crushing, Pisani nevertheless quoted the Western creditors as believing that Cuba was one of the least bad risks in Latin America.

The reason for this presumably has much to do with Soviet aid, and the impressive analysis by William Chislett in the *Financial Times* of 23 September 1983, "Why Cuba Is Scrambling for Hard Currency," gave prominence not to the possibly chimerical Cuban oil but to Soviet oil, which Cuba buys at very low prices and then resells to earn hard currency. Sixty-one million tons of oil have been earmarked for the period 1981-85 to go to Cuba, according to this report; Cuba earns $200 million a year of sorely needed hard currency by selling it. Chislett also emphasized the effectiveness of the trade embargo by the United States; this explains the frequent calls for the embargo to be lifted, though the justifications offered are usually political. The Cuban deputy trade minister, Miguel Castillo, was also quoted on the danger of rising Soviet oil prices, as the USSR itself felt the pinch: "If we reach the stage where we are paying more I suppose Washington will say we are being exploited by Moscow."

By far the most favorable assessment of the Cuban economy came from Jonathan Steele in the *Guardian*, "Cuba Marks 25 Years of Riding Economic Storms." This piece set great store by Cuba's independence of the crisis in the rest of Latin America caused by interest rates, and featured an interview with Raúl León of the National Bank. León confirmed that, in spite of its debt problem, Cuba would not rejoin the IMF or the World Bank, as other Soviet satellites had recently done, because of the influence of the United States over these organizations. Tourism and hotel construction were growing, but no major Western investment would be permitted for the same reason. In Steele's view, Cuba was "unusually favoured by the standards of the Third World."

Her living standards had been "unaffected," unlike those of her neighbors; in spite of the secret promises made by Castro which had been reported earlier in the year (mentioned above), Steele still argued that "the major result of Cuba's debt problems has been a reduction rather than an increase in Western influence."[52]

The most thorough study of the economic record of the Castro regime over the past quarter of a century came from the Havana correspondent, identified only by the initials "C. E.," of the main Swiss newspaper, the *Neue Zürcher Zeitung,* in an article headed "Cuba's Economy in the 25 Years of the Revolution: Dependence on Sugar Prices and Soviet Help." This piece gave some startling figures: Soviet aid accounts for a fourth of GDP, which in 1982 meant $6 billion, or $11-12 million a day. Apart from sugar, nickel accounted for 8 percent of exports, far more than fish, tobacco, coffee, and fruit, which in turn exceeded industrial products—a mere 2 percent of exports. A severe lack of capital due to the Western debt had led to import controls; but in spite of this there had been a 35 percent fall in hard currency earnings in the last year alone.

The first ten years of Castro's rule had seen stagnant private consumption in order to produce useful workers, according to the *Neue Zürcher Zeitung,* and Chislett, in his *Financial Times* piece, mentioned the 30,000 Cubans working abroad in a "non-military capacity" as an important potential source of foreign currency. The first Five Year Plan of 1976-80 had permitted wages to rise, but worsening terms of trade in the late 1970s had combined with the economic "blockade" to generate a crisis. According to the Cuban planning office, the country requires $1.5 billion a year of hard currency, of which 10-15 percent would be spent on consumer goods, 55-60 percent on partly finished materials, and the rest for capital goods. The general assessment by the *Neue Zürcher Zeitung* was grim: "In general however, the economic balance presents a fairly dark picture, and the prospects for the foreseeable future are also by no means rosy."[53]

Political Oppression

The Cuban-American community—in large measure a legacy of Castro's political police—continues to rankle, even in Cuba itself, where the former Peruvian embassy, according to Jonathan Steele,[54] has been converted into a public chamber of horrors, depicting the émigrés as drug addicts, homosexuals (against whom Castro launched an ongoing campaign of public humiliation in the mid-1960s), "Lumpen" and "scum" of all kinds. Steele reported this without comment. But the Communist *Morning Star* published an article, written by John

Griffiths, on 9 March 1983, called "Cubans Form Queue for a Return Flight Home." This claimed that the established Cuban-Americans resented the Mariel émigrés who had arrived recently regarding them as "escoria" (rubbish). Families lived for months in "little more than a concentration camp," while black Cubans "are experiencing racial discrimination for the first time in their lives" in the United States.

Hijackers who demand to go to Havana are used as evidence of the homesickness of the exiled community—though no proof is offered that any of these individuals have been Cuban-Americans, or that they are in any way representative if they were. Finally, we are told that "tens of thousands of those who left Cuba in 1980 have applied to return to Cuba." The number is obviously deliberately vague, and because it would be very difficult to prove the Cuban government wrong if it claimed to have received such applications, the assertion was worth risking for the *Morning Star*'s purposes. This does not alter its implausibility.

If it be true that the long queues every day outside the old Sears Roebuck store in Havana are "a sign not so much of shortages of basic items, but that people have money in their pockets," as Steele reported in the *Guardian* (with a photograph of smiling black Cubans captioned "Rations there may be, but few Third World countries can claim such success"), the explanation of mass emigration in spite of harassment becomes a political matter.

But Steele wants to have his cake and eat it, for he also distinguishes sharply between Cuba and the Soviet satellites, about which he knows more: "But is this the placidity and calm of so much of eastern Europe, which is often a mask for a deep popular resignation and sense of hopelessness? Does the superficial orderliness conceal a long-suppressed desire for change?"[55] Not, according to Steele, in Cuba.

Steele's colleague John Rettie offered the following account of the Committees for the Defense of the Revolution, the principal tools of the Cuban form of totalitarianism, with a control of private life that the Gestapo would have envied. Rettie repeats the erroneous claim that opposition to Castro within Cuba before and after the Bay of Pigs episode was "orchestrated from the US." (even Enzensberger in 1969 did not accept that, though he thought the CIA wanted the invasion to be defeated). The CDRs were thus a justified precaution against the CIA:

> So the CDRs were born, and they still watch and inform. It is hard to be sure what the popular view of them is, but it does seem that only a small minority resents them deeply. For the overwhelming majority, they are essential as long as the United States maintains its pressure.

To go to the Bay of Pigs, and to follow the story set out in the museum of how Cuba was softened up for the invasion, is to hear the story of Nicaragua today—the same tale of exile attacks, bombings, and efforts to undermine the economy, 22 years on.[56]

As so often, it is only the person who has suffered at the hands of those who are here exculpated who provides the adequate response: Armando Valladares, in the interview already quoted, said that "only a degraded minority of Communists and members of the political police act willingly [on behalf of these committees]; the others adopt a passive attitude and engage in these activities with a bad grace. All organizations of the regime are devoted to the same task: to detect and denounce the least manifestation of anti-Communism."

This account is confirmed by the article by the *Daily Telegraph*'s Fazlollah, "Cuban Walls Have Ears." It was mostly devoted to the persecution of one "José María," a student who was not so much an active opponent of the regime as an "apático." On the CDRs, which had denounced the student, Fazlollah quoted another witness (it is noticeable that Fazlollah, a critical observer of the Cuban regime, tends to have more such anecdotal evidence in his reports than those who are sympathetic, like Steele and Rettie, who both included descriptions of pretty revolutionary girls instead): "One man told me: 'If I volunteer every couple of months and donate blood occasionally when they call for help, the defence committee leaves me alone.' "[57]

According to Valladares, resistance to the regime not only exists but includes men within the party. Inevitably, very little news of this filters through to the European press. In the *Frankfurter Allgemeine Zeitung* there appeared a report on 23 April 1983 of the revelation by Valladares that death sentences and other severe penalties had been imposed on Cuban imitators of Solidarity. The *Guardian* printed the denial of these reports by the Cuban government on 17 May 1983, but even the latter had to admit that thirty-three men had received "severe sentences" for "sabotage and assassination."

The *Frankfurter Allgemeine* carried three very full reports of the International Sakharov Committee Hearings in Copenhagen on the subject of Cuba, at which Valladares presented a severe indictment of the terror, which he believed to be increasing (27, 28, 30 April 1983). In the interview in *Politique Internationale,* Valladares described the concentration camps, open farms, and open fronts, where political prisoners of various grades are kept: "The executions have never ceased in Cuba. But the government in Havana is highly adept at hiding its crimes, for if its exactions were better known throughout the whole world, the regime would lose all legitimacy."[58]

It is odd, to say the least, that the organization that should be most dedicated to publicizing such outrages, Amnesty International, appears only once (in Britain at least) to have protested at the ignoring of political oppression in Cuba in the press, and in this single case, the protest was, for once, hardly justified. On 13 January the *Daily Telegraph* published a letter from Janet Johnstone, director of the British Section of Amnesty International, objecting to the report by Fazlollah, " 'My Promise Fulfilled,' Castro Tells Cubans," of Castro's anniversary speech in the same paper on 3 January.

Fazlollah, as we have seen, is one of the few British journalists writing on Cuba not to have been captivated by Castro, and the article in question was one of the more objective pieces to appear about the anniversary celebrations. With very little space, he chose to mention, in addition to Castro's Santiago speech, the economy of Cuba since 1959, the improvement of social services, and Cuba's relations with the United States and the USSR. But he did say that "personal liberties are restricted under Communism." Because he had drawn attention to political oppression on several other occasions, it was scarcely just of Johnstone to speak of "our distress and alarm raised by the report's scant, even elusive attention to the human rights situation in Cuba."[59] It was, nonetheless, welcome from the director of an organization that so energetically denounces the violations of human rights in those Latin American countries that are closer to the United States than Cuba or Nicaragua in ideology.

Johnstone proceeded to list injustices perpetrated against political prisoners, including the "use of intimidating methods to extract self-incriminating statements" (i.e. torture), and the "continued detention of approximately 220 long-term political prisoners who had already completed their sentences without judicial procedure."[60] The release of one of these, Ricardo Bofill—who was, like Valladares, the subject of intercession by President Mitterand—generated considerable publicity in France,[61] but no Cuban has, as yet, acquired the status of Solzenit-syn or Sakharov in Western Europe. A spokesperson for the oppressed whom even the oppressors fear is still lacking in Cuba, though not for want of nobility of spirit in such figures as the poet Jorge Valls. What is striking in the letter from Amnesty is the impression it gives that the oppression in Cuba affects only hundreds; according to Valladares, in his evidence at the Shakharov Hearings, there are 14,000 political prisoners in Cuba at present, and since 1959 there have been 80,000. If these figures are correct, even approximately, they are comparable to the number of such prisoners in the whole of Eastern Europe, excluding the USSR—in a country of about 10 million!

Conclusion

Castro's Cuba has lost its revolutionary virtue in the eyes of its European admirers, but is good enough for them even as a whore. Behind the ephemera scrutinzed here, the indoctrination of the young proceeds; above the self-deceiving conceits of the journalists, the anguish of the incarcerated sometimes becomes audible. The Sandinistas have replaced Guevara as the object of wishful thinking among the anti-American left in Western Europe, and, in spite of the Falklands and Grenada, Latin America in general is of less concern to European public opinion than to the opinion formers. The majority of the latter are not deceived by Castro, but even they often fall into subtle but significant half-truths—referring to the trade embargo by the United States as a "blockade," or to the Bay of Pigs as a "precedent" for the mining of ports in Nicaragua (as the Washington correspondent of *Le Monde,* Henri Pierre, did on 19 April 1984).

No other major communist state is an island, and none is more completely insulated from societies of a different stamp, apart, perhaps, from the remoter regions of China or the Soviet Union. The low living standards caused by a stifling planned economy and expensive foreign adventures have been presented as Spartan virtue by the regime, and the European who perceives his own society as decadent will naturally find something to admire in this. But Sparta, though tougher, was also duller than Athens, and the most interesting thing most Westerners appear to find in Castro's Cuba is its leader. He has been there so long that he rarely bothers to justify his reputation for "charisma" with flamboyant gestures, at least for the Western press.

Castro is the greatest of all the many parasites upon friction between the United States and its European allies. Nothing he does matters in Europe as much as that, by merely existing, he is a thorn in the side of the United States. Hence the fickleness of his friends, who only rediscover the "informal political style" of Cuba—and the fact that he, like them but unlike most dictators, is an intellectual—when it suits them to offer a contrast to the United States. We may be sure, however, that Castro is well aware of the fickle character of his friends in the Western press, for he is more than a match for most statesmen, let alone journalists, in realpolitik. It costs him nothing to flatter the correspondents of Western Europe, and his willingness to oblige Mitterand, like his recent visit to Spain, is no less cheap.

As long as he is perceived to be civilized and generally on the defensive against his giant neighbor, Castro can count on the disapproval of Western Europe as a sufficient deterrent to any administration of the United States that might find itself provoked beyond endurance. It is to Western Europe, too, that Castro will have to turn in the event of an economic collapse so serious that the Soviet Union refuses to bail him out. It is already a success for him that he has remained respectable in Europe in a way that indigenous dictatorships of comparable longevity, such as those of Spain and Portugal, never did. How has he done it?

The interpretation of Cuban history as "the pursuit of freedom," what Benedetto Croce called "history as the story of liberty," causes European liberals to revolt against the idea that such an evolution could be halted and reversed. They search desperately for signs of this spirit in a monolithic society where even the church—traditionally perceived as reactionary by liberals, but now embraced by them as the guarantor of liberty where all else has failed—seems irreversibly weakened. The bitter truth, however, is that Cubans, in their pursuit of freedom, became the pursued, and this is a truth that Western Europeans cannot afford to ignore.

Moderator: Mr. David Asman, *Wall Street Journal*

There has been a lack of questioning of the basic facts that is often necessary in the case of the governments in Cuba and in Nicaragua. This lack of questioning leads me to doubt some of the figures that even Castro's detractors point to as being partial successes in Cuba.

A change in the attitude of the press does seem to be under way. There seems to be a real desire to get to the bottom of stories that haven't been reported because they might run against the bias of some reporters. This is occurring not to make ideological reparations per se but rather it is being done because there's a realization that there are some great stories out there that haven't been told.

Reporters who may be liberal recognize a good story even if it goes against their ideology. The desire for professional distinction is beginning to win out more and more over personal ideological bias.

Respondent: Dr. Mark Falcoff, American Enterprise Institute

There are some indications that things are changing in the European press, and that in some way it is far ahead of the U.S. press in its perspectives. There is a tendency in Europe, however, to view the history of Latin America not as the history of independent countries but as that of U.S. sins and evils. There are people and countries in Latin America that have a life of their own. It's not all what the United

States has done to Latin America. It would be as if to say that the history of Ireland can be explained solely in terms of what the English have done to Ireland, and this would be ludicrous. Ireland has an independent history, local complexities. The same holds true for Latin America.

In Europe, the United States-Cuban conflict is so personalized that there is a reluctance on the part of Europeans to give comfort to the United States by criticizing Cuba. Admiration for the nationalistic movements in countries such as Cuba is not only an outlet for expression of European nationalism, it is also a form of expressing European resentment toward the decline of European importance in world politics.

There is also a tendency to underestimate the importance of the communist regimes in Cuba and Nicaragua to the United States. In Europe, their existence is seen as almost trivial, whereas in the United States they are seen as having serious consequences.

In the case of Spain specifically, Hispanic pride plays a part in the press coverage, i.e. Cuba as a Hispanic country effectively defying the United States mitigates Cuban abuses, injustices, and so on. Additionally, there's a generalized ideological slump among Socialists with the direction that the González government is taking in Spain. Many Communists feel that it's too bourgeois and that the real radical revolution is happening in Cuba and that therefore it has to succeed.

In Germany, escapism plays a large part in influencing press coverage of Cuba. The Germans transfer their sense of national guilt to the United States by looking at their history, admitting that they did terrible things and then turning around and accusing the United States of doing even more terrible things in Latin America now.

Respondent: Dr. Joachim Maitre, Boston University

There is reason for optimism in European journalism. In general the newspapers are more positive regarding Western values. Prime Minister Thatcher and President Mitterand were taken to task by many newspapers over their hysterical reactions to the United States action in Grenada. Many newspapers recognized that the Americans not only meant well but also did well. The mood is changing and we should take note of it.

Granma, Pravda, Barricada, and the like are not newspapers in the way that we know them in the United States. They are party organs mainly written to have one function and one purpose: to announce the party line on a daily basis to all members of the Communist party.

Western journalists tend to consider such publications as a source, and they are, in outlining official government policy. However, to read and perceive these papers as one reads and perceives the *Washington Post* or the *New York Times* is absurd.

It has been reported recently in the press that the young people in Managua when they see Western journalists begin to mouth and then whisper these words, "El Frente y Somoza son la misma cosa," (The Sandinista Front and Somoza are the same thing). The whispers get louder until the journalists hear them. It is only a matter of time until the Sandinistas are recognized outside of Nicaragua, as well, for the dictators they are.

Notes

1. Hans Magnus Enzensberger, *Das Verhor von Habana* (Frankfurt am Main: Suhrkamp, 1970). The author is responsible for translations of quotations from all non-English sources used in this paper. He would like to thank Lord Thomas of Swynnerton for useful advice, and the staff of the press library of the Royal Institute of International Affairs, London, for their cooperation.
2. Enzensberger, *Das Verhor von Habana*.
3. Ibid.
4. *World Today* 25 (January 1969).
5. *Encounter,* March 1984.
6. Fidel Castro, speech in Santiago de Cuba, January 1, 1984.
7. *Times,* 7 November 1984.
8. *Le Monde,* 1 February 1984.
9. *Guardian,* 4 November 1983.
10. *Politique Internationale* 21 (automne 1983).
11. *Guardian,* 10 November 1983.
12. Ibid., 26 July 1983.
13. Ibid.
14. Ibid., 28 July 1983.
15. Ibid., 29 July 1983.
16. John Rettie in the *Guardian,* 4 November 1983.
17. *Guardian,* 29 July 1983.
18. *Times,* 27 July 1983.
19. Ibid.
20. Ibid.
21. Irving Kristol, *Reflections of a Neoconservative* (New York: Basic Books, 1983), p. 24.
22. *Politique Internationale* 21 (Fall 1983).
23. *Guardian,* 2 August 1983.
24. Ibid.
25. *Encounter,* March 1984.
26. *Guardian,* 1 August 1983.
27. Ibid.
28. *Times,* 7 November 1983.

29. *Newsweek*, quoted in *Times*, 2 January 1984.
30. *Guardian*, 3 January 1984.
31. *Financial Times*, 5 January 1984.
32. *Guardian*, 10 November 1983.
33. Ibid., 1 August 1983.
34. *Le Monde*, 31 March 1984.
35. Ibid., 23 March 1983.
36. *Guardian*, 10 November 1983.
37. *Le Monde*, 22-23 January 1984.
38. Ibid.
39. *Times*, 30 December 1984.
40. Ibid.
41. Ibid.
42. *Frankfurter Allgemeiné Zeitung*, 23 March 1984.
43. *Guardian*, 4 November 1983.
44. Ibid., 30 September 1983.
46. *Times*, 30 December 1983.
47. *Daily Telegraph*, 2 December 1983.
48. *Wiener Zeitung*, 3 January 1984.
49. *Daily Telegraph*, 24 November 1983.
50. *Financial Times*, 27 January 1983.
51. Ibid.
52. *Guardian*, 31 December 1983.
53. *Neue Zürcher Zeitung*, 10 March 1983.
54. *Guardian*, 1 August 1983.
55. Ibid.
56. Ibid., 10 November 1983.
57. *Daily Telegraph*, 14 November 1983.
58. *Politique Internationale* 21 (Fall 1983).
59. *Daily Telegraph*, January 13, 1984.
60. Ibid.
61. See, for example, *Le Monde*, 7 January 1984.

About the Contributors

Vivian W. Dudro is a recent graduate of Arizona State University, where she was Editor of the Arizona State University newspaper. She is currently a free-lance writer and has written several articles for the *National Catholic Register.*

Kevin Greene is a graduate student at the John F. Kennedy School of Government at Harvard University, concentrating on international development and finance.

Daniel Johnson currently works with Hugh Thomas at the Centre for Policy Studies (London). He is also a free-lance journalist and has written numerous articles for the *Times Literary Supplement*, the *Sun Times*, the *Listener*, the *Spectator*, and several academic journals.

William E. Ratliff is a Research Fellow at the Hoover Institution on War, Revolution and Peace at Stanford University. He has been a staff writer for the *Peninsula Times Tribune* of Palo Alto, California, and has taught political theory and international politics at Stanford and other Bay Area universities.

Carlos Ripoll is Professor of Romance Languages at Queens College of the City University of New York. Dr. Ripoll is the author of several books and many articles on Cuban culture and history, including *The Cuban Scene: Censors and Dissenters*, published in 1982 by the Cuban American National Foundation, and a bilingual anthology of Martí's thoughts.

John R. Silber has been president of Boston University since 1971. He was educated at Trinity University (San Antonio) and received his Ph.D. in Philosophy at Yale University. Dr. Silber is a leading national spokesman on educational and social issues. In July, 1983 President Reagan appointed him to the National Bipartisan Commission on Central America.

John P. Wallach is the Foreign Affairs Editor for Hearst Newspapers. He has visited Cuba and written of his experience and observations on the island, being among the first journalists to visit Cuba in 1970.

Index

Abrams, Floyd, 19, 33
Adorno, Theodor, 32
Afghanistan, 74
Africa, 7, 10, 40, 76, 77. *See also* name of country
Agromonte, Roberto, 87–88
Aguilar, Luis, 105–6
AIDS [Acquired Immune Deficiency Syndrome], 46
Alamar housing project, 118
Alfonsin, Raúl, 74
Alvarez, Santiago, 151
Amnesty International, 144, 182
Andropov, Yuri Vladmirovich, 74–75
Angola, 15–16, 25–26, 40, 48, 50–54, 61, 77, 117. *See also* Africa
Arafat, Yasir, 40
Argentina, 44, 73–74, 128. *See also* Latin America
Arms talks, 74, 75–76
Arrangements/restrictions in Cuba, 114–19
Asman, David, 184
Austin, Hudson, *See* Grenada
Austria, 176–77
Autocratic censorship, 83–94, 103–4
Avance, 95, 98

Baldwin, Hanson, 7
Ball, George W., 16–17, 23, 24
Barricada, 71, 78
Batista, Rubén, 88
Batista [Fulgencio] government, 8, 85–94, 104–5
Bay of Pigs, 9, 45, 138–39, 147, 160, 181
Begin, Menachem, 76

Bishop, Maurice, 167–68. *See also* Grenada
Blechman, Barry, 15, 24–25
Bofill, Ricardo, 182
Bohemia, 85, 86–87, 88, 89–92, 94, 96, 101
Borge, Tomás, 65
Bourne, Peter, 134, 135–36, 142–44, 146, 148–50
Brazil, 73. *See also* Latin America
Brezhnev, Leonid, 32, 74, 148
Britain. *See* Great Britain; name of British newspaper/journalist
Brittain, Victoria, 176
Bulgaria, 76
Bundy, McGeorge, 18, 36

Cambodia, 77
Cameras in Cuba, 118–19
Carter, [Jimmy] administration. *See* United States
Castillo, Miguel, 178
Castro, Fidel: alleged assassination attempts by CIA on, 136, 139–40, 147; attitude toward media of, 85, 93–94, 95, 102–3, 133–34; attitude about Nixon of, 146–48; on exporting revolution, 145–46; as an intellectual, 142, 153, 183; manipulation of press by, 129–30, 133–34, 149; and power, 141–42, 144; views of himself, 135–36, 145
Castro, Ramón, 118, 119
Castro, Raúl, 63, 133, 167
Caute, David, 135, 145
"CBS Reports", 137
CDR (Committee for the Defense of the

191